Praise for Edward Jay Epstein's

HOW AMERICA LOST ITS SECRETS

"Mr. Epstein shows that much in Mr. Snowden's story simply does not add up. . . . The picture [of Snowden] that emerges is of an odd, deeply resentful young man motivated less by high moral purpose than personal revenge."
—*The Wall Street Journal*

"Epstein reminds readers of one unsettling detail after another from the Snowden story. The popular characterization of Snowden—as an idealist motivated by patriotism even at great personal risk—takes an unrecoverable pounding in these pages." —*The Christian Science Monitor*

"In addition to giving a full and nuanced portrait of the man himself, Epstein details the shattering impact Snowden's theft and famous June 9, 2013, video announcement has had on the agency and the intelligence community worldwide. A riveting and informative work for both Snowden watchers and espionage buffs." —*Booklist* (starred review)

"Nuanced. . . . A wild and harrowing detective story and impressively evenhanded portrait of a very sticky case."
—*Kirkus Reviews* (starred review)

"Powerful and convincing." —*The Hollywood Reporter*

Edward Jay Epstein

HOW AMERICA LOST ITS SECRETS

Edward Jay Epstein is an investigative journalist and a former political science professor at MIT and UCLA. He is the author of many books, including *Inquest: The Warren Commission and the Establishment of Truth*, *The Hollywood Economist: The Hidden Financial Reality Behind the Movies*, and *The Rise and Fall of Diamonds: The Shattering of a Brilliant Illusion*. He lives in New York City.

www.edwardjayepstein.com

HOW AMERICA
LOST ITS SECRETS

HOW AMERICA LOST ITS SECRETS

Edward Snowden, the Man and the Theft

Edward Jay Epstein

VINTAGE BOOKS
A Division of Penguin Random House LLC
New York

FIRST VINTAGE BOOKS EDITION, NOVEMBER 2017

Copyright © 2017 by E. J. E. Publications Ltd.

All rights reserved. Published in the United States by Vintage Books, a division of Penguin Random House LLC, New York, and distributed in Canada by Random House of Canada, a division of Penguin Random House Canada Limited, Toronto. Originally published in hardcover in the United States by Alfred A. Knopf, a division of Penguin Random House LLC, New York, in 2017.

Vintage and colophon are registered trademarks of Penguin Random House LLC.

The Library of Congress has cataloged the Knopf edition as follows:
Names: Epstein, Edward Jay, author.
Title: How America lost its secrets : Edward Snowden, the man and the theft /
by Edward Jay Epstein.
Description: New York : Alfred A. Knopf, [2017] |
Includes bibliographical references and index.
Identifiers: LCCN 2016026940
Subjects: LCSH: Snowden, Edward J., 1983– | United States. National Security Agency/
Central Security Service. | Leaks (Disclosure of information)—United States. | Electronic
surveillance—United States. | Whistle-blowing—United States.
Classification: LCC JF1525.W45 E67 2017 | DDC 327.12730092—dc23
LC record available at https://lccn.loc.gov/2016026940

Vintage Books Trade Paperback ISBN: 978-1-101-97437-7
eBook ISBN: 978-0-451-49457-3

Author photograph © Valerie Sadoun
Book design by Maggie Hinders

www.vintagebooks.com

Printed in the United States of America
10   9   8   7   6   5   4   3   2   1

This book is dedicated to the memory of a wise teacher,

James Q. Wilson (1931–2012)

There are certain persons who . . . have a perfect right to commit breaches of morality and crimes, and . . . the law is not for them.

—FYODOR DOSTOYEVSKY, *Crime and Punishment*

Contents

HOW AMERICA
LOST ITS SECRETS

Prologue

Snowden's Trail: Hong Kong, 2014

T HE NATIONAL SECURITY AGENCY, or, as it is now commonly called, the NSA, was created on October 24, 1952, in such a tight cocoon of secrecy that even the presidential order creating it was classified top secret. When journalists asked questions about this new agency, Washington officials jokingly told them that the initials NSA stood for "No Such Agency." The reason for this extraordinary stealth is that the NSA is involved in a very sensitive enterprise. Its job is to intercept, decode, and analyze foreign electronic communications transmitted around the globe over copper wires, fiberoptic cable, satellite, microwave relays, cell phone towers, wireless transmissions, and the Internet for specified intelligence purposes. In intelligence jargon, its product is called COMINT, which stands for communications intelligence. Because this form of intelligence gathering is most effective when the NSA's targets are unaware of the state-of-the-art tools the NSA uses to break into their computers and telecommunications channels to first intercept and then decrypt their secret messages, the NSA goes to extraordinary lengths to keep them secret. Draconian laws protect this secrecy.

In the first week of June 2013, the NSA learned that there had been a massive breach. Thousands of secret files bearing on communications intelligence had been stolen from a heavily guarded regional base in Oahu, Hawaii.

The suspect was Edward Snowden, a twenty-nine-year-old civilian analyst at that base, who had fled to Hong Kong before the breach was discovered. According to a three-count criminal complaint filed by federal prosecutors in the Eastern District of Virginia, Snowden had stolen government property and violated the Espionage Act by the unauthorized and willful communication of national defense information to an unauthorized person. He also likely violated the Computer Fraud and Abuse Act by entering computer systems illicitly.

This was not a whodunit mystery. On June 9, 2013, in an extraordinary twelve-minute video made in a cramped hotel room in Hong Kong, Snowden identified himself as the person who had taken the NSA documents. Watching the video, the world saw a shy, awkward, and sympathetic-looking man wearing a rumpled shirt, rimless glasses, and a computer-geek haircut, passionately speaking out against what he termed the NSA's violations of the law and, in a shaky voice, expressing his willingness to suffer the consequences for exposing them.

Snowden had an innocent, idealistic, principled look about him, and the world was ready to congratulate him for revealing the NSA's alleged illegal collection of data inside the United States. But in fact, Snowden had stolen a great deal more than documents relating to domestic surveillance. He had also stolen secret documents from the NSA, the CIA, the Department of Defense, and the British cipher service revealing the sources and methods they employed in their monitoring of adversaries, which was their job.

By the time the theft had been discovered, in the first week of June 2013, it was impossible for the FBI, a grand jury, or any other U.S. agency to question him because he had fled the country. His first stop, Hong Kong, the economically autonomous city of 7.2 million, is a special administrative region of mainland China. Under the terms of the 1997 transfer of sovereignty from Great Britain, China is responsible for Hong Kong's defense and foreign policy, including intelligence services. He then proceeded to Russia, which has no extradition treaty with the United States. Russia granted him asylum, making it unlikely that U.S. authorities would ever have the opportunity to question him.

Snowden's escape left in its wake an incredibly important unsolved mystery: How had a young analyst in training at the NSA succeeded in penetrating all the layers of NSA security to pull off the largest theft of secret documents in the history of American intelligence? Did he act alone? What happened to the documents? Was his arrival in Russia part of the plan?

Because I had written several books on the vulnerability of intelligence services, this was a mystery—a "*how*dunit," if you like—that immediately intrigued me. Even if Snowden had acted for the most salutary of reasons, the unauthorized transfer of state secrets from the United States to an adversary country is, by almost any definition, a form of espionage.

I decided to begin my investigation of this case in Hong Kong, because it was the place to which Snowden first fled after leaving Hawaii. Snowden had planned the trip for at least four weeks, according to the mandatory travel plan he had filed at the NSA. When I spoke to my sources in the intelligence community, they could not explain Snowden's choice. It would not necessarily protect him from the reach of U.S. law, because Hong Kong had an active extradition treaty with the United States. Just a few months earlier, Hong Kong had made headlines by honoring America's request to extradite Trent Martin, a fugitive wanted for insider trading.

Nor was Hong Kong particularly convenient to Hawaii. There were no nonstop flights there from Honolulu in May 2013. Snowden flew eight hours to Narita International Airport in Japan, where he waited almost three hours. He then flew five hours to Hong Kong. Snowden could have flown to countries that do not have extradition treaties with America in far less time.

Adding to this mystery, at the time he departed Honolulu, Snowden had not yet arranged for any journalists to meet him in Hong Kong, and as far as U.S. intelligence could determine, he had no known appointments there. Even so, Snowden carried to Hong Kong digital copies he had made of the top secret NSA documents. As General Michael Hayden, who served as the head of both the NSA and the CIA, told me, "It's very mysterious why Snowden chose Hong Kong." We can assume he had a compelling enough reason for him to take the risk that he would be arrested there by Hong Kong police after U.S. authorities invoked the detention provision of its extradition treaty. It was of course possible that Snowden had traveled there to see someone he believed could protect him.

I arrived in Hong Kong on May 20, 2014—exactly one year after Snowden had arrived there aboard a Japan Airlines flight. I checked in to the Mira hotel in the Tsim Sha Tsui shopping district of Kowloon, a ten-minute ferry ride away from Hong Kong Island, where most of the foreign consulates are located.

I chose the Mira because it was the five-star hotel in which Snowden had stayed and where he had made the celebrated video admitting his role in taking the NSA documents. I asked at the front desk for room 1014, the same one that Snowden had occupied in 2013, because I wanted easy access to the hotel's service and security personnel responsible for the room who might have had contact with Snowden a year earlier. Unfortunately, that room was occupied, but I was given a nearby room that served my purpose.

Snowden had told Glenn Greenwald and Laura Poitras, the *Guardian* reporters he met in Hong Kong, that he had hidden out at the Mira hotel since his arrival in Hong Kong because he feared that the CIA might capture him. My first surprise was that Snowden had not arrived at the Mira until eleven days after he arrived in Hong Kong. As I learned from the hotel staff, Snowden had registered there under his real name and used his own passport and credit card to secure the room, an odd choice if he was hiding out. He had checked in to the hotel not on May 20, as he had told the reporters, but on June 1, 2013. He checked out on June 10.

Wherever Snowden stayed from May 20 to June 1, he apparently considered it a safe enough place from which to send Greenwald a "welcome package," as he called it, of twenty top secret NSA documents on May 25. He had now not only downloaded documents but also violated the oath he had signed when he took his job by providing them to an unauthorized party. During this period, Snowden also contacted Barton Gellman, on behalf of *The Washington Post,* via e-mail. Indeed, while he was staying someplace other than the place he claimed to be staying, he made almost all the arrangements for his journalistic coming-out. He was in contact with at least one foreign mission during this period, according to what he wrote to Gellman on May 24. In that e-mail, concerning when and how his story was to be published by *The Washington Post,* Snowden asked Gellman to include some text that would help Snowden with his dealings with this mission. But which country was he approaching? In an effort to establish Snowden's whereabouts during these "missing" eleven days, which, among other things, could shed light on why he first came to Hong Kong, I called Keith Bradsher, a prizewinning journalist who had been the *New York Times* bureau chief in Hong Kong in 2013. He had written a well-researched report about Snowden's arrival there. He proposed we meet at the Foreign Correspondents' Club.

Bradsher told me that he had known Albert Ho, who had been retained as Snowden's lawyer, for more than a decade. He had interviewed him many times, because he was a leader of a political movement in Hong Kong. Bradsher said that a few days after Snowden had revealed himself on June 9, he met with Ho and questioned him about Snowden's unknown whereabouts.

Ho told Bradsher that all of Snowden's logistics had been arranged for him by an intermediary, whom Ho called a "carer." Ho said that Snowden had been in contact with the "carer" prior to his arrival in Hong Kong on May 20. According to Ho, it was this person who had arranged accommodations for Snowden on his arrival and afterward. If so, it seemed to me that this person might be able to shed light on whom, if anyone, Snowden saw in his first eleven days in Hong Kong. Even if this person might have been unaware of the reasons for Snowden's trip to Hong Kong when he made the arrangements for him, he was still the best lead I had to learning why Snowden had come to Hong Kong. Bradsher told me that he pressed Ho for details about this mystery person over the course of several meetings but Ho would not identify him beyond saying that he was a "well-connected resident" of Hong Kong.

I called Ho's law office in Hong Kong. He politely declined to be interviewed by me, saying he had said all he was going to say about the Snowden case. I was able, though, to make an appointment with Robert Tibbo, a Canadian-born barrister specializing in civil liberties cases. Tibbo had worked closely with Ho on the Snowden case.

I met Tibbo in the tearoom at the Mandarin Oriental hotel on Hong Kong Island. Tibbo, in his early fifties, was tall, with a round face and thinning hair. He talked freely about his remarkable career. After earning a degree in chemical engineering from McGill University and working in Asia as an engineer for a decade, he went to law school in New Zealand and became a barrister in Hong Kong specializing in cases involving the legal status of refugees.

Over a leisurely tea, Tibbo made it clear that he had played a far more active role than Ho in the Snowden case. He had even personally escorted Snowden from the Mira hotel to a safe house on June 10. He did not dispute what Ho had told Bradsher. When I asked him if he could give me the name of the "carer," he said that he was bound by a lawyer-client privilege that prevented him from providing me with any details that might reveal the identity of the person who had made arrangements for Snowden. When I asked the date that he was officially retained by Snowden, he said that Snowden had signed an agreement hiring him and Ho's law firm as his legal adviser on June 10, 2013 (which was a matter of public record).

"I understand that," I said, "but I am inquiring about something that had happened before you became his legal adviser." He shook his head, as if getting rid of a pesky fly, and said that his oath precluded him from saying anything at all that might do damage to the credibility of his client. "Not even where he was staying in May in Hong Kong?" I persisted. He leaned forward and, after a brief hesitation, said, jokingly I assumed, that he would not divulge that information, "even if you held a gun to my head." We met two more times, but true to his word Tibbo would not say if he even knew the identity of the "carer."

Meanwhile, Joyce Xu, a very resourceful Chinese journalist who was assisting me in Hong Kong, had filed the equivalent of a Freedom of Information request with the Hong Kong Security Bureau asking for information about Snowden's movements in May. Thomas Ng, the secretary for security, turned down the request, adding that Hong Kong authorities do not keep records of hotel registrations. I had run into a dead end with the Hong Kong authorities on the issue of Snowden's "carer" and Snowden's whereabouts for those eleven crucial days.

At this point, I got some much-needed help from an old friend on the Obama White House staff. Before I had left New York, I asked him if he could find someone at the consulate in Hong Kong who might brief me on the Snowden case. I didn't hear from him until just a few days before I was due to return to New York. He put me in touch with a former employee of the Hong Kong consulate, who he said was "fully informed" about the efforts of the U.S. mission to locate Snowden in Hong Kong. This person was still living in Hong Kong, and he agreed to meet with me on condition that I did not mention either his name or his specific job in the U.S. mission in Hong Kong. The venue was the terrace lounge of the American Club in Exchange Square in central Hong Kong, a posh club mainly for expatriate Americans. It was on the forty-eighth floor, with a spectacular view of Victoria Harbor. Once there, I had no problem finding my source, identifying him by the description he had given me. He was sitting alone at a discreet table in the corner.

After we ordered drinks, he told me in a soft voice about the American reaction to Snowden's revelations in Hong Kong. "All hell broke loose," he said, describing the atmosphere at the U.S. mission after Snowden's video was posted on *The Guardian*'s website on June 9.

I asked about an assertion that Snowden had made concerning the U.S. consulate in that extraordinary video. Snowden had said that he could be seized at any moment by a CIA rendition team based at the U.S. consulate "just down the road" from the Mira hotel.

"Was that true?" I asked.

He rolled his eyes and said, "Snowden has a pretty wild imagination. For one thing, the U.S. consulate is not down the road from the Mira in Kowloon; it is here on Hong Kong Island. And there was no CIA rendition team in Hong Kong."

My next question concerned a second period during which

Snowden's whereabouts are clouded—the period between the time he left the Mira hotel on June 10 and the day he left Hong Kong for Russia on June 23. When I asked my consulate source whether the U.S. mission took any action to track Snowden during these thirteen days, he explained that the FBI had long maintained a contingent of "legal attachés" based at the consulate to pursue many possible violations of U.S. law including video piracy. In addition, the CIA and the Defense Intelligence Agency (DIA) had retained a handful of "China watchers" under diplomatic cover in Hong Kong. This group constituted the "intelligence mission," as he referred to it. It had developed informal relations with the Hong Kong police that, along with the NSA's electronic capabilities abroad, allowed it to track Snowden's movements after he had outed himself on the video. Because Snowden, his lawyers, and the journalists in his entourage frequently used their cell phones to text one another, it was fairly easy for the U.S. intelligence mission to follow Snowden's trail after he left the Mira hotel. He said that the Hong Kong police also knew where he was during this period. My source further suggested that the massive Chinese intelligence contingent in Hong Kong also knew, because it had close relations with the Hong Kong police.

"So everyone knew Snowden's whereabouts as he moved every few days from apartment to apartment," I interjected. He answered that it was no secret to anyone except the media and the public. "Of course we knew," he said, adding that there were also photographs of Snowden entering the office building that housed the Russian consulate. I mentioned that there was a report in a Russian newspaper that Snowden had visited the Russian consulate in late June in connection with the flight he later took to Moscow. "All we know is he entered the building," he answered, with a shrug.

That Russian consulate visit did not come as a complete surprise to U.S. intelligence. After Snowden left the Mira, his interactions with the Russian and Chinese intelligence services in Hong Kong had been closely monitored by "secret means," a term that in that context likely indicated electronic surveillance. A former top intelligence executive in Washington, D.C., subsequently confirmed this monitoring to me. All of Snowden's stealth in exiting from the Mira hotel, which included wearing a baseball cap and dark glasses, thus proved ineffective in hiding him from U.S. intelligence and presumably other intelligence services seeking the treasure trove of documents he had taken from the NSA.

As for his next destination, I could find no evidence that Snowden had made any arrangements during his monthlong stay in Hong Kong to go to any Latin American country. Before he went public on June 9, he could have easily gotten a visa in Hong Kong with his still-valid passport to go to almost any country in the world, including Cuba (for which a U.S. passport was not necessary), Bolivia, and Ecuador. Yet he did not apply for visas during this time period. Even as late as June 8, after meetings with Greenwald and Poitras, his name had still not been revealed, no criminal complaint had been issued against him, and there was no Interpol red alert for his detention. He could have walked out of the Mira hotel, caught a taxi to the Hong Kong airport, and gone on Swiss International Air Lines via Zurich to any country in South America or to Iceland. But, as in the oft-cited Sherlock Holmes clue of the dog that did not bark, Snowden's inaction in not obtaining visas during this thirty-day period suggests that he had no plans to go anyplace but where he went: Moscow.

However, the mystery that most concerned me was not where Snowden was housed in the interim between when he went public and when he went to Moscow. It was where, and in whose care, Snowden had been *before* he met with journalists at the Mira on June 3. Part of this mystery would be cleared up nearly three years later when Tibbo, still acting as Snowden's legal representative, released copies of hotel records showing Snowden had initially stayed at the Hotel ICON when he arrived in Hong Kong on May 20, before booking himself into a "Courtyard room" at Mira hotel from May 21 to May 30 (using his MasterCard). On May 30, he rebooked himself into the more elite "Club City" section of the Mira with an unidentified guest. Finally, on June 1, he booked himself alone back into a Courtyard room (using a different credit card). If these records are accurate, the hotel rooms in which Snowden stayed during his first three weeks in Hong Kong are no longer in doubt. What remains unknown is the contacts he had in Hong Kong before he met with journalists on June 3. The only gap here was filled in by Vladimir Putin, who disclosed Snowden met with Russian diplomats in Hong Kong *before* Putin proposed Snowden come to Russia on June 11. Aside from that meeting, Snowden's activities during this period were not a mystery I was going to solve on this first trip to Hong Kong. I needed to know more about his activities before he got there. After all, Snowden was not, as he himself pointed out from Moscow, an "angel descending from the heavens." He had been working for the U.S. government for the previous seven years. During that period, he had been part of America's secret intelligence regime and held a clearance for sensitive compartmented information, or SCI. Such SCI material is considered so sensitive that it must be handled within formal access control systems established by the director of national intelligence.

Nor did Snowden's breach begin with his handing over classified documents to the *Guardian* reporters in Hong Kong in June 2013 or, for that matter, in the eleven days prior to his meeting with journalists. He had, as the NSA quickly determined, begun illicitly copying documents in the summer of 2012. Such a dangerous enterprise is not born of a sudden impulse. It was, as his actions suggested, nurtured over many months. Even if he had managed to elude American intelligence from late May to early June 2013, he could not hide all the history that led to his decision to come to Hong Kong. There had to be an envelope of circumstances surrounding it, including Snowden's motivation, associates, movements, finances, and activities prior to his fleeing to Hong Kong. What was missing was not just Snowden's first eleven days in Hong Kong but the context of the alleged crime.

I first needed to find out who Edward Snowden was.

PART ONE

SNOWDEN'S ARC

I woke this morning with a new name. I had had a vision. A dream vision. A vision righteous and true. Before me I saw Gamers, Gamers shrouded in the glory of their true names.

Step forth, and assume your name in the pantheon. It's always been there, your avatar's true name. It slips through your subconscious, reveals itself under your posts, and flashed visibly in that moment of unrestrained spite; in the indulgent teabag. You've felt it, known it, recognized it.

Now realize it.

I woke this morning with a new name. That name is Wolfking.

Wolfking Awesomefox.

—EDWARD SNOWDEN, Geneva, June 12, 2008

CHAPTER 1

Tinker

It's like the boiling frog. You get exposed to a little bit of evil, a little bit of rule-breaking, a little bit of dishonesty . . . you can come to justify it.

—EDWARD SNOWDEN, Moscow, 2014

EDWARD JOSEPH SNOWDEN was born on June 21, 1983, in Elizabeth City, North Carolina. His parents were Lon Snowden and Elizabeth "Wendy" Barrett. According to their marriage records, they wed when they were both eighteen in 1979. The following year they had a daughter, Jessica.

Lon Snowden, like his father before him, served in the U.S. Coast Guard. He was stationed at its main aviation base, where his father-in-law, Edward Joseph Barrett, was an officer and rising star of the Coast Guard. While Edward Snowden was still a child, his maternal grandfather would become not only an admiral but also head of the Coast Guard's entire aviation service.

When Lon was transferred to a Coast Guard base near Baltimore in 1992, he bought a two-story house in Crofton, Maryland, a residential community very close to the NSA's headquarters building at Fort Meade. Edward, who was nine, and Jessica, who was twelve, were enrolled in local public schools in Crofton.

Jessica was a top student. After she obtained her degree at the

University of Maryland, she went on to law school, graduating with honors. Unlike his sister, Edward Snowden experienced a string of failures in his education. In 1998, after only one year of classes, he dropped out of Arundel High School; according to school records, he stopped attending classes at the age of fifteen. He later attributed his absence from school to a medical problem, mononucleosis, but according to Robert Mosier, a spokesman for Anne Arundel County public schools, there is no record of any illness. Brad Gunson, who knew Snowden before he dropped out of high school, recalled in an interview with *The Washington Post* only that he had a high-pitched voice, liked magic cards, and played fantasy video games.

Instead of completing a formal education, Snowden went his own way. Still in his teens, he became the product of a broken home. His parents were entangled in messy divorce proceedings until he was seventeen. By this time, Jessica had her own apartment. When his parents separated, Snowden's mother bought a two-bedroom condominium in Ellicott City, Maryland. She moved Edward, along with his two cats, into the condominium, while she remained in the family house awaiting its sale. According to a condominium neighbor, Joyce Kinsey, Snowden stayed home alone almost all the time. From what she could observe, he spent long hours in front of a computer screen.

At the age of eighteen, while other teens his age went to college, Snowden was still living by himself, now devoting a large part of his time to playing fantasy games on the Internet. Posting under the alias TheTrueHooHa on a website called *Ars Technica*, he showed himself to be a passionate gamer. He was especially drawn to anime, a graphically violent style of Japanese animation. These anime games had by 2002 achieved a fanatic following in both Japan and the United States. He claimed special skills at Tekken, a martial arts fighting game. He even went to anime conventions in the Washington, D.C., area. When he became a webmaster for Ryuhana Press, a website running these anime-based games, he described himself somewhat fancifully as a thirty-seven-year-old father of two children. The only truth in his description was that he was born on "the longest day of the year" (June 21).

He wrote Internet posts under his TrueHooHa alias about how he used weight lifting and intensive training to precision shape his body. He bragged to his online followers that he had reduced his "body fat percentage to between 9.5% and 10.5%" (which was less than half of the average for his age). He wrote that he wore "cool" purple sunglasses, practiced martial arts, and was a fan of Japanese cuisine. He described himself at one point, as if advertising his virtues, as having a "head of vibrant, shimmering blond hair (with volume)."

He appeared somewhat restless with his solitary life in his almost daily postings. He expressed a longing to go to Japan. "I've always dreamed of being able to 'make it' in Japan. I've taken Japanese for a year and a half," he wrote in 2002. Despite his claim of learning Japanese, there is no record of his taking any courses in Japanese. But it was perhaps part of his yearning. In pursuit of an employment opportunity in Japan, he posted, "I'd love a cushy gov job over there." Eventually, he gave up on the idea of relocating himself to Japan because, as he explained in a post, he would have to put his cats in quarantine for six months.

Snowden's father meanwhile moved to Pennsylvania with his new wife-to-be. This left Snowden with only one male family member in the area, his maternal grandfather, Admiral Barrett, who was now in the top echelon of U.S. intelligence working at the Pentagon. Barrett was there when a plane piloted by terrorists crashed into it on 9/11. He emerged unscathed.

Snowden sought to join the Special Forces through the 18X program, a U.S. Army Reserve program created in 2003 that allowed individuals who had not served in the military or completed their education to train to be a Special Forces recruit. He listed his religion on the application as Buddhist because, as he explained in a sardonic post on *Ars Technica*, "agnostic is strangely absent" from the form.

He enlisted in the army reserves on May 7, 2004, according to U.S. Army records. He reported for a ten-week basic training at Fort Benning, Georgia, which was standard for all enlistees in the infantry. In August, he began a three-week course in parachute jumping but did not complete that training. As Snowden put it in his Internet postings, he "washed out." He was discharged on September 29, 2004, ending his nineteen-week military career. Snowden would later claim on the Internet that he returned to civilian life because he had broken both legs. An army spokesman could not confirm that Snowden injured his legs or that he was in fact dropped from the program for medical reasons.

Under his TrueHooHa alias, Snowden wrote that "they [the army] held onto me until the doctors cleared me to be discharged, and then after being cleared they held onto me for another month just for shits and giggles." He attributed this treatment in the army, as he would later attribute his problems in the CIA and the NSA, to the inferior intelligence of his superiors. He wrote in his post, "Psych problems = dishonorable discharge depending on how much they hate you. Lots of alleged homos were in the hold unit, too, but they only got a general discharge at best."

If he had broken his legs, it was not evident to Joyce Kinsey, his next-door neighbor, who told me that she never saw Snowden on crutches when he returned to his mother's condominium in September 2004. Army records show that he did not receive a medical discharge. He received an "administrative discharge." Unlike a medical discharge, which is given because a soldier has sustained injuries that prevent him from performing his duties, an administrative discharge is a "morally neutral" form of separation given to a soldier when he or she is deemed for nonmedical reasons inappropriate for military service. Snowden preferred to cite a medical explanation for his severance, just as he had claimed a medical reason for dropping out of high school (and would later claim he needed medical treatment for epilepsy at the NSA).

When he returned home from Fort Benning, Georgia, he was twenty-one. He remained unemployed for several months before taking a job as a security guard at the University of Maryland's Center for Advanced Study of Language, where he was given his first security clearance. Snowden had to take a polygraph exam to get the job. According to his *Ars Technica* postings, he worked the night shift from six in the evening to six in the morning. He had higher ambitions than being a campus security guard.

He wanted to become a male model. He did not seem overly concerned about his privacy, posting pictures of himself on the Internet "mooning" for the camera. He also posted provocative modeling pictures of himself on the *Ars Technica* website. He commented on his own beefcake-style pictures, "So sexxxy it hurts" and "I like my girl-ish figure that attracts girls." He approached a model agency called Model Mayhem, which recommended a photographer. He had some concern about that photographer because he, as Snowden wrote in a post, "shoots mostly guys." Snowden said he was "a little worried he might, you know, try to pull my pants off and choke me to death with them, but he turned out to be legit and is a pretty damn good model photographer." He posted the photographs on the Internet. The lack of any paid job offers dashed Snowden's hopes for a model-ing career.

Around this time, he began dating Lindsay Mills, an extremely attractive nineteen-year-old art student at the Maryland Institute College of Art. Jonathan Mills, Lindsay's father, was an applications developer at the Oracle Corporation. According to him, Snowden met his daughter on an Internet dating site. Snowden and Mills had much in common. They both had divorced parents who gave them a great deal of latitude in conducting their personal lives. Both of them were keenly interested in perfecting their bodies through exercise and diet regimes. Mills's only paid employment over the next eight years would be as a fitness and yoga instructor in Maryland. When they first met, they both had ambitions to be models, and neither of them had inhibitions about posing provocatively for photographers. They both also had a desire to travel to exotic places, including cities in Asia. Mills had spent four months in Guilin, China, before meet-ing Snowden.

As bleak as his prospects as a high-school dropout might have seemed, Snowden had an unexpected stroke of good fortune in the spring of 2006. The CIA offered him a $66,000-a-year job as a CIA communications officer. "I don't have a degree of ANY type. In fact, I don't even have a high school diploma," Snowden boasted in May 2006 on the website *Ars Technica* under his alias. He added, with only a slight exaggeration, "I make 70K."

How did Snowden get the job? The CIA's minimum requirements in 2006 for a job in its clandestine division included a bachelor's or master's degree and a strong academic record, with a preferred GPA of 3.0 or better.

The CIA needed technical workers in 2006. But even if Snowden applied only in this capacity, which entailed a five-year employment agreement, the minimum requirement for an intelligence technology job was an associate's degree awarded by a two-year community college in electronics and communications, engineering technology, computer network systems, or electronics engineering technology. Candidates had to have had a final GPA of at least 3.0 on a 4.0 scale from a fully accredited technical school or university. Snowden, as we've seen, did not meet these standards. If a candidate lacks these qualifications, the CIA can make an exception only if he or she has at least two years' civilian or military work experience in the telecommunications and/or automated information systems field that is comparable to one of the requisite degree fields. Snowden in no way qualified in this way either.

Under extraordinary circumstances, even the minimum requirements might be waived if the applicant had a distinguished military career and an honorable discharge. Snowden, however, did not complete his military training at Fort Benning and received only an administrative discharge.

The CIA, to be sure, had needed computer-savvy recruits to service its expanding array of computer systems since 1990. By 2006, however, there was no shortage of fully qualified applicants for IT jobs who met the CIA's minimum standards. Most of them had university course records, work experience at IT companies, computer science training certificates from technical schools, and other such credentials. The CIA, like the NSA, also obtained technicians with special skills for IT jobs from outside contractors. So it had no need for employing a twenty-two-year-old dropout who did not meet its requisites. According to Tyler Drumheller, a former CIA station chief in Europe, the only plausible way that Snowden, with no qualifications, was allowed to jump the queue was that "he had some pull."

In 2006, Snowden's grandfather, who had attained the rank of rear admiral, was certainly well connected in the intelligence world. After twenty years' service in the Coast Guard, Barrett had joined an interagency task force in 1998, which included top executives from the CIA, the FBI, and the Drug Enforcement Administration. It had been set up to monitor any gaps in the U.S. embargo on Cuba, and Barrett, as one of its leaders, was in constant liaison with the

CIA. By 2004, he had joined the FBI as the section head of its aviation and special operations. In this capacity, he supervised the joint CIA-FBI interrogation of the prisoners in the Guantánamo base in Cuba, which involved him in the rendition program for terrorists.

Barrett could certainly have played a role in furthering his only grandson's employment. The CIA, however, has not disclosed any information about who, if anyone, recommended Snowden. All that is known is that in 2006 the CIA waived its minimum requirements for him.

Later Snowden pointed out from Moscow that in 2006 the federal government employed his entire family. His father was serving in the Coast Guard; his mother was an administrative clerk for the federal court in Maryland; his sister was a research director at the Federal Judicial Center; and Admiral Barrett was still a top executive at the FBI. In a sense, Snowden had entered the family business.

CHAPTER 2

Secret Agent

Sure, a whistleblower could use these [NSA computer vulner-
abilities], but so could a spy.

—EDWARD SNOWDEN, Moscow, 2014

THE SUDDEN TRANSFORMATION of Snowden in 2006 from a
night watchman on a university campus to an employee for
the CIA provided him with a powerful new identity and one much
closer to the avatars he adopted for his fantasy games. It was bur-
nished so deeply in his self-image that he cited it eight years later,
in exaggerated fashion, in Moscow. When Brian Williams, then an
NBC anchorman, began an hour-long television interview with
Snowden in 2014 by saying, "It seems to me spies probably look a
lot more like Ed Snowden and a lot less like James Bond these days,"
Snowden approvingly smiled and told him, "I was trained as a spy
in sort of the traditional sense of the word." Snowden further confirmed his interviewer's point, stating, "I lived and worked undercover overseas—pretending to work in a job that I'm not [in]—and
even being assigned a name that was not mine."

In reality, Snowden's employment at the CIA was far more prosaic. When he joined the CIA, he did not have the required experience in maintaining secret communication systems, so the CIA sent

him to its information technology school for six months to train as a communications officer, not a spy. After completing his training, he was dispatched to the CIA station in Geneva. He worked there for the next two years as one of dozens of information technologists servicing the CIA's communication channels in Switzerland. He was stationed there, according to Swiss registry records, under his own name from March 2007 to February 2009. He was identified as a U.S. State Department employee in Geneva because Switzerland does not allow any intelligence officers to operate in its country. Officially, he was attached to the permanent U.S. mission to the United Nations, which employed hundreds of U.S. government functionaries in Switzerland. It was a thin cover; the Swiss government was aware that the CIA maintained its base in Geneva and posted its employees at the U.S. mission.

Although Snowden would claim in a video he made in Hong Kong that he had served as a "senior adviser for the Central Intelligence Agency," he was merely a telecommunications support officer, or TSO in CIA parlance, which was a junior-level job at the CIA. He worked as part of a team of information technologists under the supervision of senior CIA officers, according to a former CIA officer in Geneva. The job of these TSOs was to protect the security of the CIA's computer systems through which the CIA station in Geneva sent and received its secret communications.

As far as is known, Snowden made very few friends at the eight-hundred-person mission. The only person to have publicly reported knowing him in Geneva during this period is Mavanee Anderson, a young and attractive summer intern at the U.S. mission from May to August 2007. She described befriending Snowden, who, according to her, said that he was in the CIA and also demonstrated to her his martial arts skills. She later recalled in interviews that he was "a bit" prone to brooding and voiced growing dissatisfaction with the CIA.

The job in Geneva did have its benefits, however. It provided him with a generous housing and travel allowance. In many ways, it was the "cushy government job" he had said he was seeking in his Internet posts. He rented a four-room apartment and had his girlfriend, Lindsay Mills, now twenty-one, join him there.

According to his posts on the *Ars Technica* website, he took full advantage of his compensation to live the high life. He gambled on financial developments by buying and selling options, which are contracts that allow speculators to bet on the directions of the market without buying the actual stocks, bonds, or commodities. He also bought a BMW sports car on which, he wrote, he disabled the speed control so he could exceed the legal limit. He described in his posts racing motorcycles in Italy and traveling around Germany with an Estonian rock star (whom he did not further identify). He also continued his avatar life in Internet gaming; the alias he chose for that was Wolfking Awesomefox. He also indulged in a fantasy gun sport called Airsoft, a variation of paintball, in which participants used realistic-looking pistols to splatter each other with paint.

Snowden's good fortune came to an abrupt end in 2008. He suffered a massive loss in his options speculations. He wrote in a post that he had "lost $20,000 in October [2008] alone," a sum that represented almost a third of his annual salary. He blamed the U.S. financial system, posting on *Ars Technica* that Ben Bernanke, the Federal Reserve chairman, was a "cockbag." He also bet against any further rise in the stock market index, asking a user with whom he was chatting on the Internet in December 2008 to "pray" for a collapse of stock prices. When his correspondent asked him why he wanted him to pray for a decline, Snowden responded, "Because then I'll be filthy fucking rich." But Snowden lost this bet.

Snowden lashed out at others on the Internet over these setbacks. He termed those who questioned his financial judgment "fucking retards." As with other setbacks, he blamed them on government officials in *Ars Technica* posts. Because the CIA was engaged in 2008 in highly sensitive operations to gather banking data in Switzerland— one of which Snowden later disclosed to *The Guardian*—any Internet discussion by a CIA employee of financial losses could serve as a beacon to an adversary intelligence service on the prowl for a source. If any party was looking for disgruntled U.S. employees, Snowden's Internet chatter about bad choices in gambling could have aroused its interest.

That Snowden used his TrueHooHa alias for these Internet postings would not prevent a sophisticated espionage organization from quickly uncovering his true identity. He was listed by his true name on the roster of the U.S. mission to the UN. By consulting personnel records, one would further discover that he did not actually work for the State Department. Because it was no secret that the U.S. mission in Geneva housed the CIA station for all of Switzerland, any outsider would think it probable that this brittle gambler who played the options market worked for the CIA.

Even though it cannot be precluded that Snowden was spotted in Geneva by another intelligence service, there is no evidence, at least that I know of, to suggest that he was approached by one. Nor is there reason to believe that if he had been contacted by a foreign service in 2008, he would have responded positively. Despite his indiscreet posting about his outside activities, he apparently still respected the boundaries of secrecy that had been clearly defined in the oath he had taken at the CIA. For example, after *The New York Times* published an article revealing secret American intelligence activities in Iran on January 11, 2009, Snowden railed against the newspaper on the Internet under his TrueHooHa alias. He wrote, "This shit is classified for a reason.... It's because this shit won't work if Iran knows what we are doing." He clearly recognized that revealing intelligence sources was extremely damaging. As for the *Times*, he said, "Hopefully they'll finally go bankrupt this year." When another Internet user asked him if it was unethical to release national security secrets, he answered, "YEEEEEEEEEES."

As with every CIA officer, Snowden had to undergo a two-year evaluation and take a routine polygraph test. It was then, in December 2008, that his superior at the CIA placed a "derog" in his file, the CIA's shorthand for a derogatory comment, in an unfavorable evaluation. The reason remains somewhat murky. According to a *New York Times* story by the veteran intelligence reporter Eric Schmitt, Snowden's superior had suspected that Snowden "was trying to break into classified computer files to which he was not authorized to have access." Schmitt evidently had well-placed sources in the CIA. He said that he interviewed two senior American officials who were familiar with the case. According to what they told Schmitt, the CIA superior had decided to "send Snowden home." Officially, however, according to a reply by a CIA public affairs officer to the *Times*, Snowden had not been fired or accused of attempting to "break into classified computer files to which he did not have authorized access."

A former CIA officer who had also been at the U.S. mission in Geneva explained the discrepancy to me. He said that the spin the CIA put on the story was "necessary containment." After the Snowden breach occurred in June 2013, the CIA had a problem that could, as he put it, "blow up in its face." If Snowden had been fired but allowed to keep his security clearance in 2009, the CIA's incompetence could be partly blamed for the NSA's subsequent employment of him. If he had broken into a computer to which he was not authorized, he should have been fired if not arrested.

What this spin glossed over, according to this former CIA officer, is the part about Snowden's behavior that concerned his superior. Technically, Snowden, as a CIA communications officer, was authorized to use the computer system. The problem was that Snowden had deliberately misused it by adding code to it. This code could have compromised the security of the CIA's "live system." So while what the CIA public affairs officer quoted in the *Times* story said was correct, it clouded the issue.

During his time in Geneva, Snowden had received no promotions or commendations for his work. He was threatened with a punitive investigation unless he agreed to quietly resign from the CIA. "It was not a stellar career," Drumheller, the former CIA station chief, told me in 2014.

Snowden blamed his career-ending "derog" on an "e-mail spat" with a superior. From Moscow, he wrote to James Risen of the *Times* that his superior officer ordered him not "to rock the boat." Further, he complained that the technical team at the CIA station in Geneva had "brushed him off," even though he had a legitimate grievance. When he complained about a flaw in the computer system, he said that his superior took vengeance on him. He said he added the code to the system to prove he was right. He attributed the "derog" in his file to the incompetence, blindness, and errors of his superiors. According to Snowden, he was a victim. This would not be the last time he faulted superiors for their supposed incompetence. He would later say that the NSA experts who examined the documents that he had stolen were "totally incapable."

In any case, in February 2009, Snowden not only had a career-damaging "derog" in his file but faced an internal investigation of his suspicious computer activities. According to Drumheller, such an internal investigation would not be undertaken lightly or because of an "e-mail spat." He said that such an investigation was "a big deal" involving the CIA Office of Security in Washington and possibly the FBI. It would also result in the temporary suspension of Snowden's security clearance. This left Snowden with little real choice. If he wanted to avoid that investigation, he had to resign from the CIA, which he did in February 2009. That was the end of the security investigation.

He was clearly bitter, posting on *Ars Technica* on January 10, 2009, "Obama just appointed a fucking POLITICIAN to run the CIA!" (He was referring to Leon Panetta, President Clinton's former chief of staff.) Snowden attributed the origins of his antipathy to U.S. intelligence to his 2007–9 experiences in the CIA. He later told *Vanity Fair* that the 2009 incident in the CIA convinced him that working "through the system would lead only to reprisals."

Snowden, if not yet a ticking time bomb, was certainly a disgruntled intelligence worker before he ever got to the NSA.

CHAPTER 3

Contractor

Private contractors don't clear employees. The government does.

—ADMIRAL MICHAEL MCCONNELL,
former vice-chairman, Booz Allen Hamilton

S NOWDEN, aged twenty-five, returned from Europe and moved into his mother's condo. Not only was he unemployed now, having resigned from the CIA, but his financial state had been hurt by the huge losses he had suffered playing the options market in Geneva and by the fact that he did not qualify for any CIA benefits. His vision of himself as a secret agent, the unstoppable Wolfking Awesomefox, might have also suffered. According to the narrative he later supplied to *The Guardian*, he had become deeply concerned about the immoral way in which the CIA conducted its intelligence operations in Switzerland.

"Much of what I saw in Geneva really disillusioned me about how my government functions and what its impact is in the world. I realized that I was part of something that was doing far more harm than good," Snowden told *The Guardian*. By way of example, he said he learned that the CIA had gotten a Swiss banker drunk enough to be arrested when he drove so the CIA could compromise him. Snowden, who did not drink himself, was appalled at this ploy. Despite his growing antagonism toward the U.S. government, he had not given up on, if not becoming a secret agent, working in the netherworld of secret intelligence.

There was still a back door through which he could reenter the spy world. Private corporations hired civilian technicians to work for spy agencies as independent contractors. By 2009, the CIA, the NSA, and other U.S. intelligence services had outsourced much of the job of maintaining and upgrading their computer systems to these private companies. They supplied the NSA with most of its system administrators and other information technology workers. This arrangement allowed the NSA to effectively bypass budget limits and other restrictions limiting how many NSA technicians it could recruit. Instead of being on the NSA's own payroll, these people nominally worked for, and received their paychecks from, private employers. In fact, many of these outside contractors worked full-time for the NSA.

Snowden applied in April 2009 to one of these private companies, a subsidiary of the Dell computer company. To diversify out of manufacturing computers, Dell had recently gone into the business of managing government computer systems for the NSA and other intelligence services. As a leading specialist in the field of corporate cyber security, Dell had no problem obtaining sizable contracts from the NSA's Technology Directorate. In 2008, the NSA had in effect outsourced to Dell the task of reorganizing the backup systems at its regional bases. Dell had to find thousands of independent contractors to work at these bases. In 2009, it was seeking to fill positions at the NSA's regional base in Japan, and Snowden applied. Relocating would be no issue for him because he had a longtime interest in going to Japan.

He had little problem obtaining the job. He had a single compelling qualification: like all other CIA officers, he had been given a top secret clearance. For an outside contractor such as Dell, such a security clearance was pure gold. If a potential recruit lacked it, Dell needed to wait for a time-consuming background check that would have to be conducted before it could deploy him or her at the NSA. If a recruit already had the clearance, as Snowden did, he could begin working immediately.

Snowden still had his security clearance, despite his highly problematic exit from the CIA, because the agency had instituted a policy a few years earlier that allowed voluntarily retiring CIA officers to keep their clearance for two years after they left. This "free pass," as one former CIA officer called the two-year grace period, had been intended to make it easier for retiring officers to find jobs in parts of the defense industry. This accommodation, in turn, made it easier for the CIA to downsize to meet its budget.

Not only did Snowden retain his clearance, but unlike when he had applied for his job at the CIA in 2006, he could now list on his résumé two years of experience in information technology and cyber security at the CIA. Dell could check only a single fact: that Snowden was employed at the CIA between 2006 and 2009. His CIA file, which contained the "derog," was not available to Dell or any other private company because of government privacy regulations. Even though the CIA had "security concerns" about Snowden, it could not convey them to either Dell or the NSA without violating the privacy rules. "So the guy with whom the CIA had concerns left the Agency and joined the ranks of the many contractors working in the intelligence community [IC] before CIA could inform the rest of the IC about its worries," Michael Morell, then CIA deputy director, explained. "He even got a pay raise."

Obviously, this was a glitch in the security system. As a result of it, though, Snowden entered the secret world of the NSA only five months after being forced out of the CIA.

For the next forty-five months, Dell assigned him various IT tasks at the NSA. In June 2009, he was sent to Japan to work in the NSA complex at the U.S. Yokota Air Base, which is about two hours by car from downtown Tokyo. He moved into a small one-bedroom apartment in Fussa, just outside the sprawling base.

His initial job for Dell was teaching cyber security to army and air force personnel. In this capacity, he instructed U.S. military officers stationed at the base in how to shield their computers from hackers. Such security training had been required for military personnel dealing with classified material after several successful break-ins to U.S. military networks by China, Russia, and other adversary nations. It was not a challenging or interesting job.

But Snowden found diversions in Japan. In July 2009, Lindsay Mills joined him there. She had become an amateur photographer, specializing in arty self-portraits. She also saw herself as a global tourist, writing in her blog after arriving in Japan that she had traveled to seventeen countries. Like Snowden, she also deemed herself, tongue in cheek, a "super hero." In this sense, her Internet avatar was a match for Snowden's Wolfking Awesomefox.

In Japan, Mills and Snowden spent time with another American couple, Jennie and Joseph Chamberlin, who also worked at the Yokota base. Jennie, a sergeant in the public affairs section of the U.S. Air Force, had been at art college with Mills and called herself in her blog the Little Red Ninja. Joseph Chamberlin was a decorated U.S. Navy pilot who now flew highly sensitive intelligence-gathering missions from the Yokota base. Jennie described Lindsay in her blog as her "super-model friend." The two couples also went on expeditions in Japan together. As far as is known, the Chamberlins were the only Americans at the base with whom Snowden socialized. On August 17, 2009, the foursome attempted to walk up Mount Fuji, but they got lost en route and wound up in the Mount Fuji gift shop. Jennie described the misadventure in her blog: "Our adventure started off a little rocky with our attempts to find the interstate. Alas, our iconic mountain was obscured by cloud. A short stop at the Mt. Fuji combination soba noodle stand/gift shop was enough to whet our appetite for the further exploration that is to come." Photographs taken that day show Snowden wearing Hawaiian shorts and a black tank top emblazoned with an eagle and the letters USA. They also show Mills wearing safari shorts, a brown sweater, and what appears to be an engagement ring. "Ed was looking rather red-necky," Lindsay commented on one photograph. Snowden described her, in turn, as "nerdy." They never made it to the top of Mount Fuji.

Snowden also sought to advance himself by getting credit toward a college certificate by enrolling in a summer online course at the University of Maryland's Asia program, which had a regional campus on the Yokota base. Known as UMUC, it had a contract with the government to provide military personnel with such educational opportunities. Snowden would later claim that he was taking courses for a graduate degree in computer sciences, but William

Stevens, the assistant registrar of UMUC, who I spoke to at the base in 2016, told me that the program in 2009 did not provide graduate courses in computer sciences. According to the program's record, while Snowden had enrolled as a student in the summer of 2009, he received neither any credits nor a certificate.

In October 2009, Dell assigned Snowden a job in which he had direct access to the NSA's computers. He was now a system administrator, which is essentially a tech-savvy repairman. Dell was working on a backup system code-named EPICSHELTER. For this contract, Dell was transferring large chunks of data from the NSA's main computers in Maryland to backup drives in Japan so that the system could be quickly restored if there was a communications interruption. Because most of the classified data was in its encrypted form, it had little value to any outside party. Snowden's job was to maintain the proper functioning of computers, but as a system administrator he also had privileges to call up unencrypted files. He sat in front of a computer screen all day looking for any problems in the transferring of files to backup servers.

The work was highly repetitive and exceedingly dull. Snowden found time to search for anomalies in the system, and he claimed to have spotted a major flaw in the security system in late 2009. He discovered that a rogue system administrator in Japan could steal secret data without anyone else's realizing that it had been stolen. Snowden brought that to the attention of his superiors, as he later said.

The emergence of a rogue system administrator was not that far-fetched in 2009. Hacktivists such as Julian Assange had adopted the battle cry "Sysadmins of the world, unite." Instead of asking them to "throw off their chains," as Marx did, he asked them to send classified documents about secret government activity to the WikiLeaks site. Snowden, as a "sys admin," was aware he had the power to do so. He recalled in Moscow in 2014, "I actually recommended they [the NSA] move to two-man control for administrative access back in 2009." To make his point even clearer, he added, "A whistleblower could use these things, but so could a spy." Not without irony, Snowden became that rogue system administrator some three years later. In fact, he later used the very vulnerability he pointed out to steal NSA documents at Dell.

In September 2009, still on the Dell payroll, Snowden made a ten-day trip to India. He later said he was on an official visit "working at the US embassy." Hotel records show that he arrived at the Hyatt Regency in New Delhi on September 2 from Japan and at 3:30 p.m. on September 3 checked into the Koenig Inn, an annex to Koenig Solutions, a school that gave crash courses on programming and computer hacking. According to Rohit Aggarwal, head of the school, Snowden stayed there until September 10 while taking classes with a private instructor. It cost $2,000 in tuition and fees, which Snowden prepaid from Japan with his personal credit card. Even though Snowden later said he only took courses in "programming," the school's records show that during that week he took intensive courses in sophisticated hacking techniques. The course was titled "Ethical Hacking," but that was a euphemism for teaching the techniques of illicit hacking. The course provided tutoring on hackers' tools such as SpyEye and Zeus, which are used to circumvent security procedures. It also demonstrated how these hacking tools could be customized by criminals and spies to break into files, plant surveillance programs, impersonate system administrators, assume the privileges of system administrators in a network, and capture the passwords of others. On September 11, Snowden, according to hotel records, left India for Japan. While the stated purpose of the hacking training was to allow security consultants to detect intruders, it also prepared Snowden to be, if he chose to be, an intruder in the NSA system.

One problem with working as a contractor is that the standard two-year contracts are not necessarily renewed. Nor is there much possibility for advancement for IT workers. As one contractor told me, "It is a dead-end job with great pay." In the fall of 2010, Snowden's contract in Japan with Dell was nearing an end.

Dell offered Snowden, and he accepted, a new position in the United States. He rented a modest suburban house shaded by a sakura cherry tree in a suburb of Annapolis, Maryland. Lindsay Mills meanwhile was attending a two-week fitness training course at a retreat that qualified her to be a yoga instructor. She had been living on and off with Snowden during the previous two years abroad, including while he worked at the CIA in Switzerland and the NSA in Japan, and now she moved in with Snowden again. The twenty-five-year-old Mills posted on Instagram, "Finally in our first US place together." She also put pictures online of him in bed with her, affectionately referring to him in her posts as a "computer crusader."

He worked on problem solving for corporate clients at Dell headquarters in Annapolis. In preparation for his new corporate role, Snowden shaved off his facial hair and, with Lindsay's help, bought a Ralph Lauren suit. His corporate clients were assisting the NSA, the CIA, and the DIA. Consequently, Snowden dealt with a wide range of intelligence officers and gave presentations on the vulnerabilities in computer security at the DIA-sponsored Joint Counterintelligence seminar. In February 2011, he attended a black tie Valentine's Day gala sponsored by corporate members of the Armed Forces Communication and Electronics Association. The guest speaker was Michael Hayden, who had headed the CIA when Snowden was abruptly forced out two years earlier. Nevertheless, Snowden joined the queue to have his photo taken with the former director, a perk of the charity event.

These dealings in no way mitigated his resentment of the intelligence establishment. What began at the CIA in 2009 as objections to what he saw as the incompetence of his superiors grew into well-articulated disapproval of the way the U.S. government conducted its intelligence. He found NSA surveillance particularly worrisome, later telling *The Guardian*, "They [the NSA] are intent on making every conversation and every form of behavior in the world known to them." He claimed after defecting to Moscow that he had voiced his concerns about what he considered illicit surveillance to ten NSA officials, "none of whom took any action to address them." The NSA can find no record of these complaints, but if Snowden had indeed complained to these officials while working for Dell, his superiors at Dell either didn't notice or didn't care that they had a very disgruntled employee on their hands.

Snowden also made no secret on the Internet of his anger at the U.S. government and the corporations that served it. He railed on the *Ars Technica* site against the complicity of private corporations, such as Dell, that assisted the NSA. In his online posts in 2010, Snowden expressed loathing for the assistance that corporate America was providing the intelligence community. "It really concerns me how little this sort of corporate behavior bothers those outside of technology circles," he wrote under his TrueHooHa alias. He said he feared that America was already on "a slippery slope," and he suggested, perhaps adumbrating his own later actions, that this corporate assistance to U.S. intelligence "was entirely within our control to stop."

What the "computer crusader" expressed in these angry Internet postings was an almost obsessive concern over individuals' freely submitting to government authority. "Society really seems to have developed an unquestioning obedience towards spooky types," he wrote on *Ars Technica* without mentioning that he himself worked for a corporation that assisted spy agencies. He asked rhetorically on this public forum whether the sinister slide toward a surveillance state "sneaked in undetected because of pervasive government secrecy."

The outright contempt he expressed toward this "government secrecy" did not prevent him from seeking even more secret work at Dell for the intelligence services. In February 2011, after his CIA security clearance ran out, he applied to renew it. The new clearance now required a new background check and filling out the government's 127-page Standard Form 86.

Since 1996, background investigations for the NSA, like much of the computer work at the NSA, had been outsourced to a private company. It had proceeded from the effort of the Clinton administration to cut the size of government by privatizing tasks that could be more efficiently done by for-profit companies. U.S. Investigations Services, or USIS, as it is now called, which won the contract for background checks, was initially owned by the private equity fund Carlyle Group, which later sold it to another financial group, Providence Equity Partners. For the private equity and hedge funds, profits were the measure of success. To increase its profits from the contract with the NSA, USIS had to move more quickly in concluding background checks because it did not get paid more for extensive investigation. In 2006, the government learned these background checks were often prematurely ended. In Snowden's case, because the CIA did not share its files with a private concern, USIS did not have access to Snowden's CIA files, and it therefore did not learn about the threatened security investigation. Nor did it learn from the Internet, where he always employed an alias, that he was a disgruntled employee. So Snowden's new clearance was approved in the summer of 2011, allowing him to continue working for Dell on secret intelligence projects.

Meanwhile, in August 2011, Mills began her own blog titled *L's Journey*. In it, she described herself as "a world-traveling pole-dancing super hero." Many of her posted pictures were provocative poses of herself in her underwear and various states of undress. She wrote, "I've always wanted to be splashed on the cover of magazines, with my best air-brushed look." Her wish would be gratified two years later in a way she likely did not anticipate.

For his part, Snowden seemed happy to encourage her fantasy about being a superhero. He even gave her a *Star Trek*–inspired head visor. Despite all the concerns he voiced about privacy, he did not seem to mind her provocative posts. On the contrary, he took photographs of her, telling her at one point that her photographs were not "sexy" enough.

Snowden was soon offered a new position by Dell at the NSA's Kunia regional base in Hawaii. Dell, which was in the process of expanding its government consulting business, wanted him to be a system administrator on the NSA's backup system. The NSA needed this system before it could upgrade new security protocols that would audit suspicious activity in real time. In Hawaii, as in Japan, system administrators still worked alone. Snowden knew from his experience in Japan that this solo work in an unaudited workplace provided an opportunity for a system administrator to steal documents. So he might also have realized that as a solo system administrator in Hawaii, he would have this opportunity. Whether this was on his mind or not, on March 15, 2012, he accepted this offer. Dell agreed to pay all his relocation expenses and provide him with a housing allowance.

He found a 1,559-square-foot house in Oahu, located at 94-1044

Eleu Street in the middle-class suburb of Waipahu. It was part of the Royal Kunia development, which contained three hundred similar-looking homes. According to Albi Matco, the manager of the community association for the development, many of the residents worked at military facilities in the area. The corner house Snowden rented was comfortable enough, with three bedrooms, a walk-in closet, a living room with a high ceiling, and a single-car garage, but in no way lavish. It did not even have a backyard. He moved in on April 2, 2012, which entailed a brief separation from his girlfriend, Mills, who had committed herself to attending a girlfriend's wedding the following month. After he left for his new assignment, she wrote on Instagram, "Sex toy party and then saying goodbye to my man— well not goodbye so much as see you in two months."

CHAPTER 4

Thief

We begin by coveting what we see every day.

—HANNIBAL LECTER, *The Silence of the Lambs*

IN HAWAII IN 2012, Snowden was living a very comfortable life. He was earning just over $120,000 a year from Dell. His housing allowance covered the rent and the lease on his car. He worked five days a week at the NSA base. The commute, as I timed it, took only ten minutes. Driving past a sign marked "Restricted Area: Keep Out," and the security booth where NSA guards checked his credentials, he left his car in the outdoor lot for the Kunia Regional Security Operations Center. (When I drove into the base in 2016, I was detained nearly two hours at the security booth before being turned back.)

Snowden worked in a three-story reinforced concrete building called "the tunnel," even though it was above the ground. It had been built during World War II to serve as an aircraft assembly plant. During the war, it was entirely covered with earth and shrubbery to proof it against Japanese bomber attacks. In 1980, the NSA converted it to its regional base in Hawaii for its intelligence gathering. Its lack of windows and the dirt covering gave it the appearance, when I viewed it in 2016, of an oblong-shaped anthill. Workers, both military and civilian, entered through an exterior staircase in the center of the mound. Snowden said in describing the atmosphere, "You're in a vaulted space. Everybody has sort of similar clearances, everybody knows everybody. It's a small world." He said that to relieve the tediousness of the work, every two months or so his fellow workers would circulate a picture of a naked person that showed up on their screens as part of the NSA's surveillance of foreign suspects. He explained, "You've got young enlisted guys, 18 to 22 years old [who have] suddenly been thrust into a position of extraordinary responsibility where they now have access to all of your private records. In the course of their daily work they stumble across . . . an intimate nude photo of someone in a sexually compromising position."

He knew that copying any files, including photographs, was a violation of NSA rules. But he did not report this illicit activity to the NSA, even though he later claimed that it occurred regularly. He joked in his Moscow interview with *The Guardian* that some of the nudes were "extremely attractive" and that viewing them was, as he put it, "the fringe benefits of surveillance positions."

Snowden identified with the Libertarian Party, and at the NSA he made no effort to conceal his political support of its causes. He became an active partisan of Congressman Ron Paul, the leading figure in the party in 2012. "He's so dreamy," Snowden posted on the *Ars Technica* site in March 2009 (just after he registered to vote in North Carolina, though he no longer lived there). Paul was running in the 2012 Republican presidential primaries, and Snowden made a contribution of $500 to his election committee. Snowden's attraction to Paul's libertarian ideology was not that surprising. At the core of Paul's worldview was a deep hostility to the intrusion of the government into private lives. Snowden shared this hostility, as was clear from his Internet postings. Like other Libertarians, Snowden believed that citizens should not be "shackled" by federal law. He later addressed from Moscow via an Internet hookup a libertarian gathering at which Ron Paul also spoke. "Law is a lot like medicine," he said. "When you have too much it can be fatal." Like Paul, Snowden ardently opposed any form of gun control, as did Lindsay Mills in her online postings.

Like other Libertarians, Snowden, a contractor for the government, saw the government as an adversary. "The [American] government," he later said, "assumed upon itself, in secret, new executive powers without any public awareness or any public consent and used them against the citizenry of its own country to increase its own power, to increase its own awareness." Most relevant to his future activities at the NSA, Snowden wholeheartedly agreed with Paul's position on the dangers inherent in government surveillance of U.S. citizens. Paul described the CIA, the organization that had forced Snowden out, as nothing short of a "secret government" and said that "in a true Republic, there is no place for an organization like the CIA." He also railed against NSA surveillance.

As is clear from Snowden's Internet postings, he, like Ron Paul, had doubts about the competence of the intelligence agencies of the U.S. government. Snowden's own disillusionment about the government might have begun with his rejection and perceived mistreatment by the Special Forces of the U.S. Army. It was almost certainly reinforced by his ouster from the CIA. He later told *The Guardian* that he was disillusioned as early as 2007 when he learned about the CIA's methods in compromising Swiss citizens. His critical view of the U.S. government only hardened during the years he worked at the NSA. He described his NSA superiors as "grossly incompetent," as he later explained to a journalist from *Wired* magazine in Moscow. At the NSA, he said employees were kept in line by "fear and a false image of patriotism." He said that he saw his fellow workers cowed into "obedience to authority" and his superiors induced to break the law. He became particularly concerned with what he called the "secret powers" of the NSA. He saw them as "tremendously dangerous." By this time, Snowden was fully aware that the NSA conducted domestic surveillance because he had used his privileges as a system administrator in 2012 to read the NSA inspector general's report on a 2009 surveillance program.

Nevertheless, Snowden continued to work at the NSA, where he was, as he put it, "making a ton of money." Mills joined him in his "paradise" in June 2012, shortly before his twenty-ninth birthday. Just before leaving Annapolis for Hawaii, Mills posted a seminude picture of herself on her blog, *L's Journey*. In it, her face was covered with a blanket. The caption under it read, "Trying to avoid the changes coming my way." In Honolulu, she found "E.," as she called Snowden in her blog, "elusive." She found that he preferred to stay at home and avoided meeting other people to the point that her friends "were not quite sure that E. existed." Lindsay's fellow performers in the Waikiki Acrobatic Troupe told me in 2016 that they rarely, if ever, saw Snowden at the practice sessions. Andrew Towl, a juggler with the group, did briefly meet Snowden once. It was on a hike with Lindsay in Oahu. Towl said he asked Snowden what he was doing in Hawaii and Snowden answered tersely, "I work with computers," and continued walking. Even though Mills had dated Snowden for eight years, most of her other friends, except for Jennie and Joe Chamberlin in Japan, had not met him. Next door neighbors I spoke to caught brief glimpses of him entering or leaving his house but did not engage him in a conversation as Snowden tended to avoid eye contact. If he had other social interactions in Hawaii, no one he met came forward and spoke of meeting him, even after he became world famous.

Two days after his twenty-ninth birthday dinner on June 21, Mills described him playfully as a "goof." She wrote in her blog, "The universe is telling me something and I'm pretty sure it's saying get out, Fuck you Hawaii." In early July, she summed up her shaky situation with Snowden in another blog, writing, "I moved to Hawaii to continue my relationship with E. [but] it has been an emotional roller coaster since I stepped off the plane." She diverted herself by organizing a pole-dancing studio in the four-hundred-square-foot garage of the house. She also found her own friends in physical fitness and dance groups. She joined a New Age yoga studio called Physical Phatness, as well as a local acrobatic performance group, and, on Friday nights, pole danced at the Mercury lounge in downtown Honolulu. Unlike Snowden, she enjoyed socializing, writing in her blog, "We lovingly crammed a large group into a small corner of a delicious Japanese restaurant and filled our bellies with sushi, tempura, and good conversation."

That same July, Snowden had other things on his mind, including an attempt to advance himself. Although his position at Dell as a system administrator was a well-compensated one, especially for a twenty-nine-year-old with no formal education, it carried little prestige. He sat from 9:00 a.m. to 5:00 p.m. in a windowless room watching a bank of monitors in the so-called tunnel. Many of those who worked with him were, as he described them, "eighteen year old soldiers." Presumably, they had little interest in discussing with him the weightier issues of the world. Working as an outside contractor was also a dead-end job that hardly matched the vision he had of himself in his Internet postings. In real life, in a cubicle in the NSA, he was decidedly not the Wolfking Awesomefox heroic image he had of himself in his dream vision.

Snowden now decided to apply for a position in the NSA itself. He apparently believed that if he scored high enough on its entrance exam, the NSA would invite him to join it as a Senior Executive Service officer, or SES, which was the civilian equivalent in rank and pay to a flag officer in the U.S. armed forces. "I'm still amazed that a twenty-eight-year-old thought he could get an SES position," a civilian contractor working for the NSA during the same period told me, "Snowden had a very overinflated view of his self-worth." To enhance his chances of getting the SES job, Snowden in the summer of 2012 illicitly hacked into the NSA's administrative files and stole the answers to the NSA exam. As the NSA's subsequent postmortem would determine, it was the first known document that Snowden took without authorization at the NSA.

It was not the first time, however, that he had used his hacking skills to attempt to advance himself. At the CIA in 2009, as he later said in Moscow, he had added text to his annual CIA evaluation in what he termed "a non-malicious way" to prove a point. His CIA superior took a much darker view of that incident when the hack was detected, calling for an investigation. It was the threat of that investigation that, it will be recalled, in effect ended Snowden's CIA career. At the NSA, his intrusion was not detected for almost a year. "He stole the [NSA] test with the answers, and he took the test and he aced it," the former NSA director Michael McConnell recounted in a 2013 interview. "He then walked into the NSA and said you should hire me because I am this good on the test."

The reason why he attempted to gain entry into the upper ranks of the NSA in the late summer of 2012 is less clear. If his Internet posting and libertarian riffs are an indication of his state of mind then, he was hostile to the surveillance activities of the NSA. If so, it made little sense that he would seek a permanent career there. If this is considered in light of the career move he made six months later (in March 2013), which, as he himself admits, was for the express purpose of getting at tightly held documents stored on computers that were not available to him in his job at Dell, then he might have been seeking wider access in 2012 for a more nefarious purpose than an NSA job.

In any case, despite the near-perfect scores, the NSA did not offer him a Senior Executive Service job. "It was totally unrealistic for Snowden to expect to get an SES position," a former senior NSA officer told me. Snowden's ambitions might have been disappointed in this instance, but it did not prevent him from later claiming that he had been a senior adviser to the CIA and also a senior adviser to the Defense Intelligence Agency.

Instead of an SES position, the NSA offered him a lowly G-13 job as an information technology worker, which was not an improvement on his job at Dell. He took this slight as evidence of the NSA's incompetence, subsequently joking to a reporter in Moscow that his ability to steal the test answers should have been seen as a qualification for the NSA job. In September 2012, he turned down the NSA offer. If he was to advance himself now, he had to find a new way.

CHAPTER 5

Crossing the Rubicon

What I came to feel is that a regime that is described as a national
security agency has stopped representing the public interest and
has instead begun to protect and promote state security interests.

—EDWARD SNOWDEN, Moscow, 2014

SOON AFTER Snowden failed to get an SES job at the NSA in September 2012, he intensified his rogue activities. As we've seen,
part of Snowden's job as a system administrator under contract to
Dell was transferring files held at Fort Meade to backup computers
in Hawaii. He "was moving copies of that data there for them," said
Deputy Director Ledgett, "which was perfect cover for stealing the
[NSA] data" through the fall and winter of 2012. The security measures at the Hawaii base presented no obstacles to him because, as
a system administrator, he had privileges that allowed him to copy
documents that had not been encrypted. Indeed, it was part of the
process of building the backup system. The flaw he had pointed to
in Japan, in which system administrators working solo could safely
steal files, also existed in Hawaii, as we know. This time, however,
instead of bringing it to the attention of the NSA, he used it to steal
files.

Snowden could be confident that his thefts of documents would
go undetected. Real-time auditing of the movement of documents,

which was done at NSA headquarters in Fort Meade and most of the NSA's regional facilities, had not yet been installed at the Hawaii base, because a lack of bandwidth prevented the safe upgrading of the software. This auditing software was scheduled to be installed after the backup system was completed in 2013. The Kunia base was one of the last NSA bases that did not monitor suspicious transfers of files on a real-time basis. Snowden was aware of this deficiency; he later pointed out in his interview in *Wired* that the NSA base where he worked did not have an "audit" mechanism. This security gap allowed Snowden, using his system administrator's credentials, to copy classified data to a thumb drive without anyone's being able to trace the copied data back to him. According to the NSA's subsequent damage assessment, he stole many thousands of pages while working for Dell in 2012 before he contacted journalists. Ledgett subsequently reported that the NSA analysis of the fifty-eight thousand documents that were given by Snowden to journalists in June 2013 showed that most of them were taken while he was still working at Dell.

This theft was made even more serious by the interconnection of NSA computers with those of other intelligence agencies. Prior to the 9/11 attacks in 2001, "stovepiping" had protected NSA data on its computers from networks used by other intelligence services. After the 9/11 Commission concluded that part of the reason U.S. intelligence agencies were unable to "connect the dots" in advance of the attack was related to this practice, the NSA stripped away a large part of its stovepiping. As a result, the NSANet, which Snowden had access to at Dell in 2012, became a shared network with "common access points," as the former NSA director Michael Hayden described them to me, which made them the equivalent of "reading rooms" in a library. They served as a means for NSA workers to exchange ideas about the problems they were encountering on various projects for the intelligence community. In maintaining them, system administrators, or "system admins," like Snowden, acted as the "librarians." If a system administrator copied data from this network, no one knew.

For Snowden, the NSANet, which included CIA and Defense Department documents, provided a rich hunting ground in the fall and winter of 2012. Many of the documents he took off the NSANet revealed operations not only of the NSA but also of the CIA and the Pentagon. By taking them, he had come to a Rubicon from which there would be no return. He later explained in an e-mail to *Vanity Fair* from Moscow, "I crossed that line."

As far as is known, Snowden was not sharing documents with any other party prior to May 2013. He was not even yet in contact with Poitras, Greenwald, or any other journalists. Presumably, Snowden was collecting them on drives—despite the risks that possessing such a collection of secrets might entail—for some future use.

Why would Snowden jeopardize his career and, if caught, his freedom by undertaking this illicit enterprise? He might by now have had strong ideological objections to the NSA's global surveillance. As he said later in Moscow, "We're subverting our security standards for the sake of surveillance." Ordinarily, though, even ideologically opposed employees don't steal state secrets and risk imprisonment. If they are disgruntled, they seek employment elsewhere. Certainly, Snowden, with his three years' experience working for Dell, would have little problem finding a job as an IT worker in the booming civilian sector of computer technology. Instead, he sought to widen his access to NSA documents. This behavior suggests that he might have had another agenda. One possible clue to it is the first document he took: the NSA exam. The answers to the questions in it represented to him a form of tactical power. Those answers could empower him to obtain a more important job in the NSA itself that would allow him to burrow deeper into the executive structure of the agency. Holding such a job would unlock the door to documents containing the NSA's sources stored in areas not available to Dell contractors like himself.

His later actions demonstrated that he equated the possession of such secrets with personal power. For example, after he arrived in Moscow in 2013, he bragged to James Risen of the *Times* that he had access to secrets that gave him great leverage over the NSA. He told him specifically his access to "full lists" of the NSA's agents and operations in adversary countries could, if revealed, close down the NSA's capabilities to gather information in them.

Such a fascination with the power of government-held secrets has always been a core concern of radical Libertarians. In his 1956 book, *The Torment of Secrecy: The Background and Consequences of American Security Policies*, the sociologist Edward Shils brilliantly dissects the fascination with secrecy among individuals who fear that government agencies will use covert machinations against them. In Shils's concept, this counterculture is "tormented" by the government's possession of knowledge unavailable to them. Members of this culture tend to believe that the agencies that hold these secrets, such as the FBI, the CIA, and the NSA, can control their lives; they also believe that obtaining such secrets will give individuals power over government.

Snowden himself was concerned with a coming "dark future," which he later described as follows: "[The elites] know everything about us and we know nothing about them—because they are secret, they are privileged, and they are a separate class . . . the elite class, the political class, the resource class—we don't know where they live, we don't know what they do, we don't know who their friends are. They have the ability to know all that about us. This is the direction of the future but I think there are changing possibilities in this."

To change the "dark future," someone would have to know the secrets of the "elites." Snowden saw himself as one of the few individuals in a position to seize state secrets from those elites. He had a SCI (sensitive compartmented information) clearance, a pass into an NSA regional base, and the privileges of a system administrator. This position allowed him to steal state secrets and whatever power that went with them. And if he moved to a position that gave him greater access, he would, in this view, amass even greater power.

Whatever his actual agenda in 2012, we know that he tested possible reactions to a leak exposing NSA surveillance in the United States. He asked fellow workers at the NSA base in 2012, according to his own account, "What do you think the public would do if this [secret data] was on the front page?" He asked this question at a time when a large number of State Department and U.S. Army classified documents had been posted on Julian Assange's WikiLeaks website. These WikiLeaks revelations made, as Snowden knew they would, front-page headlines. His "question" was only rhetorical. No covert NSA document had ever been published in the press as of 2012. One reason why NSA documents remained secrets, as all intelligence workers at Dell were told when they signed their oath to protect NSA secrets, was that the unauthorized release of communications intelligence documents would violate U.S. espionage laws. Even so, there was no shortage of activists overseas, such as Assange, who would be willing to publish NSA documents revealing its global surveillance activities. Cyberpunks, as these activists called themselves, tended to be hostile to the NSA because they believed (correctly) that it monitored their activities on the Internet. This anti-NSA view was well represented at the Chaos Computer Club convention in Berlin in 2012. In addressing these cyberpunks, Assange and his followers at WikiLeaks declared that the main enemy in cyberspace was the NSA. The NSA documents Snowden had taken were far more explosive than anything Assange had posted to date because they contained NSA intelligence source material.

In the late fall of 2012, Snowden further tested his newly found powers. Using an alias, he reached out to some of the leading hacktivists. It opened a door for him to the darker side of cyberspace.

aimed at paralyzing companies, including PayPal and MasterCard, that refused to process donations for WikiLeaks, which these Anons believed were stifling the freedom of the Internet. Because hacktivists often use illicit means to redress their grievances, such as denial-of-service attacks, theft of passwords, and hacking into computers, they must conceal their true identities to avoid the retribution of the FBI and other law enforcement agencies. This requires them to operate on the dark side of cyberspace, which has become known as the dark net. Fortunately for hacktivists, the dark net is accessible to anyone.

It is a place frequented by those who want to avoid laws, regulations, and government surveillance. Its denizens include cyber saboteurs, industrial spies, purveyors of illegal contraband, spammers, pranksters, identity thieves, video pirates, bullies, slanderers, drug dealers, child pornographers, money launderers, contract killers, inside traders, anarchists, terrorists, and the intelligence services of many countries.

Sue Halpern, writing about it in *The New York Review of Books*, noted, "My own forays to the dark Net include visits to sites offering counterfeit drivers' licenses, methamphetamine, a template for a US twenty-dollar bill, files to make a 3D-printed gun, and books describing how to receive illegal goods in the mail without getting caught. There were, too, links to rape and child abuse videos."

To operate effectively on the dark net, one often needs a mask of anonymity. But it is not easy to completely hide one's tracks in cyberspace. The way that the Internet ordinarily works is that whenever an individual sends e-mails or instant messages or visits a website, his or her identity can be referenced by the IP address assigned to him or her by the Internet service provider. If dark net users' IP addresses are discoverable, they obviously cannot remain anonymous. So, to evade this built-in Internet transparency, dark side users have come to rely on ingenious software to hide their IP addresses. The most commonly used software for this purpose is Tor, which was first called the Onion Router, because it moves IP addresses through multiple layers. Tor software hides the IP address by routing messages through a network of Tor-enabled relay stations, called nodes. Each node further obscures the user's IP, even from the next node in the network. This scrambling allows messages to exit the chain of Tor nodes without an easily discoverable IP. By doing so, it "anomizes" each user of the dark side.

Because of the anonymity it provides, Tor became the software of choice for individuals and organizations who wanted to hide their identities. For example, Tor software made possible Silk Road, which acted as an exchange for drug dealers, assassins, safecrackers, and prostitutes until it was closed down by the FBI in 2013. It was created by Ross Ulbricht, a Libertarian who wore a Ron Paul T-shirt, as a website where "people could buy anything anonymously, with no trail whatsoever that led back to them." (Ulbricht received a life sentence for running this criminal enterprise in May 2015.)

Tor software was also employed by Private Bradley Manning (now Chelsea Manning) to transfer some fifty thousand diplomatic cables and military reports from his laptop to Assange's WikiLeaks website. Eventually, Manning was identified by a fellow hacker, convicted by a military court for violations of the Espionage Act, and sentenced to thirty-five years in prison. Tor enabled WikiLeaks to publish other secret data, such as material acquired in the theft of Sony's files, allegedly by the North Korean intelligence service, in 2015. It was the means for guaranteeing anonymity to the IT workers who responded to Assange's by now famous clarion call to unite. It allowed system administrators who opposed the "surveillance state," as well as other disgruntled employees of government agencies or corporations, to send documents they copied to the WikiLeaks website without revealing their IP addresses.

Because WikiLeaks did not know the identity of its sources, it could not be legally compelled to reveal them. "Tor's importance to WikiLeaks cannot be overstated," Assange said in an interview with *Rolling Stone* in 2012. Indeed, without the anonymity provided by its Tor software, WikiLeaks could not have easily entered into a document-sharing arrangement with major newspapers, including *The Guardian, The New York Times, Der Spiegel, Le Monde,* and *El País.* Through the magic of Tor, these newspapers simply attribute their sources to WikiLeaks, which, in turn, made Assange a major force in international journalism.

Ironically, Tor was a creation of U.S. intelligence. In the early years of the twenty-first century, the U.S. Naval Research Laboratory and the Defense Advanced Research Projects Agency developed it to allow American intelligence operatives to cloak their movements on the Internet. They could anonymously manipulate websites operated by Islamic radicals, for example, and create their own Trojan horse sites to lure would-be terrorists and spies. As it turned out, that use of Tor software had a conceptual flaw. If U.S. intelligence services used it, the targets could figure out that anyone visiting a site without an IP address was using Tor software to hide it. If Tor was exclusively used by U.S. intelligence services, the targets could further deduce that all the anonymous visitors were avatars for American intelligence. It would be analogous to undercover police using pink-colored cars that civilians did not use.

To remedy this flaw, the U.S. government made Tor software open source in 2008 and freely available to everyone in the world. It even provided funding for its promulgation, with the State Department, the National Science Foundation, and the Broadcasting Board of Governors financing Tor's core developer. The public rationale for this generosity was that Tor could serve as a tool for, as the State Department called it, "democracy advocates in authoritarian states." While Tor software remained a useful tool in covert operations by the CIA, the DIA, and the FBI, it was anathema to the NSA because it made it more difficult for it to track potential targets.

As Tor software became widely used by adversaries (as well as common criminals), the NSA sought to find vulnerabilities in it. "It should hardly be surprising that our intelligence agencies seek ways to counteract targets that use Tor software to hide their communications," explained an NSA spokesperson. The NSA's adversaries also took an interest in identifying Tor users because they might include political dissidents and potential spies.

Tor software also took on a cultlike importance to hacktivists concerned with the U.S. government's tracking their activities. Catherine A. Fitzpatrick provides an illuminating insight into the mind-set of these hacktivists in her 2014 book, *Privacy for Me and Not for Thee*. She describes them as largely "radical anarchists" who believe "the state is all-powerful, that law-enforcement is so strong that it will prevail anyway, and that they are a persecuted minority." As a refuge against the surveillance of the state, and in particular the NSA, they not only attempt to hide their own identities but also use encryption to obscure their messages. Their goal is to free their movements "of any interference from law-enforcement." In this mind-set, according to Fitzpatrick, "they believe government intelligence agencies will stop at nothing to stop them from absolute encryption."

Tor software was a means to defeat the NSA, but for it to be successful, there needed to be such a proliferation of Tor servers that the NSA could not piece together IP addresses. The problem was that the Tor Project, as they called it, was still a very tiny operation in 2012. It employed fewer than a hundred core developers, who were located mainly in Germany, Iceland, Japan, Estonia, and the United States. Its staff worked mainly out of a single room in Cambridge, Massachusetts.

The guiding spirit behind the Tor movement in the private sector was Jacob Appelbaum, a charismatic twenty-eight-year-old who had grown up in Northern California. Like Snowden, he had dropped out of high school. Appelbaum identified himself to his followers on the Internet as a "hacktivist" battling state surveillance. For him, as for many in the hacktivist culture, the main enemy was the NSA. After all, the NSA had a vast army of computer scientists working to defeat Tor software. Appelbaum was well connected in this culture, having been the North American representative for WikiLeaks before he moved to Berlin in 2013. He also managed WikiLeaks's cyber security when it released the classified documents it obtained from Manning in 2010. He was so well regarded among hacktivists that Assange chose him as his keynote speaker replacement at the Hackers on Planet Earth (HOPE) convention in New York City. Assange told *Rolling Stone*, "Jake [Appelbaum] has been a tireless promoter behind the scenes of our cause." For its part, *Rolling Stone* titled its profile of Appelbaum "Meet the Most Dangerous Man in Cyberspace." (Assange needed a replacement for this particular event because he feared if he came to New York, he would be arrested for releasing the Manning files on WikiLeaks.)

In Berlin, Appelbaum went to extreme lengths to protect himself from American surveillance. For example, when George Packer interviewed him for *The New Yorker* in 2014, he insisted on meeting with Packer naked in a sauna so he could be sure Packer did not have a recording device (other than his notebook). Appelbaum stated repeatedly in interviews that he was being spied upon by America. While his claims might have sounded paranoid to his interviewers, as a character in Joseph Heller's *Catch-22* famously said, "Just because you're paranoid doesn't mean they aren't after you."

Runa Sandvik, a close associate of Appelbaum's, also worked tirelessly to extend Tor's cloak of anonymity in the private sector against the surveillance of the NSA and other would-be intruders of privacy. A Norwegian national in her mid-twenties, she wrote a well-followed blog on Internet privacy for *Forbes* in 2012, in which she identified herself as a privacy and security researcher working at the intersection of technology, law, and policy. Appelbaum and Sandvik both came in contact with Snowden before he went public and while he was still working for the NSA in Hawaii.

In 2012, Snowden became involved in the effort to encourage the use of Tor software to protect privacy. He made no secret of his concerns about electronic interceptions. According to an anonymous co-worker, he even wore a jacket to work with a parody of the NSA insignia, which, instead of merely depicting the NSA eagle, showed the eagle clutching AT&T phone lines. He had also become a member of the Electronic Frontier Foundation, the digital rights organization that was helping finance Tor. He saw Tor software as a remedy. "Without Tor," he later wrote, "when you walk the streets of the Internet, you're always watched." His efforts on behalf of Tor were not limited to symbolic gestures. In 2012, he set up a two-gigabyte server called "The Signal," which he described as the largest Tor relay station exit node in Honolulu. He apparently paid for it himself.

Through his work as a system administrator for Dell, he found documents revealing NSA efforts, not yet successful, to defeat Tor's ability to camouflage a user's identity on the Internet. He found that the NSA was attempting to build backdoor entry ways into Tor software. One of the NSA documents that he illicitly downloaded, titled "Tor Stinks," described the agency's continuing efforts to penetrate Tor servers. In addition, he downloaded NSA documents describing programs begun in 2012 that aimed at searching the Internet for the cyber signatures of foreign parties suspected of hacking into U.S. government systems.

He also made efforts to directly contact Sandvik. She recalls first hearing from Snowden in November 2012. He first wrote to her under the alias Cincinnatus but later supplied his real name and mailing address in Hawaii because he wanted her to mail him authentic computer stickers from the Tor Project that he could use as "swag," as he wrote her, to attract further interest in Tor software in Hawaii. As a result, she knew his identity seven months before he went public in Hong Kong. He would later tell Sandvik from Moscow that he had been "moonlighting" by working to advance the Tor Project. He added, with some understatement, that his moonlighting was "something the NSA might not have been too happy about."

On November 18, 2012, while still working for Dell at the NSA, his dual role led him to begin organizing a "CryptoParty" aimed at finding new recruits for Tor. The CryptoParty movement had been started in 2012 by Asher Wolf, a radical hacktivist and anarchist living in Melbourne, Australia. She promoted the get-togethers not unlike the Tupperware parties of the 1950s. The party organizer, usually with a representative of the Tor Project, advertised the party on the Internet. Attendees were encouraged to bring their own laptops so they could install Tor as well as encryption software in them. The attendees would then be instructed on how to use it. Finally, those converted to Tor software would be told to proselytize about its virtues by holding their own CryptoParty. Wolf's idea was to use these gatherings to expand the realm of Tor.

Snowden called his fete the Oahu CryptoParty. It had its own web page. He told Wolf that it would be the first CryptoParty in Honolulu. She wrote back advising him to "keep it simple." (Wolf later said she did not know he was working at the NSA.)

Snowden apparently had no inhibitions in staging a party that the leadership of the NSA might consider subversive of its battle against Tor. He even invited fellow NSA workers in Hawaii, as well as others in the local computer culture. He asked Sandvik, who was living in Washington, D.C., at the time, to participate, proposing that she co-host the party with him. He scheduled it for December 11, 2012, in Honolulu. According to Sandvik's account, Snowden informed her that he "had been talking some of the more technical guys at work into setting up some additional fast servers" for Tor. His "work" place at the time was the NSA. So, if he was telling the truth, he had already attempted to find co-workers at the NSA who might be interested in attending an anti-NSA surveillance presentation.

Sandvik not only agreed to be Snowden's co-presenter but made the Oahu CryptoParty a Tor-sponsored event. Sandvik flew to Honolulu on December 6, 2012. It was a fourteen-hour flight and a relatively expensive one. She later told *Wired* magazine that the invitation from Snowden coincided with her plan to take a "vacation in Hawaii." Whatever her reason, it brought her in direct contact with a Tor supporter with access to the computers of its main enemy, the NSA.

On December 11, following Snowden's instructions, Sandvik arrived shortly before 6:00 p.m. at the Fishcake gallery in downtown Honolulu. She proceeded through a maze of furniture display rooms to BoxJelly, a public space. She was then directed to a small back room in which there were folding chairs and worktables already set up for the event. Rechung Fujihira, the owner of BoxJelly, told me that Hi Capacity, a "creative collective" of computer buffs, had arranged the logistics for the event. As he recalled, Snowden had requested their help for the CryptoParty.

Sandvik found Snowden waiting for her with Lindsay Mills, whom he introduced to Sandvik as his girlfriend. He told Sandvik that Mills was there to make a video of the event. Mills did not mention the party in her blog. But that Snowden brought her and introduced her to Sandvik suggests that he did not keep secret from her his activities to further Tor.

The event started at 6:00 p.m. sharp. By Sandvik's count, about twenty people gradually filled the room. She reckoned that about half of the attendees were from Snowden's workplace. Snowden began the presentation by giving reasons why Internet users needed to defend their privacy by using both encryption and Tor software. According to one attendee who asked not to be identified by name, Snowden, while not revealing that he worked for the NSA, spoke with such precise knowledge about government surveillance capabilities that the attendee suspected Snowden worked for the government. Snowden next introduced Sandvik, who took the podium and discussed the work of the Tor Project, stressing the importance of expanding the Tor network. Following their presentations, Snowden and Sandvik took questions from the audience.

The Oahu CryptoParty, according to Sandvik, ended about 10:00 p.m. No one objected to Mills's making a video of the meeting, even though it was dedicated to the idea of protecting personal privacy. The video was not posted on the Internet, so presumably Snowden wanted it for his own purposes. Afterward, Sandvik went to a local diner called Zippy's for a late dinner. She left Hawaii two days later.

Not all the hacktivists that Snowden invited were able to attend. Parker Higgins, for example, a prime mover in the Electronic Frontier Foundation and founder of the San Francisco CryptoParty, wrote back to him that he was unable to attend the December CryptoParty because of the high price of the airfare that month between San Francisco and Honolulu. He added that he would try to attend Snowden's next CryptoParty, which was scheduled for February 23, 2013. (Higgins would make headlines in 2013 by flying a chartered blimp over the NSA's secret facility in Utah and photographing it from the air.)

Snowden's double duty continued: downloading secret documents while remaining in touch with some of the leading figures in the Tor Project under his various aliases. He also continued to invite activists to his CryptoParties, and he openly advertised them on the Internet until 2013. The CIA's former deputy director Morell, who reviewed the security situation at the NSA in 2014 as a member of President Obama's NSA Review Committee, found that the NSA in the post–Cold War age had encouraged its technical workers to freely discuss challenges that arose in its computer operations. "The idea was to spread knowledge and learn from the successes of others," Morell wrote, "but it created enormous security vulnerability, given the always-existent risk of an insider committed to stealing secrets." According to a former intelligence executive, this new "open culture," exemplified by largely unrestricted entry to the NSANet by civilian contractors, fit the culture of the young civilians on the "geek squads" who now ran the NSA's computer networks.

It was remarkable that even in such an "open culture," Snowden's

CryptoParty, Tor station, and other anti-NSA activities could go unremarked upon. After all, ten or so NSA workers attended the first party, and it is not unlikely that many of them recognized him as their co-worker. If so, they knew (as did Sandvik and Mills) that the Tor advocate "Cincinnatus" was Snowden. He had also not been shy in contacting notable enemies of the NSA via e-mail, such as Jacob Appelbaum, Parker Higgins, and Asher Wolf. If anyone, including the security staff of the NSA, had been on the lookout for dissident intelligence workers, this well-advertised gathering and its organizer might have been of interest.

In 2014, I asked a former top NSA executive whether such activities on behalf of Tor by an NSA employee would arouse the attention of the NSA's own "Q" counterespionage unit. He answered, "Snowden was not an NSA employee." Because Snowden was a contract employee of Dell's residing in the United States, the NSA could not legally monitor his private activities or intercept his communication. To do so would require a court-approved FBI request. So Snowden/Cincinnatus was free to operate openly in recruiting NSA workers, hacktivists, and computer buffs for his events. Ironically, adversary intelligence services searching for disgruntled intelligence workers had no such constraints.

CHAPTER 7

String Puller

It wasn't that they put it on me as an individual—that I'm uniquely qualified [or] an angel descending from the heavens—as that they put it on someone, somewhere.

—EDWARD SNOWDEN, Moscow, 2013

DOWNLOADING NSA documents was not Snowden's only rogue activity while working at the NSA for Dell in 2012. Three weeks after the CryptoParty, Snowden began anonymously contacting a high-profile journalist. He used the same alias, Cincinnatus, that he used with Sandvik and to advertise the Oahu CryptoParty. The journalist to whom he wrote on December 1, 2012, was Glenn Greenwald, the previously mentioned Rio-based columnist for *The Guardian*.

Greenwald had not always been an activist journalist. He had been a litigation lawyer at the elite New York firm of Wachtell, Lipton, Rosen & Katz. He was also an entrepreneur, owning part of Master Notions, a company that, among other things, had a 50 percent financial interest in the pornographic website HJ (an acronym that originally stood for "Hairy Jock"). All did not go well with this enterprise. In 2004, Greenwald became involved in an acrimonious lawsuit with his other associates in HJ. As a result, he had a number of open legal judgments filed against him, including an $85,000 lien by the IRS.

After resigning from his law firm in 2005, he moved to Rio de Janeiro and began a new career as a blogger for the Internet magazine *Salon*. He wrote fierce, and often brilliant, polemics against U.S. government surveillance and other perceived intrusions on personal privacy. The extent of his bitter antagonism toward the activities of the "surveillance state," as he called it, was reflected in the title of his 2006 book, *How Would a Patriot Act? Defending American Values from a President Run Amok*. His position on surveillance was unrelenting, even when it came to the president. "By ordering illegal eavesdropping, the president had committed crimes and should be held accountable for them," Greenwald wrote. When Barack Obama became president in 2009, Greenwald also attacked him for breaking the law by "ordering illegal eavesdropping." Because of his opposition to Obama, he contributed money to the libertarian campaign of Ron Paul, the same candidate to whom Snowden gave money.

In August 2012, he had transferred his provocative blog, which had amassed a following of nearly one million readers (including Snowden), from *Salon* to *The Guardian*. The British newspaper shared his powerful anti-surveillance position, having first published the WikiLeaks documents that had been illicitly leaked by Manning and published by Assange in 2010.

Greenwald was an activist as well as a journalist. He joined the board of directors of the Freedom of the Press Foundation (eventually Runa Sandvik would join too). It had been set up expressly to funnel money to both Assange's WikiLeaks site and the defense fund for Manning after he was arrested. Such a financial intermediary was necessary because American credit card companies were blocking money transfers to these two causes in 2012. This "blockade" was taking its toll on WikiLeaks. According to Assange, "WikiLeaks had been cut off from more than 90 percent of its finances." The Freedom of the Press Foundation came to its rescue. John Perry Barlow, one of the songwriters for the Grateful Dead, was one of its chief financial backers. "The first serious info war is now engaged," Barlow declared. "The field of battle is WikiLeaks." He served with Greenwald and Poitras on its board.

Snowden was an avid reader of Greenwald's screeds against the government. If he were to assume the role of a modern-day Prometheus, delivering forbidden NSA secrets to the public, Greenwald would be a logical candidate to break the story. Snowden could safely assume that Greenwald would be sympathetic to exposing NSA surveillance from his many blogs, tweets, and YouTube comments on the subject. For example, on November 13, 2012, just eighteen days before Snowden contacted him, Greenwald had written a blog for *The Guardian* asserting that the United States was "a surveillance state run amok." In it, echoing very closely what Snowden said at his CryptoParty, Greenwald wrote, "Any remnants of internet anonymity have been all but obliterated between the state and technology companies." Citing a story in *The Washington Post,* he continued, "Every day, collection systems at the National Security Agency intercept and store 1.7 billion e-mails, phone calls and other types of communications."

As a result, Greenwald called for action in that blog posting, writing, "The US operates a sprawling, unaccountable Surveillance State that, in violent breach of the core guarantees of the Fourth Amendment, monitors and records virtually everything even the most law-abiding citizens do." That same week, Snowden invited Runa Sandvik to co-host his CryptoParty.

One problem for Snowden in reaching out to Greenwald was Greenwald's lack of any encryption for his e-mails. Communicating with a journalist like Greenwald who famously attacked the very organization for which Snowden worked was itself a risky undertaking, especially if he wanted to pass classified NSA documents to him. If his e-mails were intercepted by the NSA in Brazil (where Greenwald lived) and where the NSA was not restricted by U.S. law, he could lose his job or even be arrested. As Cincinnatus, he told Greenwald that he needed to immediately encrypt his computer. To make his point, he cited Greenwald's November 12, 2012, blog. In it, Greenwald noted that General David Petraeus, then the CIA director, had been caught in a sex scandal because his personal e-mails had been intercepted. Snowden wrote to Greenwald that Petraeus would not have been exposed if he had used encryption. Snowden sent Greenwald instructions on how to install the necessary encryption software and a link to a twelve-minute video on encryption (which might have been the same video he used at his CryptoParty a few weeks earlier).

Greenwald did not manage to encrypt his computer, however, and Snowden, unwilling to deal with Greenwald through an unencrypted channel, broke off contact with him in January 2013. Even so, he did not give up his plan of using Greenwald in his enterprise. He merely sought an intermediary who used encryption.

He chose Laura Poitras. He knew she and Greenwald were founding board members of the Freedom of the Press Foundation. Greenwald had written about her extensively. For example, he wrote an entire blog about her confrontation with the U.S. government and her plans to make a documentary about the "US Government's increasing powers of domestic surveillance [through] its expanding covert domestic NSA activities."

Since 2011, Poitras had been diligently filming the construction of a massive NSA repository for data in Bluffdale, Utah. In the antisurveillance culture, the structure had become symbolic of the powers of the NSA. In fact, it was the same NSA site that Parker Higgins photographed from a blimp in the fall of 2013 and posted on the Internet after Poitras had released her documentary about the NSA's use of the Bluffdale repository for domestic spying.

Aside from her connections with Greenwald, Poitras had other impressive credentials. Born in 1964 in Boston, she came from a wealthy family that donated large sums of money to philanthropic causes, including $20 million for research on bipolar disorders. After graduating from the New School for Public Engagement in 1996, she pursued a career as an activist filmmaker. Her focus quickly became exposing NSA surveillance. One of her short documentaries about the NSA's domestic surveillance program was featured on the *New York Times* website and attracted enormous attention in 2012. As a dedicated opponent of the surveillance state, she participated in public events with William Binney, the ex-NSA whistle-blower, and Jacob Appelbaum. In April 2012, for example, she made a presentation at the Whitney Museum in New York with Binney and Appelbaum. She had become such a leading activist against the NSA by December 2012 that Appelbaum, after lauding her work, interspersed clips from her short film in his keynote address at the Chaos Computer Club convention of hacktivists in Berlin that month.

Snowden also closely followed her rise in this world. By simply googling Poitras's name in January 2013, he would have learned about her connections with Greenwald, Appelbaum, Binney, Assange, and other leading figures in the anti-surveillance camp. When asked later by Poitras why he had chosen her to help him, Snowden replied, "I didn't. You chose yourself." The problem for Snowden was anonymously drawing her into his enterprise.

Poitras was living in Berlin in January 2013, which made her vulnerable to NSA surveillance. To get to her through an encrypted channel, Snowden chose a circuitous approach. On January 11, he wrote to Micah Lee in Berkeley, California. Given Lee's residence in the United States, as Snowden knew, the NSA would be legally barred from monitoring his communications without a warrant. He used Lee, who was the chief technology officer at the Freedom of the Press Foundation, as the encrypted gateway to Poitras. Lee was also well-connected to others whom Snowden had contacted for his CryptoParty. Lee had been an associate of Runa Sandvik's at Tor and was a prominent member of Noisebridge, an eclectic anti-government hackers' commune based in Northern California, of which Appelbaum was also a member.

To contact Lee, Snowden chose the alias Anon108. Anon is an alias frequently used by members of the Anonymous commune of hacktivists. "I'm a friend," Snowden wrote to Lee. "I need to get information securely to Laura Poitras and her alone, but I can't find an email gpg key for her." The "gpg" encryption key he asked for, more commonly called a PGP key, was the so-called public key for an encryption system called Pretty Good Privacy, or, for short, PGP. This encryption system required both a public and a private key. Snowden asked Lee to provide the former one, because Poitras had the latter one. Lee wrote to Poitras about Anon108. The next day, with the approval of Poitras, Lee supplied Poitras's public key to Snowden, or, as he knew him, Anon108.

With it, Snowden contacted Poitras directly. He asked her as a first step to open an anonymous e-mail account using Tor software. Poitras later wrote about this initial contact, "I was at that point filming with several people who were all being targeted by the [U.S.] government." Many of the people she was filming, including Appelbaum, Assange, Binney, and the former NSA employee Thomas Drake, could attract interest by U.S. or foreign intelligence services.

Snowden asked Poitras to take out a new enciphering key to use exclusively for her liaison with him. It provided them both with an extra layer of protection from any surveillance by law enforcement. Presumably, she accommodated his requests because she anticipated that the anonymous person would use this encrypted channel to send her highly sensitive material.

On January 23, Snowden wrote to Poitras under yet another alias. This time he called himself Citizen Four. He wrote, "At this stage I can offer nothing more than my word." He then said falsely, "I am a senior government employee in the intelligence community." She had no way of knowing at this "stage" that despite giving her his "word," he was not who he claimed to be. He was not a "government employee," he was not a "senior" official, and he was not a member of the "intelligence community" (which is composed of the intelligence services of the U.S. government). He would later also claim to her that he had been "a senior adviser to the CIA" and "a senior adviser to the DIA." That was untrue, too. In January 2013, he was merely a contract employee of Dell's working as a computer technician at the NSA base in Hawaii.

Snowden told her in his initial e-mail that he was well acquainted with her career as an anti-surveillance activist. He said that he had read Greenwald's account in *Salon* that past April, a blog in which Greenwald detailed the forty times in which Poitras was searched by U.S. authorities. The story also said that Poitras believed she was on a special watch list and under constant U.S. government surveillance. She had come under such scrutiny by U.S. authorities, it turned out, because of her documentary about American military abuses of civilians in Iraq in 2006, titled *My Country, My Country*. While filming it, she was at a place close to an insurgent ambush of U.S. troops in Iraq. Her presence at the ambush site led army intelligence officers to suspect (without any evidence) that she might have been tipped off by the insurgents. She firmly denied the charge, and the government never substantiated it. Even so, because of this incident, since

2006 she had been kept on a list that caused authorities to search her at airports. As a result, she took elaborate countermeasures to evade any possible surveillance of her communications.

Snowden knew about this incident because Greenwald described it in great detail in a blog that Snowden read (as he later told Greenwald). "Poitras is now forced to take extreme steps—ones that hamper her ability to do her work," Greenwald wrote. "She now avoids traveling with any electronic devices. She uses alternative methods to deliver the most sensitive parts of her work—raw film and interview notes—to secure locations. She spends substantial time and resources protecting her computers with encryption and password defenses. Especially when she is in the US, she avoids talking on the phone about her work, particularly to sources. And she simply will not edit her films at her home out of fear—obviously well grounded—that government agents will attempt to search and seize the raw footage." She claimed, as she told journalists, she was the victim of "Kafkaesque government harassment."

Snowden was duly impressed with her concerns about government surveillance, which he agreed was ubiquitous. Indeed, he later described her as "more paranoid when it comes to electronic security than I can be." He meant it as a compliment. Such functional paranoia or "operational security," as Greenwald would call the precautions that she took, dovetailed with Snowden's growing conviction that universal encryption was necessary to defeat the surveillance state. It also made her the perfect channel for Snowden to safely pass some of the classified documents he stole to Greenwald and other journalists.

It was not difficult to get her to cooperate in his plot. He wrote, for example, "The surveillance you've experienced means you have been 'selected'—a term which will mean more to you as you learn how the modern SIGINT [signals intelligence] system works." Just as she had been "chosen" by her work to act as his conduit, according to Snowden, she had been chosen by the NSA as a target because of her work. The idea of her being "selected" by an invisible signals intelligence agency, the NSA, could only excite her longtime concerns about being watched by the government.

"Your victimization by the NSA system means that you are well aware of the threat that [the NSA's] unrestricted, secret abilities pose for democracies," he continued. "I hope you understand that contacting you is extremely high risk and if you are willing to agree to the following precautions before I share more, this will not be a waste of your time." Further playing on her concern, he asked her to confirm to him "that no one has ever had a copy of your private key and that it uses a strong pass phrase." Such precautions were necessary because "your adversary is capable of one trillion guesses per second." That "adversary" was, as she knew from her previous film, the NSA. At this point, she knew she was entering into a dangerous liaison with an unknown party in pursuit of NSA secrets. She wondered if he might be part of a plan to entrap her or her contacts like Assange and Appelbaum, as she noted in her diary. "Is C4 a trap?" she asked herself, referring to her Citizen Four source. "Will he put me in prison?"

To elude this "adversary," Snowden stressed to Poitras that she would have to adopt a conspiratorial frame of mind. "If the device you store the private key and enter your pass phrase on has been hacked, it is trivial to decrypt our communications," he explained. "If you publish the source material, I will likely be immediately implicated." If her correspondent could be "immediately implicated," it meant that he was a person authorized to handle these secrets. So Poitras knew, as early as January 2013, that she was creating an encrypted channel for someone with access to NSA secrets who would be incriminated by providing them to her.

The key source for Poitras's previously referred to short video was Binney. Like her new source, he had been authorized to handle NSA secrets. Binney had been an NSA technical director until he had retired in 2001. The NSA's domestic surveillance program that Binney told the press about years before being interviewed in Poitras's film was called Stellarwind. It involved data mining domestic communications and financial transactions that had been authorized by President George W. Bush in 2001 after 9/11 as commander-in-chief under the war powers given to him following the attacks. It indeed led to a major exposé on domestic spying by *The New York Times* in December 2005.

Binney had never provided Poitras with any NSA documents

to back up the charges he made that Stellarwind was an unlawful domestic surveillance operation. He could not have done so without violating his sworn oath and, for that matter, U.S. anti-espionage statutes. Binney made it clear to her and other journalists that he was not a lawbreaker. But her new source, C4, was willing to do what Binney (and other insiders) had refused to do. He was offering in these e-mails to provide her with secret government documents, even though it would implicate him as an outlaw. To further whet her appetite, he told her that these up-to-date NSA documents would fully substantiate the allegations that Binney made in her film. Even more important, he said Binney's 2001 disclosures were still relevant to her cause. "What you know as Stellarwind has grown," he wrote to her. "The expanded special source operations that took over Stellarwind's share of the pie have spread all over the world to practically include comprehensive coverage of the United States." In fact, as Snowden knew from the Inspector General report he had read, the NSA had terminated Stellarwind almost a decade earlier. President Bush ended it after top officials of the Justice Department insisted that he did not have the legal authority for the domestic part of Stellarwind. Instead, he asked Congress to revise FISA to meet the objections of the Justice Department. The result was the FISA Amendment Act of 2006. Unlike the previous Stellarwind program, it did not permit domestic surveillance. It specified that the government could not target any person in the United States or anywhere else in the world under this authority. Nor could it target any foreign person, even one residing outside of the United States, to acquire information from a particular known person inside the United States. As the act recognized that information about U.S. citizens might mistakenly be intercepted by the NSA, it required that such data about Americans be minimized and reviewed bimonthly by a Justice Department task force. Although the NSA program in place in 2013 was not the comprehensive domestic surveillance that Snowden claimed it to be, Poitras had no way of knowing at this early state that her source was misleading her.

He offered to substantiate her worst fears about the growth of NSA surveillance: "I know the location of most domestic interception points, and that the largest telecommunication companies in the

US are betraying the trust of their customers, which I can prove." He even proffered evidence implicating President Barack Obama in illegal surveillance. "There is a detailed policy framework, a kind of martial law for cyber operations, created by the White House. It's called presidential policy 20," he wrote to her. It was an eighteen-page directive that Obama had signed four months earlier in October 2012. Snowden was offering to reveal to her up-to-date evidence of a surveillance state in America presided over by the president himself. It was what she had been searching for over the past three years. How could she, as an activist filmmaker, resist such a sensational offer?

He further explained to her that he had placed great trust in her discretion. "No one, not even my most trusted confidante, is aware of my intentions, and it would not be fair for them to fall under suspicion for my actions," he said.

Poitras must have found it flattering that a total stranger was willing to disclose to her in e-mails what he would not tell even his "most trusted confidante" about his intentions to commit an illicit breach of U.S. national security. It also put her under enormous stress. She noted in her journal that the pressure made her feel as if she were "underwater." "I am battling with my nervous system. It doesn't let me rest or sleep. Eye twitches, clenched throat, and now literally waiting to be raided."

Snowden was also taking an extraordinary risk. After all, he had no way of knowing who else she told about him. She had long been concerned, with good reason, that the U.S. government was out to get her. An unknown person offering to supply her with secret documents could be attempting to entrap her. So Snowden could not preclude the possibility that she would consult with others about the offer he was making her. Because her current documentary project included interviews by her with Assange, Appelbaum, and three ex-NSA executives, intelligence services with sophisticated surveillance capabilities might also have taken a professional interest in her communications, as Poitras herself had suspected. Even if Snowden was somehow able to use his position as a system administrator at Dell to ascertain that the NSA did not have Poitras under surveillance, he could not be sure that other agencies, such as the Russian and Chinese intelligence services, were not monitoring his communications with her. It was, however, a chance Snowden was willing to take.

Snowden, in any case, did not intend to conceal his identity for more than a few months. He told Poitras he had a specific purpose in allowing her to name him in her ongoing film project. Indeed, he said it was essential in his plan to prevent others, including presumably his "most trusted confidante," from being suspected by law enforcement of helping him in his enterprise. He prevailed on her to accommodate his plan, saying, "You may be the only one who can prevent that, and that is by immediately nailing me to the cross rather than trying to protect me as a source." His choice of the imagery of crucifixion suggested that like Jesus Christ he was willing to sacrifice himself for the sake of others.

In keeping with their operational security arrangement, Snowden said that he would first send her an encrypted file of documents that she would not be able to read. Only after his conditions were met and "everything else is done," he said, "the key will follow." He was now pulling the strings. To get that key, she had to follow his instructions.

One of his conditions was that she help him recruit Greenwald and other outlets for his disclosures. "The material provided and the investigative effort required will be too much for any one person," he wrote to Poitras. He next directed her to contact Greenwald. "I recommend that at the very minimum you involve Greenwald. I believe you know him." (Snowden apparently did not tell her that he had unsuccessfully attempted to reach out to Greenwald before he had contacted her.)

His continued interest in Greenwald was understandable. Aside from Greenwald's opposition to what he called the "Surveillance State," he was a gateway to *The Guardian*. That publication had become an important player in the business of disclosing government documents by publishing a large part of the U.S. documents supplied to WikiLeaks, as we have seen. By breaking whistleblowing stories about U.S. intelligence, it had also greatly increased the circulation of its website. As an establishment newspaper, it also gave these WikiLeaks stories credibility with the media. So despite Greenwald's inability to create an encrypted channel, Snowden still needed him. He had no reason to believe that Greenwald would turn down the opportunity for a whistle-blowing scoop for *The Guardian*. After all, the classified documents Snowden would provide him would also give credence to both Greenwald's book and his many blogs denouncing U.S. government surveillance.

Aside from Greenwald and Poitras, Snowden sought an outlet inside the American establishment. So he had Poitras write to Barton Gellman, the Pulitzer Prize–winning reporter for *The Washington Post*. Poitras had met Gellman in 2010, when they were both fellows at NYU's Center on Law and Security. Poitras had requested help in encrypting her computer from Karen Greenberg, the executive director of the center, who took her "by the hand" to meet Gellman, Greenberg's resident expert on encryption software. Born in 1960, Gellman graduated from Princeton in 1981 and became an award-winning investigative reporter for the *Miami Herald,* the *Post,* and *Time* magazine. He was also the author of *Angler: The Cheney Vice Presidency*. If Gellman could be drawn into the enterprise, he could provide Snowden with a gateway to the prestigious American paper credited with bringing down President Richard Nixon in the Watergate scandal.

Poitras, as the go-between for Snowden, immediately contacted Gellman. After telling him she was involved in a story about NSA surveillance, she suggested that they meet in New York City.

For their rendezvous, Poitras took a number of precautions to evade anyone attempting to follow her. She had Gellman first meet her in one coffee shop in lower Manhattan. When he arrived, she had him follow her on foot to another coffee shop, following her anti-surveillance tradecraft. Once assured no one was watching them, she ordered coffee for herself and Gellman. Over coffee, she told Gellman about Snowden, whom she described as her anonymous source. She said that he was willing to supply Gellman with documents that would expose domestic surveillance, if Gellman agreed to write a story on it for the *Post*. Even though Gellman had left the staff of the *Post* in 2010, he had previously written several stories on that subject for the newspaper, and he was also highly regarded by the editors there. Gellman was interested in Poitras's offer (although he would consult a friend at the Justice Department about the legality of publishing NSA documents).

Snowden had now laid the groundwork for at least two possible outlets. Poitras, however, was having some difficulty in bringing Greenwald in on the plan. Like Snowden, she did not trust writing to him in unencrypted e-mails, and because Greenwald lived in Brazil, she still had not found an opportunity for a face-to-face meeting with him.

That opportunity arose in mid-April 2013. Greenwald had flown to the United States to give the lead speech at an event in Yonkers, New York, sponsored by the Council on American-Islamic Relations, a pro-Muslim civil rights organization. He had delivered the keynote speech at its previous meeting in San Jose, California, where his impassioned depiction of the American "Surveillance State" received a rousing ovation from the attendees. He was invited to speak at this award dinner for its East Coast chapter.

Poitras flew from Berlin to New York to see him. On April 19, 2013, she arranged to meet Greenwald at noon in the restaurant of the Marriott hotel where Greenwald was staying. When Greenwald arrived at the restaurant carrying a cell phone, she explained to him that the NSA could surreptitiously turn his cell phone into a microphone and use it to eavesdrop on their conversation. She told him to go back to his room and leave his phone there. When he returned, phoneless, she took further precautions by having them change tables several times. Greenwald accepted these tactics because, as he later said, she was in charge of their "operational security."

When they finally settled at a table in the nearly empty restaurant, she showed Greenwald e-mails she had received from Citizen Four. Greenwald, as he recounted, made "no connection" to the "long-forgotten emails" he had received from Snowden under the alias Cincinnatus. Reading the e-mails that Snowden had sent to Poitras, he was impressed with the "sincerity" of the anonymous correspondent.

When Poitras showed Greenwald Citizen Four's mission statement in which he said his motive was to end the U.S. "surveillance state," Greenwald was further impressed with the source. The surveillance state Snowden described closely dovetailed with the surveillance state that Greenwald had described himself in his speech at the Council on American-Islamic Relations dinner in 2012. Of course, the similarity of the phrasing might not have been entirely coincidental. Greenwald's 2012 speech had been put on YouTube and widely circulated on the Internet just a few days before Snowden first wrote to him on December 1, 2012. Snowden identified himself as a privacy advocate, which was also how Greenwald often identified himself in his speeches. He also echoed other concerns Greenwald had publicly expressed, including defending American privacy from government intrusions.

Snowden promised the leaks he would supply would provide dramatic results. He asserted in one of his e-mails to Poitras that the "shock" of the documents he would give Greenwald would result in the public's learning about the secret "mechanisms through which our privacy is violated." According to Snowden's assessment, following that initial uproar, they could achieve another objective in their common cause. "We can guarantee for all people equal protection against unreasonable search," he wrote. In light of this convergence of views, it is not surprising that Greenwald was fully convinced of Citizen Four's bona fides. He said to Poitras, "He's real," and he agreed to help break the story in *The Guardian*.

Poitras now revealed to Greenwald that Citizen Four would deliver an entire trove of secret documents to them in six to eight weeks. According to this timetable, the Greenwald scoop and the "shock" Citizen Four promised would come in early to mid-June 2013.

At this point in April, Snowden was in full control. Although his job at Dell involved endlessly monitoring largely meaningless encrypted messages in the NSA tunnel, he had been able to get three major journalists to react favorably to his proposal. None of them knew his name, position, age, location, or where precisely he worked. Nor did they know the means by which he planned to obtain the secrets that he dangled before them. They also did not know where, or even if, they would meet their source. Their total knowledge about him was the description he improperly gave of himself: a "senior government employee in the intelligence community" (Greenwald speculated that he was a disgruntled CIA station chief).

Even though they were operating largely in the dark, these three journalists acted as almost any other ambitious reporter would if he or she were offered a major scoop about illegal acts of the government. In addition, the information was in line with what they had previously investigated or written about. None of these journalists had any reason to doubt at this point that their anonymous source was anything but the sincere whistle-blower he claimed to be. They could not have known from his anonymous e-mails that aside from the whistle-blowing documents he promised them, he was in the process of stealing a large number of other documents that concerned the NSA's sources and methods in foreign countries. These documents, to which Snowden never referred in his correspondence with them, had little if anything at all to do with domestic spying on American citizens.

CHAPTER 8

Raider of the Inner Sanctum

They think there's a smoking gun in there that would be the death of them all politically.

—EDWARD SNOWDEN, Moscow, 2014

T HE NIGHTMARE OF THE NSA is a penetration. As the CIA, the FBI, and the NSA found out in the 1990s, no intelligence service is invulnerable to it. Any employee of a large intelligence organization can turn, or be turned, against it. Among the more than ten thousand intelligence workers employed by the NSA, it is a near certainty that over time more than one of them will become dissatisfied with their work. A worker may have a personal grievance about salary, lack of promotion, or treatment by his or her superiors. Disenchantment with the NSA may also proceed from idealistic objections. The NSA is in the business of secretly intercepting messages, and an insider could come to find its spying activities at odds with his or her own beliefs about the violation of privacy. For any of these reasons, a disgruntled insider could go rogue. He or she then might attempt to right a perceived wrong by disclosing NSA secrets to another party. That party might then induce or blackmail the rogue employee into disclosing further secrets.

To guard against this, the NSA has developed a well-organized system for stratifying its data so that obtaining critical secrets required a rogue employee to burrow into its heavily protected inner sanctum. As part of this system, the NSA divides its data into different tiers depending on the importance of the secrets to its operations. The first tier, Level 1, is mainly administrative material. This data would include FISA court orders and other directives its employees might need to check on to carry out their tasks. Level 2 contains data from which the secret sources have been removed. This tier, available to other intelligence services and policy makers, includes reports and analysis that can be shared. Level 3 contains documents that cannot be shared outside a small group of authorized individuals, because they disclose the secret sources through which the NSA surreptitiously obtained the information. This third tier includes, for example, compiled lists of sources in China, Russia, Iran, and other adversary countries. It also discloses the exotic methods the NSA uses to get some of this data. Level 3 documents also include reports on specific NSA, CIA, and Pentagon operations unknown to adversaries. These Level 3 documents are described by NSA executives as "the Keys to the Kingdom," because they could invalidate America's entire intelligence enterprise if they fell into the hands of an adversary. And, as far as is known, prior to 2013, there had been no successful theft of any Level 3 documents.

Because of their extreme sensitivity, Level 3 documents were not handled by most of the private firms providing independent contractors. At Dell, Snowden had access mainly to Level 1 and Level 2 data (which he could, and did, download from shared sites on NSANet). These lower-level documents had whistle-blowing potential because they concerned NSA operations in the United States. They did not reveal, however, sources that the NSA used in intercepting the military and civilian activities of foreign adversaries.

Snowden quit his job at Dell as a system administrator on March 15, 2013, to take another job working for the NSA in Hawaii at Booz Allen Hamilton. Unlike other outside contractors that serviced the NSA, the firm he now chose specialized in handling the NSA's Level 3 data.

When Snowden applied to Booz Allen earlier in March 2013, the company had no opening for a system administrator at the National Threat Operations Center, an NSA unit in which it dealt with Level 3 data. It did have an opening for an infrastructure analyst, a lower-paying job involving monitoring threats from China, Russia, and other adversaries. Despite a cut in pay, Snowden took that job. "Snowden was an IT guy, not a SIGINT analyst," a former NSA Signals Intelligence officer pointed out. "He was working as a contracted infrastructure analyst for NSA's Information Assurance arm, . . . [which, ironically as it turned out] protects classified U.S. communications from potential intruders." Steven Bay, the manager at Booz Allen who hired and supervised Snowden, recalled that the first "red flag" came up soon after Snowden began his training, when "Snowden began asking about a highly classified mass-surveillance program" to which Snowden did not have access (although Bay did). In retrospect, Bay realized that Snowden had applied for the job for a specific reason. "He targeted our [Booz Allen] contract directly," Bay said. "Somehow he figured out that our contract, and what we did on that contract, were the types of gates he needed to get access to."

Snowden subsequently told the *South China Morning Post* that he took this job to "get access to lists of machines all over the world the NSA had hacked." If so, he was after the keys to the NSA's kingdom of global surveillance. Booz Allen held those keys. "He targeted my company because we enjoy more access than other companies," Booz Allen's vice-chairman Michael McConnell said with the benefit of hindsight. As a result of the theft, he appraised, "an entire generation of intelligence was lost." McConnell, a former NSA director, was in a position to know.

Snowden's sudden career change had both advantages and disadvantages for the enterprise he was planning. The main advantage was that he would have proximity to the computers in which were kept the "lists" he sought of NSA global sources. The main disadvantage, aside from a cut in salary, was that he would no longer be a system administrator. This change meant he would no longer have privileges to bypass password restrictions or temporarily transfer data. Instead, as an infrastructure analyst, he would not have password access, at least during the two-month-long training period, to the computers that he had not been specifically "read into," which did not include those computers that stored the Level 3 lists. Access to these tightly controlled compartments was limited to only a handful of analysts at the center who had a need to know.

Because the new job entailed handling higher-level secret documents, Booz Allen had stricter requirements for applicants than Dell. To slip by them, Snowden had engaged in a minor subterfuge. He wrote on his application that he was expecting a master's degree from the online division of Liverpool University in England. In fact, he had not completed a single course at Liverpool and would not be receiving any sort of a degree from it. Booz Allen did not verify this and had agreed to hire him as a trainee-analyst. It did not change that decision even after it found out about his subterfuge.

According to Admiral McConnell, Snowden never actually worked in the Booz Allen offices, which are housed in a skyscraper in downtown Honolulu. Instead, he was immediately assigned to work at the NSA's highly sensitive National Threat Operations Center at the Kunia base, the same location where he had worked for Dell.

Before he could begin working there, however, he needed to fly to Maryland to take a mandatory orientation course at the NSA. The course was given in an eleven-story building, with a sheer wall of black glass, on the NSA's 350-acre campus at Fort Meade. He arrived there from Hawaii on April 1, 2013. Like every other Booz Allen contractor who worked at the NSA's center, Snowden was required to sign the "Sensitive Compartmented Information Nondisclosure Agreement." In this document, Snowden acknowledged that he had been granted access to sensitive compartmented information, called SCI, as part of his work and that he understood that any disclosure of that information to an unauthorized person would violate federal criminal law. He was also told, as were all new contract employees at Booz Allen, that its disclosure could damage the interests of the United States and benefit its enemies. In signing the document, he swore an oath not to divulge any of this information without first receiving written approval from U.S. authorities. So less than two months before he downloaded sensitive compartmented information, he was fully aware of what the consequences of divulging this information would be. By this time, as we know, he had already agreed to deliver classified data to three journalists.

Snowden believed that bringing complaints to NSA lawyers or supervisors was, as he put it, "playing with fire." "When I was at NSA," Snowden later said in Moscow, "everybody knew that for anything more serious than workplace harassment, going through the official process was a career-ender at best."

Nevertheless, on April 5, 2013, while still in the training facility in Maryland, he apparently sought to establish a paper trail for himself. He wrote a letter to NSA's Office of the General Counsel asking whether or not NSA directives take precedence over acts of Congress. A lawyer from the Office of the General Counsel responded three days later, addressing Snowden as "Dear Ed." The lawyer said that acts of Congress take precedence over NSA directives. He also suggested that "Ed" phone him if he needed any further clarification. Presumably, Snowden had asked the question to elicit a reply he could later use to bolster his claim that the NSA had ignored or rejected policies regarding NSA directives. Instead, the "Dear Ed" response was of little use to Snowden, because it did not dispute his point that NSA directives must lawfully conform to the acts of Congress. The NSA lawyer never heard back from "Ed."

Snowden completed his orientation course at Fort Meade on Friday, April 12, 2013. While he was in Maryland, he took time off to pay visits to both of his divorced parents. It would be the last time he would see either of them in the United States.

He returned on April 13 to Hawaii. One domestic task he had to attend to was helping Mills pack up their possessions, which they stored in boxes in the garage. The lease on their house was up on April 30, 2013, and they had to move. According to Mills, they found a temporary rental just a few blocks away.

On Monday, April 15, Snowden began on-the-job training as an analyst at the National Threat Operations Center. He would not complete the course. After he began the training, he prepared his exit by writing to Booz Allen and saying he needed a brief medical leave in May to undergo treatment for epilepsy symptoms. As far as is known, he did not suffer from epilepsy. Booz Allen required a minimum of one month's notice for foreign travel. By making the request, he lessened the likelihood that it would arouse undue suspicion when he departed for Hong Kong with stolen documents on May 18. This brief window left him some four weeks to take the lists that he coveted.

Snowden carried out the heist with precision reminiscent of a *Mission: Impossible* movie caper. First, he needed to get passwords to up to twenty-four compartments at the National Threat Operations Center that he had not been read into. Even in the "open culture" of the NSA, this was not an easy challenge. He would be asking one or more intelligence professionals to break strict NSA rules that not only prohibited them from disclosing their passwords to an unauthorized party such as himself but required them to report any unauthorized person who asked to use their passwords. Remarkably, he accomplished this incredible feat. He gained access to twenty-four compartments containing the NSA's most closely guarded secrets in a matter of a few weeks.

Next, he had to find the lists he was seeking in a vast ocean of data. For this task, he used software applications called spiders to crawl through the data and find the files he was after. He deployed these robotic spiders, which presumably had been programmed in advance, soon after he began working at the center. According to the subsequent NSA damage assessment, Snowden's spiders indexed well over one million documents. Many of those that he copied and moved were from Level 3 sensitive compartmented information, according to the NSA analysis. The spiders also made his penetration relatively safe. As previously mentioned, the Hawaii base did not have a real-time auditing system. So alarm bells did not go off in the security office when he indexed documents.

Finally, Snowden had to find a way to transfer this data to a computer with an opened USB port. This task was complicated by a security precaution. Most of the computers at the center had had their ports sealed shut to prevent unauthorized downloads. Making the transfer even more difficult, he was working as an analyst in training in an open-plan office with closed-circuit security cameras. But it was not impossible. System administrators sometimes used service computers that had unsealed ports to back up data before they did maintenance work. Even though Snowden was no longer a system administrator, he could still perhaps befriend a system administrator or even steal or borrow a service computer.

Whatever the NSA's and Booz Allen's security measures, Snowden succeeded in getting the files. In a matter of a few weeks, he managed to download hundreds of thousands of Level 3 documents to an unsealed computer. He also took some less sensitive documents from the administrative file (which contained mainly Level 1 documents) at the end of April. These later acquisitions included an order from the FISA court issued on April 25, 2013.

He had completed the operation by May 17, the last day he would ever enter the NSA facility. He transferred the data he had amassed on the service computer, including the lists of the computers in Russia and China that the NSA had succeeded in penetrating, onto storage devices, which he later said were thumb drives. Then he coolly walked past the security guards at the exit, who only seldom performed random checks on NSA employees.

He carried out the entire operation with such brilliant stealth that he left few if any clues behind as to how he obtained his colleagues' passwords to multiple compartments, moved the data from many different supposedly sealed computers to an opened service machine, or downloaded these documents to multiple thumb drives without arousing suspicion. The NSA would not discover the theft for fifteen days.

His departure from Hawaii was also well prepared. Lindsay Mills had departed that morning for a planned two-week visit to the outer islands. This trip allowed him to pack his belongings without saying anything to her that might be difficult for her to later explain. He simply left a note that she could show to authorities saying that he was away on a "business trip." He informed Bay that he would have to go in for epilepsy tests on the following Monday and Tuesday. If the results weren't good, he might have to be out even longer.

CHAPTER 9

Escape Artist

I'm not self-destructive. I don't want to self-immolate and erase myself from the pages of history. But if we don't take chances, we can't win.

—EDWARD SNOWDEN, Moscow, 2014

THE NEXT EVENING, May 18, Snowden drove to Honolulu International Airport. He left his leased car in the parking lot. He took with him only carry-on baggage, including a backpack and a laptop with a Tor sticker on it. "I took everything I had on my back," he said, referring to the backpack. He also said that he took enough cash to pay for his fugitive life and he took the thumb drives containing the NSA's keys to the kingdom.

At this point, of course, Snowden was not wanted by the authorities. He had provided his employer and the NSA with a medical excuse for his absence from work so he would not be immediately missed. He had a valid passport, a credit card, and ID. Snowden's destination was Hong Kong. After crossing the international date line, Snowden waited about three hours in the transit zone of Narita. He then boarded a plane to Hong Kong. After the four-hour flight from Narita, he arrived in Hong Kong early in the morning on May 20.

He had visited Hong Kong at least once before, with Lindsay Mills, when he was stationed in Japan. According to Albert Ho, his

Hong Kong lawyer, Snowden stayed at a residence arranged for him in advance by a party whom Snowden knew prior to his arrival. As noted earlier, for the next ten days, Snowden did not use his credit card or leave any paper trail to his location. Wherever he was, "his first priority," as he later told Greenwald, was to find a place safe from U.S. countermeasures. He brought with him a large number of electronic copies of NSA documents marked TS/SCI/NOFORN, which stood for "Top Secret, Sensitive Compartmented Information, and No Foreign Distribution." According to government rules, data carrying these labels could not be removed from a government-approved "SCI facility." But Snowden, who brought them with him into this semiautonomous zone in China, broke these rules.

Wherever Snowden was staying, apparently he believed he was relatively safe. "That whole period was very carefully planned and orchestrated," Snowden later told *The Guardian* in Moscow. On May 22, he sent an e-mail to Bay (who did not know he had left Hawaii) saying that his epilepsy tests came back with "bad" results, and he needed further medical attention. Here Snowden communicated directly first with Gellman and then with Greenwald. He e-mailed Gellman under the alias "Verax."

Already, via Poitras, he had provided Gellman with PowerPoint slides from an NSA presentation about a joint FBI-NSA-CIA operation code-named PRISM. He believed it qualified as whistle-blowing because it revealed that the NSA, in intercepting e-mails, tweets, postings, and other web interactions about foreign terrorists, incidentally also picked up data about Americans. According to the rules imposed on the NSA, whatever information was accidently picked up about Americans was supposed to be eliminated and information about Americans collected because they were in contact with a foreign target was supposed to be minimized by periodic reviews. Even so, it was likely some data was not expunged in this process. So PRISM could cause embarrassment for the NSA.

Snowden had not yet made arrangements to meet journalists, but now he proposed that Gellman join him in Hong Kong. In attempting to convince him of the urgency of the trip, he wrote that he had reason to believe that "omniscient State powers" imperiled "our freedom and way of life." He noted, with a touch of modesty, "Perhaps

I am naive." He also added dramatically, "I have risked my life and family." Even so, Gellman declined coming to Hong Kong. (According to Greenwald, Gellman could not make the trip, because lawyers for *The Washington Post* were uneasy with having a reporter receive classified documents in a part of China.)

On May 24, 2013, Snowden attempted to apply more pressure on Gellman by telling him that the story about the PRISM program had to be published by the *Post* within seventy-two hours. Gellman could not accede to such a condition, because the decision of when to publish a story was made not by him but by the editors of the newspaper. He told Snowden that the earliest the story could be published was June 6, 2013, which was well past Snowden's deadline.

Snowden next turned to Greenwald in Brazil. Both Poitras and Micah Lee had made great efforts to tutor Greenwald on encryption protocols, with Lee's sending Greenwald a DVD by FedEx that would allow him to receive both encrypted messages and encrypted phone calls. Even then, Greenwald was unable to fully install it. As a result, Greenwald still had not met Snowden's requisites on encrypting his computer.

With Gellman uncertain, Greenwald was now essential to Snowden's plan. If he was to have any newspaper outlet, he needed to persuade Greenwald to come to Hong Kong. At this point, he took matters into his own hands. On May 25, Snowden somewhat aggressively e-mailed Greenwald, saying, "I've been working on a major project with a mutual friend of ours. You recently had to decline short-term travel to meet with me." Although he did not specify the "short-term travel" to which he referred, he added pointedly, "You need to be involved in this story." He suggested that they immediately speak on the phone via a website that encrypts conversations. Snowden began the call by complaining, "I don't like how this is developing." He made it clear that he, not the journalist he had selected, was pulling the strings. If Greenwald wanted the scoop, he had to follow Snowden's instructions, which included dividing the scoops between *The Guardian* and *The Washington Post*. According to his plan, Gellman would break the PRISM story in the *Post*, and Greenwald would break the "mass domestic spying" story in *The Guardian*. In addition, he insisted that *The Guardian* publish his personal manifesto alongside its story. As he envisioned it, the media event would also include a video component in which Greenwald would interview him.

Greenwald agreed to this micromanaging, so Snowden said he would send him what he called a "welcome package" of documents to demonstrate his good faith. His plan also required a face-to-face meeting. Snowden told him, "The first order of business is to get you to Hong Kong." The whole conversation lasted two hours, according to Greenwald.

Snowden sent him twenty classified NSA documents labeled "Top Secret." He also included in the package his personal manifesto, which asserted that the NSA was part of an international conspiracy of intelligence agencies that were working to "inflict upon the world a system of secret, pervasive surveillance from which there is no refuge."

Meanwhile, Snowden told Poitras he was sending her a number of NSA documents, including a FISA warrant that had been issued less than a month earlier. He wanted that FISA warrant to serve as the basis of Greenwald's scoop. It was perfect whistle-blowing material for *The Guardian* because it ordered Verizon to turn over all its billing records for ninety days to the NSA. It was as close to a smoking gun as anything he had copied at the NSA. It would also get attention because James Clapper, the director of national intelligence, had stated before Congress just two months earlier that the NSA did not collect phone data in America. This warrant would allow *The Guardian*, in the best tradition of gotcha journalism, to catch Clapper in an apparent lie.

Continuing his string pulling, Snowden instructed Poitras not to show the FISA warrant to Greenwald until they were safely aboard a plane to Hong Kong. That would prevent Greenwald from releasing the story previously. He also sent Poitras an entire encrypted file of NSA documents, saying it would "include my true name and details for the record, though it will be your decision as to whether or how to declare my involvement." He did not send her the key to decipher the file, saying, "The key will follow when everything else is done." He further told her that he preferred that her new film focus on him as the sole perpetrator of the leak so that no one else at the NSA would be suspected.

Poitras and Gellman were not the only journalists involved in the news event. Poitras also asked Appelbaum to help her interview Snowden about the NSA's operations. She later said that she needed someone with technical expertise in government surveillance to test the bona fides of Citizen Four. She believed that Appelbaum, who had participated in her anti-NSA presentations in 2012, qualified for the position.

Snowden previously had contact with Appelbaum. Appelbaum had communicated with Snowden under his Oahu CryptoParty alias about an obscure piece of software just a few weeks after Snowden had met with Runa Sandvik in Hawaii in December 2012. Appelbaum, in fact, had worked with Sandvik as a core developer of Tor software. Snowden allowed Appelbaum to put detailed questions to him concerning the secret operations of the NSA before he met with Poitras and Greenwald in Hong Kong. Indeed, Poitras joined him in asking Snowden via encrypted e-mails such questions as "What are some of the big surveillance programs that are active today and how do international partners aid the NSA?" "Does the NSA partner with other nations, like Israel?" and "Do private companies help the NSA?" Snowden answered all the questions to the satisfaction of Appelbaum and Poitras. (The interview was published on July 8, 2013, with Snowden's approval on the website of *Der Spiegel*, the German weekly, which had also published the WikiLeaks documents.)

As the days ticked away while Snowden was waiting for Greenwald in Hong Kong, Greenwald was awaiting a green light to go there from Janine Gibson, the editor of the *Guardian* website, who was based in New York. Under Gibson's leadership, *The Guardian*'s website had effectively "gone into the business of publishing government secrets," as the *Guardian* columnist Michael Wolff pointed out. Most of the documents had been supplied by Bradley Manning via WikiLeaks. Few if any of these previous documents *The Guardian* published were highly classified, and none were SCI top secret documents. The NSA documents Greenwald had received from Citizen Four were another matter. They contained the sort of SCI communications intelligence data that no major newspaper had ever published before. Their disclosure might result in journalists' being imprisoned, because both British law and U.S. law criminalized the disclosure by anyone of communications intelligence. As a lawyer, Greenwald recognized this danger. On the other hand, the NSA documents were far more explosive than the WikiLeaks material and promised an even greater spike in circulation. So Greenwald assumed that Gibson would be willing to authorize their publication and provide the expenses for his trip to Hong Kong.

He flew from Rio to New York on May 30 to meet in person with Gibson, who had concerns about publishing what were purported to be top secret documents that came from an anonymous source. She was certainly not willing to go along with Citizen Four's demand that *The Guardian* publish his personal manifesto alongside the documents. Aside from its shrill and alarming tone, it sounded, as she told Greenwald, "a bit Ted Kaczynski-ish," referring to the mathematician known as the Unabomber who had maimed or killed twenty-six people with anonymous mail bombs between 1978 and 1995. Kaczynski had also demanded that newspapers publish his personal manifesto. Gibson explained to Greenwald, "It is going to sound crazy to some people." Her concern was that it would detract from the credibility of the rest of the story. Snowden had also written to Greenwald to explain his position. "Even the Constitution is subverted when the appetites of power demand it," Snowden said. Paraphrasing President Thomas Jefferson, he continued, "Let us speak no more of faith in man, but bind him down from mischief by the chains of cryptography." Snowden, showing his cultlike faith in encryption, substituted "cryptography" for Jefferson's word "constitution." Gibson was unmoved. The stolen NSA documents were another matter. They were an enormous scoop that could have a greater impact than the WikiLeaks scoop.

Gibson authorized Greenwald's trip to Hong Kong on the condition that he take with him a *Guardian* staffer in whom she had confidence, the Scottish-born Ewen MacAskill, a sixty-one-year-old veteran journalist who had been the Washington bureau chief for *The Guardian*. His assignment was to evaluate the bona fides of the anonymous source in Hong Kong for Gibson. Greenwald accepted her terms. Poitras, who would be accompanying them, would be paying her own way.

In case *The Guardian* failed to publish the story, Snowden had a contingency plan in place. While Greenwald was negotiating with Gibson, Snowden arranged for Micah Lee, Poitras's associate at the Freedom of the Press Foundation, to build a personal website for him. Writing to Lee from Hong Kong, first under his alias Anon108 and later under his real name, Snowden said that he planned to post his "anti-surveillance manifesto." He would also use it to post "a global petition against surveillance." Snowden had Lee name the site "SupportOnlineRights.com." According to Lee, the website would be built with a "dead man's switch," which would automatically trigger the release of NSA documents if Snowden was arrested. It was not clear whether Lee was doing this work as a freelancer or in his capacity as the chief technology officer for the Freedom of the Press Foundation. The website Lee built for Snowden proved unnecessary when Poitras e-mailed him on June 1 that *The Guardian* had approved the trip and she and Greenwald were booked on a Cathay Pacific flight to Hong Kong. They would arrive the next day.

In his preparation to go public in Hong Kong, Snowden showed himself fully capable of orchestrating what would become a major news story. He not only picked the journalists who would break it but also instructed each of them as to the timing, sequence, and content of their initial disclosures. In the security of his unknown residence in Hong Kong, he also worked to carefully separate the purloined NSA documents into two very different caches. "I carefully evaluated every single document I disclosed," Snowden explained to the *Guardian* journalists in early June. The documents in this first cache were selected to serve what he termed the "public interest." In the hands of journalists, these selected documents, and the story he fashioned to accompany them, would burnish his image in the public consciousness as a whistle-blower. He did not turn over the second cache, telling Greenwald, "There are all sorts of documents that would have made a big impact that I didn't turn over."

By the time he received the message from Poitras, Snowden had finished his preparations for the journalists. With selected documents copied on a thumb drive, he moved from the residence where he had been staying for ten days to a venue for meeting the reporters. The place he chose, as noted earlier, was the Mira hotel in the Kowloon district of Hong Kong, where he checked in under his own name. He e-mailed Poitras his name and the address of the hotel; there was no longer any reason to hide his true identity.

CHAPTER 10

Whistle-blower

They elected me. The overseers . . . The [American] system failed comprehensively, and each level of oversight, each level of responsibility that should have addressed this, abdicated their responsibility.

—EDWARD SNOWDEN, Moscow, 2013

WHILE SNOWDEN in Hong Kong was attempting to reel in the journalists, Lindsay Mills returned to Honolulu from her "island-hopping" trip to find their house partially flooded and Snowden nowhere to be found. In a brief note Snowden left her, he said he was away on a business trip and indicated that, at least temporarily, their eight-year relationship was on hold.

"I feel alone, lost, overwhelmed, and desperate for a reprieve from the bipolar nature of my current situation," she wrote in her journal on June 2 (which would be June 3 across the international timeline in Hong Kong). "I've nearly lost my mind, family, and house over the past few weeks." She also noted in her online journal, "Oh and I physically lost my memory [SIM] card with nearly all my adventure photos," as well as other personal data. The loss would make it difficult to reconstruct her past activities with Snowden.

In Hong Kong, if Snowden were following Lindsay's online journal, he would have read that his girlfriend had returned home, lost her data, and needed a "reprieve" from the situation in which he had put her. But because they were exchanging private text messages by then, he would not have needed to consult her public journal. Snowden was certainly aware that he would soon be the object of a manhunt that could involve those with whom he was acquainted. He instructed Poitras to mask their e-mail communications in cyberspace "so we don't have a clue or record of your true name in your file communication chain." Such precautions were necessary, he explained to her, because "every trick in the book is likely to be used in looking into this." The journalists arrived the evening of June 2.

The Mira hotel can be entered by guests both through a ground-floor lobby with a restaurant and a smaller third-floor lobby that connects to the Mira shopping mall. The instructions that Snowden sent Poitras on her arrival were an exercise in control: "On timing, regarding meeting up in Hong Kong, the first rendezvous attempt will be at 10 a.m. local time. We will meet in the hallway outside of the restaurant in the Mira Hotel. I will be working on a Rubik's cube so that you can identify me. Approach me and ask if I know the hours of the restaurant. I'll respond by stating that I'm not sure and suggest you try the lounge instead. I'll offer to show you where it is, and at that point we're good. You simply need to follow naturally." According to Greenwald's account, Snowden changed the plan to the upper lobby. "We were to go to the third floor," Greenwald writes. "We were to wait on a couch near a 'giant alligator,'" which Poitras said was a room decoration. (A hotel executive told me that the hotel knew of no plastic alligator on the third floor but possibly it had been temporarily parked there by a hotel guest.) They were then to give the recognition signal. Although these instructions provided the atmospherics of "an international spy thriller," as Greenwald described them, Snowden hardly needed any spy tradecraft to recognize Greenwald and Poitras because there were many photographs of them on the Internet.

In any case, they gave the recognition signal, twice, in the designated place, and a young man walked over to them holding a Rubik's Cube. Greenwald noted, "The first thing I saw was the unsolved Rubik's Cube, twirling in the man's left hand." The man said, "Hello," and introduced himself as "Ed Snowden."

Greenwald was particularly surprised by Snowden's boyish looks.

"The initial impression was one of extreme confusion," Greenwald wrote in his book. "I was expecting to meet somebody in his sixties or seventies, someone very senior in the agency, because I knew almost nothing about him prior to our arrival in Hong Kong." His initial confusion was understandable. Snowden, it will be recalled, had falsely identified himself to them in an e-mail as a senior member of the intelligence community.

Snowden led Greenwald and Poitras to the nearby elevator, and they went through various corridors of the hotel to his room on the tenth floor. It was mainly occupied by a king-sized bed, but it also featured a sleek writing desk in the corner, two chairs, and a modernistic lamp. The bathroom was behind a glass partition, which could be closed off by a black louver blind. There was also a small refrigerator in which Snowden asked them to stow their cell phones.

Snowden, as we know, had already told Poitras that he wanted her to make a documentary of the meeting. She therefore wasted no time in mounting her camera on a tripod. "Minutes after meeting, I set up the camera," she said. Snowden told her, "When you are involved in an action which is likely to get you indicted, you typically don't have a camera rolling in the room." Nevertheless, he allowed her to film his actions for the next eight days. One possible reason is that he had no intention of standing trial. In any case, as Poitras found out, Snowden was anything but camera shy. Over the next week, she would shoot over twenty hours of Snowden's activities in that small room. It was essentially a one-man show, a presentation of him, by himself, for the appreciation of a global public. Poitras knew virtually nothing about her subject until ten minutes before she began filming him. She had not even googled him, because she was concerned that her Internet search might alert the NSA and law enforcement authorities. In an over-the-top waiver of his own privacy, he allowed her to film him washing in the bathroom, preening his hair in the mirror, napping on his bed, getting dressed, and packing his bag. He even permitted her to film a private computer exchange between him and Mills (who was in Honolulu). That day Mills informed Snowden that two government investigators had come to their home in Hawaii, asking her about Snowden's whereabouts. When he had failed to show up for work on June 3 it evidently set off alarm bells at Booz Allen and the NSA. Snowden expressed anger to the journalists in the room at the NSA's intrusions on the privacy of his girlfriend.

Snowden also performed his security procedures on camera, including stuffing bed pillows under the door to block any eavesdroppers and throwing a red blanket over his head, which he called jokingly his "magical cloak of power." He explained to Greenwald that he donned his "cloak" when he turned on his laptop to prevent any hidden cameras in the room from spotting his password. He also checked the hotel phone for bugs. It was not without irony that he went through these security rituals to protect his data as he allowed Poitras to film NSA data on his computer screen. Because he planned to use these journalists as his outlets to go public in a few days, the security measures he performed while on camera would only serve a temporary purpose.

The centerpiece of the planned video would take the form of an interview with Greenwald. Snowden himself provided the talking points. The filming would eventually provide Poitras with a feature-length documentary, *Citizenfour*, which would be commercially released in October 2014 and win an Academy Award for her.

The next day, Ewen MacAskill, whom Poitras had not wanted Greenwald to bring to the initial meeting, joined Poitras and Greenwald in Snowden's room. Snowden insisted that MacAskill also go through the ritual of stowing his cell phone in the minibar refrigerator. Not without irony, Snowden's own phone can be seen on his bed recharging. Although MacAskill was sent by Gibson to the event to verify the source's bona fides, he had apparently hardly been briefed. The questioning went as follows:

MACASKILL: Sorry, I don't know anything about you.
SNOWDEN: OK, I work for—
MACASKILL: Sorry, I don't know even your name.
SNOWDEN: Oh, sorry, my name is Edward Snowden. I go by Ed.

MacAskill went on to ask him to enumerate the various positions he held during his career in intelligence. Snowden was not entirely truthful in describing himself. He said that he had been a senior adviser to the CIA, when he had been just a telecommunications support officer. He also said he had been a senior adviser at the Defense Intelligence Agency, even though, according to that intelligence service, he was never employed there. (He did speak at an interagency counterintelligence course the DIA had sponsored.) He said he had a $200,000-a-year salary from Booz Allen when, according to Booz Allen, it was $133,000. It is understandable that he wanted to impress these *Guardian* journalists in light of his young age and boyish appearance, even to the extent of meretriciously claiming in the video that he had been personally given the "authority" at the NSA to intercept President Obama's private communications, which, according to an NSA spokeswoman, was not true. No NSA employee, and certainly no civilian contract worker, was given the authority to spy on the president of the United States, she insisted. Such career enhancements reinforced the fact that Snowden altered reality when it suited his purpose with journalists.

Snowden had greatly exaggerated or misrepresented the positions he held with the CIA and the DIA, but no effort was made by the team of journalists to verify the information. Instead, MacAskill wrote to Janine Gibson in New York, "The Guinness is good." It was a prearranged code by which MacAskill certified Snowden's credibility for *The Guardian*. Gibson told Greenwald to proceed with the story. Snowden had already provided Poitras and Greenwald with thumb drives on which he had loaded the documents he wanted them to use.

Greenwald wrote his first story about NSA transgressions based almost entirely on the FISA warrant involving Verizon's cooperation that Snowden had copied from the administrative file. Before the story could be published, however, the *Guardian* policy required relevant American government officials be given the opportunity to respond. Gibson made the requisite call to the White House national security spokesperson, Caitlin Hayden, who arranged a conference call with the FBI's deputy director, Sean Joyce, the NSA's deputy director, Chris Inglis, and Robert Litt, the legal officer for the Office of the Director of National Intelligence. After duly taking into account the response of these three officials, which included the admonition by Litt that "no serious news organization would publish this," Gibson gave the green light to publish the story.

The story broke on June 6. "NSA Collecting Phone Records of Millions of Verizon Customers Daily," proclaimed the *Guardian* headline. Under Greenwald's byline, it said, "Exclusive: Top secret court order requiring Verizon to hand over all call data shows scale of domestic surveillance under Obama." Along with it was the FISA order. The PRISM story broke hours later in *The Washington Post*. Written by Gellman and Poitras, it claimed that the NSA and the FBI were tapping directly into the central servers of nine leading U.S. Internet companies, which were knowingly participating in the operation. The latter allegation turned out to be not entirely true, because some of the Internet companies cited in the story denied that they had knowingly participated. The back-to-back publication of these two stories by *The Guardian* and the *Post*, however, provided the explosive "shock," at least in the global media, that Snowden had predicted.

Snowden's identity had not been revealed in either the *Guardian* or the *Post* story on June 6. Snowden, however, insisted on outing himself. He explained to Greenwald that he needed to "define himself" before the U.S. government "demonized" him as a spy. That self-definition would be accomplished by a twelve-minute video titled "Whistleblower." Poitras extracted much of the material for the video from the twenty or so hours she had shot. In the filmed interview, Snowden voiced many of the same statements he had made in his manifesto, so he no longer needed to post that on the Internet. When he insisted on the immediate airing of the video, Greenwald told him that by going public in this way, he was saying "fuck you" to the American government. Snowden replied, "I want to identify myself as the person behind these disclosures."

On June 9, the video was posted on the *Guardian* website with the Freedom of the Press Foundation getting an on-screen credit. "My name is Ed Snowden," the extraordinary disclosure began. He then described how the NSA was watching U.S. citizens. Even though the NSA press spokesperson subsequently disputed some of his more dramatic claims, such as his assertion that he had the authority at the NSA "to wiretap anyone, even the president," the press largely accepted his claims as established facts. As for American surveillance, he declared, "I don't want to live in a society that does those sorts of things."

The *Guardian* story accompanying the video carried the headline "Edward Snowden: The Whistleblower Behind the NSA Surveillance Revelations." Overnight, Snowden became a global celebrity and, to much of the world, a hero.

The next morning he packed his belongings into a backpack and moved, without notifying the front desk, to another room Poitras had rented at the Mira. Complicated schemes, especially when they involve transferring state secrets to unauthorized parties in a foreign country, do not necessarily go as planned. That was true of Snowden's escape plan. Snowden had no plan to stay put and face the music. On the morning of June 10, though, there was apparently a problem. Robert Tibbo and Jonathan Man, the lawyers who, along with Albert Ho, had been retained for Snowden by an unidentified party, received an emergency phone call early in the morning telling them to help Snowden move to a safe location. Although Tibbo would not identify the person who had called, the message had been relayed to Man and him through Ho's office. When Tibbo called Snowden offering to help him move, Snowden told him, "I can make myself unrecognizable."

Tibbo and Man immediately proceeded to the mall adjacent to the Mira hotel, where they met Snowden. After he signed a document appointing Ho's law firm as his "legal adviser," the three of them slipped out via the mall exit. Tibbo and Man planned to move Snowden to the apartments of refugees who were their clients.

Snowden's credit card had been frozen, so it is not clear who paid his sizable hotel bill. According to hotel records, it was paid by another credit card. Poitras, who had taken a room at the hotel, might have used her own credit card, or Snowden might have had another benefactor in Hong Kong. In any case, the lawyers escorted Snowden to a prearranged residence.

"I am in a safe house for now," Snowden wrote to Greenwald on June 11. The situation might not have been totally under his control, because he added, "But I have no idea how safe it is."

Greenwald flew back to Brazil that day. Soon afterward, he would resign from *The Guardian*. In February 2014, he became the cofounding editor of *The Intercept*, an online publication dedicated to investigative journalism, which was backed by the Internet billionaire Pierre Omidyar.

Poitras remained in Hong Kong, where she moved, along with the *Guardian* reporter MacAskill, to the five-star Sheraton Hong Kong Hotel & Towers, which, like the Mira hotel, was on Nathan Road in Kowloon. *The Guardian* paid the bill. Her next task was to set up what turned out to be Snowden's final interview in Hong Kong. It was scheduled for June 12.

The journalist chosen was Lana Lam, a young Australian reporter working for the *South China Morning Post*. Tibbo had suggested Lam to Snowden. She had served as Tibbo's outlet on previous news stories, and, as he told me, he found her to be a totally reliable journalist. He brought her to Poitras's suite at the Sheraton in Kowloon. First, Lam had to agree to the conditions of the interview, which included submitting the story to Poitras for Snowden's approval. Next, as Lam put it, Poitras "confiscated" her cell phone. Finally, after a ten-minute wait, Poitras took her to another room and sat her before a black laptop. The laptop, which had a Tor sticker on it, had on its screen an online chat room where she was connected by Poitras to Snowden.

"Hi Lana, thanks for coming for this," Snowden said from his safe house. He told her that the NSA had intercepted data from at least sixty-one thousand different computers in Hong Kong, China, and elsewhere. To expose what he called America's "hypocrisy" in accusing China of cyber espionage, he supplied her with relevant NSA documents. "Last week the American government happily operated in the shadows with no respect for the consent of the governed, but no longer," he said. "The United States government has committed a tremendous number of crimes against Hong Kong [and] the People's Republic of China as well." Under Poitras's close supervision, Lam was allowed to ask Snowden more questions about the NSA's interception of communications in Hong Kong and China. He told her, "I have had many opportunities to flee Hong Kong, but I would rather stay and fight the United States government in the courts." That bit of braggadocio would not be proven out.

Greenwald, Poitras, and MacAskill in their reporting did not concern themselves with any of the mechanics of the largest theft of top secret documents in the history of the United States. In the entire filmed interview at the Mira hotel, for example, they did not ask their source how he managed to get access to the documents. Lam, however, asked him about how he widened his access. When she asked him why he had switched jobs from Dell to Booz Allen Hamilton in March 2013, his answer provided her with a real scoop: "My position with Booz Allen Hamilton granted me access to lists of machines all over the world the NSA hacked." Snowden told her that he deliberately went to Booz Allen Hamilton to get access to the "lists" revealing the NSA's sources in foreign countries. This admission could further complicate his legal situation in Hong Kong because it suggested that he meant to steal documents even before he had known their content. In fact, to protect himself, he restricted Lam from publishing this part of the interview until *after* he had departed Hong Kong. (It was not published until June 24, a day after he arrived in Russia.) This condition indicated to Lam that as early as June 12, if not before, he was planning on leaving Hong Kong.

His interview with Lam didn't reveal how he had learned about these "lists" before taking the job. Nor did he reveal to her what he planned to do with these lists. He made it clear to her, however, that he had not disposed of all his secret documents. "If I have time to go through this information," he said, "I would like to make it available to journalists in each country to make their own assessment, independent of my bias, as to whether or not the knowledge of US network operations against their people should be published." So as late as June 12, Snowden was still reading and assessing the files he had stolen from the NSA four weeks earlier.

Poitras vetted the Lam interview. Soon afterward, she suspected that she was being followed. That was likely, because by June 14 all the intelligence services in Hong Kong knew that she was in contact with Snowden.

"I was being tailed," Poitras recalled in an interview with a *Vogue* reporter in Berlin in 2014. "The risks became very great," she said in describing her situation in Hong Kong. So, on June 15, she left Hong Kong and flew back to Berlin, where she began editing her footage of the Snowden interview.

Meanwhile, Snowden, organizing his own exit from Hong Kong, placed a call to Julian Assange.

CHAPTER 11

Enter Assange

Thanks to Russia (and thanks to WikiLeaks), Snowden remains
free.

—JULIAN ASSANGE, *Newsweek,* 2015

JULIAN ASSANGE had made a brilliant career of trafficking in
state, military, and corporate secrets. Born on July 3, 1971, in
Queensland, Australia, Assange began his hacking career while still
a teenager. Using the alias Mendax ("the untruthful one"), he had
hacked into the computers of the Pentagon, the U.S. Navy, NASA,
Citibank, Lockheed Martin, and Australia's Overseas Telecommunications Commission before he was twenty. At the age of twenty-five,
he pleaded guilty to twenty-five charges of hacking in Australia but
was released on a good behavior bond. In 2006, with the spread of
Tor software, he co-founded WikiLeaks, a website in which secret
documents could be anonymously sent and posted. The site received
little public attention until Bradley Manning sent it several hundred thousand lowly classified U.S. military and State Department
documents in April 2010. With these stolen documents, WikiLeaks
became a media sensation, and Assange, the runner-up for *Time*'s
Man of the Year for 2010, became a leading figure, along with Appelbaum, in the global hacktivist underground.

In November 2010, however, he ran into a legal problem in Sweden. A judge in Stockholm ordered his detention on suspicion of rape, sexual molestation, and unlawful coercion. He denied the charges but was arrested in London on a European arrest warrant. In December, he was released on a $312,700 bail deposit (supplied by his supporters) and confined to Ellingham Hall in Norfolk, England. While awaiting the outcome of the extradition proceedings, he lived there with Sarah Harrison, his twenty-eight-year-old deputy at WikiLeaks. A graduate of the elite Sevenoaks School in Kent, Harrison served as Assange's liaison with the outside world. Although she was officially given the title "investigative editor" of WikiLeaks, she worked so closely with Assange during this period that the British press carried stories saying she was his paramour. Harrison worked on a WikiLeaks documentary titled *Mediastan,* which concerned further publicizing WikiLeaks's exposé of embarrassing U.S. secrets in the former Soviet Union. It was a project that took her to Russia and provided her with a Russian visa.

In June 2012, after the extradition order was upheld, Assange jumped bail and fled to the Ecuador embassy in London. For the next year, his only visible means of income was a weekly program from the embassy. It was sponsored in 2012 by RT television, a Moscow-based, English-language news channel funded by the Russian government, which would also finance and release *Mediastan.* This sponsorship suggests that the Russian government saw potential value in the document-gathering activities of WikiLeaks.

Snowden telephoned Assange at his refuge at the Ecuador embassy on June 10, 2013. According to Assange, Snowden needed help for his exit plan. He wanted Assange to use WikiLeaks's "resources" to get him out of Hong Kong. Assange considered it a surprising request, because Snowden had not given any of the stolen documents to WikiLeaks. In their discussion, according to Assange, Snowden claimed that one reason he decided to take the secret NSA documents was the brutal treatment of Bradley Manning after he was arrested in 2010 by the U.S. government. "Snowden told me they had abused Manning in a way that contributed to his decision to become a whistle-blower," Assange said in an interview in 2015.

If Manning's mistreatment was Snowden's motive, it was a sharp departure from the position Snowden had taken in his postings on the *Ars Technica* site in January 2009. He complained in a post there about the detrimental consequences to U.S. intelligence of leakers' revealing "classified shit" to *The New York Times,* and he suggested as punishment "those people should be shot in the balls." Either he had a change of heart, or he was telling Assange what he believed he wanted to hear.

Assange counseled Snowden to go directly to Russia. "My advice was that he should take asylum in Russia despite the negative PR consequences," he told the London *Times* in 2015. He said, "Snowden was well aware of the spin that would be put on it if he took asylum in Russia." So a story would be released presumably by WikiLeaks, coinciding with his departure, asserting that Snowden was "bound for the republic of Ecuador via a safe route." When Snowden asked how he would carry out the plan, Assange told him that he would immediately dispatch one of his senior staff members to help him engineer his escape to Russia. That senior staff member was Sarah Harrison.

After speaking to Snowden, Assange called Harrison, who was in Melbourne. She had gone there a month earlier to help organize Assange's somewhat quixotic election campaign for president of Australia. Assange told her to forget the campaign and go to Hong Kong. She was to use WikiLeaks's resources to save Snowden from "a lifetime in prison." Presumably, Assange told her that he had advised Snowden to proceed to Russia. Harrison later said that she didn't even bother to pack her clothing after hearing from Assange. She caught the next plane to Hong Kong and arrived there on June 11— the same day that Snowden texted Greenwald he was in a safe house and before Snowden's explosive interview with Lam. Harrison had her own connections in Hong Kong. Her two younger sisters, Kate and Alexandra, lived there and were part of the expatriate community. She also had an older brother, Simon, who headed Avra, a ship brokerage and commodity trading company, headquartered in Singapore, but he frequently traveled to Hong Kong on business.

Like Poitras, Sarah Harrison took great care to shield her movements. She did not have a Twitter, Facebook, or any other social media account. She did not own a cell phone for fear of being tracked by an intelligence service. When she traveled, she bought "burner" phones locally and disposed of them before any calls could be traced back to her. Upon arriving in Hong Kong, she avoided meeting Snowden face-to-face out of concern about the surveillance of American intelligence there. Instead, for thirteen days in Hong Kong she worked through intermediaries. Her task was not only to arrange Snowden's escape route but also to create diversions to camouflage his real destination. Under Assange's tutelage, she had made deceptive ploys an integral part of her tradecraft. "We were working very hard to lay as many false trails as possible," she later told an interviewer in Berlin.

According to Assange, she booked decoy flights for Snowden to Beijing and New Delhi. She also used Snowden's credit card number to pay for the flight to India; because the card was blocked, she knew there was a high probability that it would come to the attention of U.S. intelligence. According to Harrison, she booked no fewer than a dozen such decoy tickets to confuse Snowden's possible pursuers in U.S. intelligence. The only actual ticket she bought for Snowden, according to an Aeroflot official, was one to Moscow at the last minute. She bought a ticket for herself on the same flight, leaving on June 23.

The source of the money for the Assange-Harrison operation is unclear. Subsequently, Harrison said she was setting up secret bank accounts to help organize such transborder escapes. Assange said she was using "WikiLeaks's resources." Harrison said the "WikiLeaks team" helped fund Snowden's flight to Russia from Hong Kong, as well as her own flight there. But WikiLeaks was not an organization with spare cash in June 2013. Assange had forfeited his own bail by fleeing to the embassy of Ecuador, offending many of his financial supporters in Britain. He had also all but exhausted his bank account. Aside from money that dribbled in from Poitras's six-month-old Freedom of the Press Foundation, the only steady source of funds for WikiLeaks in 2013 was the previously mentioned payments Assange received from the Russian government's RT television.

Mounting pressure was brought on the Hong Kong government to take action against Snowden. On June 16, the U.S. government informed the Hong Kong authorities that it had filed a criminal complaint against Snowden and would be seeking his extradition.

Because Hong Kong had a vigorously enforced extradition agreement with the United States, as mentioned above, it was expected that Snowden would be taken into custody. But China had the final say in any extradition decision. In fact, China had explicitly been given the right of vetoing any extraditions for any reason in the formal 1999 agreement between Hong Kong and the United States. Because the Chinese president, Xi Jinping, had just met with President Obama in California, China also had an interest in avoiding embarrassing public demonstrations on behalf of Snowden. According to a well-placed official in Hong Kong, China's liaison office in Hong Kong told the Hong Kong Authority in no uncertain terms that Snowden had to be out of Hong Kong by June 23.

On June 19, Snowden had a meeting with Tibbo, the barrister who would handle any eventual court case, and Man and Ho, the Hong Kong solicitors who had been retained for him. It took place in a small apartment where, according to Ho, they ate pizza while they discussed Snowden's options.

Tibbo wanted Snowden to remain in Hong Kong, allow himself to be arrested, seek bail, and fight extradition in court. Tibbo said he planned to mount a powerful legal defense against extradition by using a provision in Hong Kong's extradition treaty with the United States that protects fugitives from persecution on political grounds. After he told Snowden that it would entail a long court battle, Snowden asked him if he could avoid even being arrested.

Tibbo explained that Hong Kong courts, which closely follow British law, would certainly issue an arrest warrant for him immediately after the United States formally filed charges against him. Those charges could come within hours, he reckoned. Soon afterward, Snowden would be temporarily jailed, and his computers, electronic gear, and thumb drives would be seized and placed in the custody of the court. Tibbo would immediately seek his release on bail but could not guarantee an outcome because Snowden, who had fled U.S. jurisdiction, might be considered a flight risk. If so, Snowden could remain incarcerated during the long court battle. During the litigation, Snowden would have a platform to make his case against U.S. surveillance. Indeed, Tibbo's strategy involved building massive public support for Snowden's cause. Once the U.S.

government filed charges, though, Snowden could further expect it would invalidate his passport to go anywhere except for his return to the United States, and Interpol would issue a red alert to all its members. Because his case involved national security secrets, he had also to consider that the Hong Kong court could deny him any use of the Internet until his extradition case was settled. If Snowden wanted to leave Hong Kong, he had to act swiftly.

Tibbo, although evasive on the point when I interviewed him, might not have known about the escape Harrison was planning. He did not know that Snowden's other alternatives were not good. He had no money, and his credit card had been blocked. He had no visas to go to any other country, and Interpol would issue its own border alert as soon as the United States filed its charges. At that point, Hong Kong airport authorities would be officially notified and could prevent him from leaving the city. Even if he somehow got out, he would be an international fugitive. Tibbo counseled Snowden to seek redress in the Hong Kong courts.

Snowden, though, had no intention of allowing himself to be arrested. Despite what he had told Lana Lam only one week earlier, at least for publication, about his determination to seek justice in the Hong Kong courts, he had not planned to use Hong Kong as anything more than a temporary stopover on his escape route. Two months later and safely in Moscow, he made this point clear in a lengthy interview with Alan Rusbridger, the editor of *The Guardian*. He told him that it had never been part of his plan to use Hong Kong to escape the legal consequences of his act. "The purpose of my mission [to Hong Kong] was to get the information to journalists." If so, he had merely been using Tibbo, Man, and Ho to provide him with temporary cover while, following the instructions of Assange, Harrison laid down the smoke screen for his escape to Moscow.

CHAPTER 12

Fugitive

If I end up in chains in Guantánamo, I can live with that.

—EDWARD SNOWDEN, Hong Kong, 2013

DURING HIS INTERVIEWS with Poitras and Greenwald in June, Snowden said stoically, "If I am arrested, I am arrested." His fatalistic words notwithstanding, Snowden had made plans to seek a haven from American justice well before his meeting them. As early as May 24, 2013, he had suggested to Barton Gellman that he was making arrangements with a foreign government. To that end, he asked Gellman to insert an encrypted key in the Internet version of the NSA exposé that Snowden proposed he write for *The Washington Post*. He told him the purpose of the encrypted key was to assist him with a foreign government. Snowden did not identify any foreign government to Gellman, but Gellman said he knew that Snowden wanted to "seek asylum" overseas. He decided against assisting him. "I can't help him evade U.S. jurisdiction—I don't want to, and I can't," he later explained. "It's not my job. It's not the relationship. I am a journalist."

Although Gellman suspected that Iceland might be the foreign government in question, Snowden, as it turned out, had never contacted the consulate of Iceland while he was in Hong Kong. "We had heard nothing from Snowden," an Iceland government official told *Vanity Fair.*

Snowden also did not contact the government of Ecuador while in Hong Kong. In mid-June, while Harrison was laying down false tracks for Snowden in Hong Kong, Assange in London asked Fidel Narváez, who was a friend of his and the legal attaché in the London embassy of Ecuador, to issue a document that Snowden could use. But this document was not delivered to Snowden in Hong Kong (and it was later invalidated by Ecuador). There are no direct flights to Ecuador from Hong Kong. If Snowden had really planned to go to Ecuador without stopping in a country allied with the United States, he would have had to fly to Cuba. He would need a Cuban travel document to do that, which he could have obtained from the Cuban consulate anytime during his month in Hong Kong. But he did not obtain it. Nor did he acquire a visa to go to any other country in Latin America or elsewhere while in Hong Kong. So where was he headed?

Whatever foreign government with which Snowden was dealing earlier presumably did not have an extradition treaty with the United States. Almost all other countries that did not have active extradition treaties with the United States could not be directly reached by air. With three notable exceptions, the flights to most of these countries had stopovers in a country that was an ally of the United States, where officials could seize Snowden. The three exceptions were China, North Korea (via China), and Russia.

The only one of these three countries that Snowden is known to have had contact with directly during his thirty-three-day stay in Hong Kong was Russia. The Russian president, Vladimir Putin, revealed these contacts in a televised press briefing in September 2013. Putin did not provide the date of these contacts, but he provided an intriguing clue. Snowden was identified to him, according to Putin, not by name but merely as an "agent of special services." If his name was not given to Putin, it might have been because Snowden's first meeting with the Russians had taken place before Snowden became a household name on June 9, 2013.

For his part, Snowden was evasive when discussing his contacts with Russia while still in Hong Kong. When Lana Lam asked Snowden on June 12, 2013, whether he had already requested asylum from the Russian government, he deferred, saying, "My only comment is that I am glad there are governments that refuse to be intimidated by great power." The Russian government was clearly not intimidated by the threats of reprisals by the United States, as the Obama administration would learn after Snowden's arrival in Russia on June 23. Snowden could only have known that with certainty on June 12 if he had been in contact with Russian officials prior to his interview with Lam.

If Putin's own description of Snowden's interactions with the Russians in Hong Kong is to be believed, the decision to facilitate Snowden's escape to Russia had been kicked all the way up the Russian chain of command to Putin. Presumably, this decision-making process began earlier than June 21, when Snowden was said to have gone to the consulate. But how much earlier? Because Snowden had arrived in Hong Kong on May 20, his contacts with Russian officials could have occurred in May. Such a contact with the Russians would fit with Snowden's telling Gellman on May 24 that he needed his help in dealing with the diplomatic mission of a country that Snowden did not identify.

In any case, Putin said an American "agent of the special services" had contacted Russian diplomats because he wanted assistance. The agent, Snowden, of course, needed assistance to escape from Hong Kong. The decision to accept him in Russia, given the international ramifications, would have to be made at a much higher level than the Russian mission in Hong Kong.

Nine days before Snowden boarded Aeroflot Flight SU213 to Moscow on June 23, the United States had filed a criminal complaint against him. It had also officially alerted Interpol when it unsealed the complaint on June 21. It had invalidated his U.S. passport except to return to America (although he still had it in his possession at the Hong Kong airport). Because by this time he was the most famous visitor in Hong Kong, his passage through passport control on June 23 might have reflected the acquiescence of the Hong Kong authorities to the reported request of China to be rid of Snowden by that date.

According to one Aeroflot official, ordinarily all international passengers are required to have a valid passport as well as a visa to the country of final destination. Snowden had neither a valid passport nor a visa. Still Snowden was able to board the flight to Moscow. Aeroflot, a state-controlled airline, presumably responds to the Russian government on matters where Putin has given his approval.

Snowden first met Harrison in person on June 23. She was waiting for him in the car that Jonathan Man had arranged to take him to the airport that morning. Snowden was dressed in a gray shirt and khaki slacks. Harrison was dressed in jeans and flip-flops. She said she had chosen this dress style so that they would blend in at the airport with vacationing tourists. She had financed the trip, and she was apparently now calling the shots. Harrison's concern was that they might be arrested at the airport, so Man accompanied them through passport control. He was able to do this because he bought a ticket on the cheapest available international flight. Harrison had given Man a phone number to call if they got arrested. When she and Snowden boarded the flight at 12:45 p.m., Harrison effectively became Snowden's second "carer"—a job that would require her presence in Moscow for the next four months.

Snowden had pretty much remained silent until the plane took off. The first full proper sentence she heard from him as they headed for Moscow, as she recalled, was "I didn't expect that WikiLeaks was going to send a ninja to get me out."

Meanwhile, Assange continued creating "distractions," as he put it. On June 24, a booking was made for Snowden on an Aeroflot flight to Cuba, and this information was relayed to the foreign press organization in Moscow, resulting in over a dozen reporters flying to Havana on the flight. Snowden, of course, never showed up for it. "In some of our communications, we deliberately spoke about that [flight] on open lines to lawyers in the United States," Assange said. One subsequent piece of his misinformation was that Snowden was flying to Bolivia on the private plane of the Bolivian president, Evo Morales (who was then in Moscow for a meeting). That misinformation had the desired effect. U.S. allies in Europe, including France, Spain, and Portugal, refused to allow that plane to fly through its airspace, forcing the plane to land in Austria. This misinformation resulted in an international incident but did not change the fact that Snowden was still in the custody of Russian authorities.

Snowden came to realize that those assisting him, including Assange and Harrison, were taking serious risks. "Anyone in a three-mile radius [of me] is going to get hammered," he later said in 2015 to a reporter from *Vogue*. (After finally leaving Snowden in Moscow on November 3, 2013, Harrison moved to Berlin, where she set up an organization to provide, as she termed it, "an underground railroad" for other fugitives who had made available documents exposing government secrets.)

Snowden was sequestered in the transit zone of the Moscow airport for thirty-seven days. A Russian intermediary provided him with a Russian classic to read while awaiting asylum. It was Fyodor Dostoyevsky's *Crime and Punishment*, whose protagonist, Rodion Romanovich Raskolnikov, is a dissenter who believes breaking the law is morally justified by the unfair abuses of the political system.

Snowden received official sanctuary in Russia on August 1, 2013. His public statements in Hong Kong that he was willing to go to prison so that others could live freely in a democratic society were, as it turned out, mere rhetoric. Instead of risking prison, he had successfully escaped to a country in which he would be treated as a hero for defying the U.S. government. He had not sacrificed himself; he had transformed himself. He had risen from being a lowly technician in Hawaii whose talents went largely unrecognized to the status of an international media star in Moscow. In his new role, he could make Internet appearances via Skype to prestigious gatherings, such as the TED conference, where he would be roundly applauded as an Internet hero, as well as be paid a $20,000 fee for just his electronic participation. He would be beamed into dozens of ACLU meetings where he was celebrated as a defender of American liberty. He would describe to sympathetic audiences in Germany, Norway, and France the unfairness of the American legal system, asserting that it was denying him a "fair trial." He would now make front-page news by granting interviews to *The New York Times, The Washington Post, The Nation*, and other publications. He would join Poitras and Greenwald on the board of directors of the Freedom of the Press Foundation. He would be the subject of an Oscar-winning documentary, the hero of the 2016 Hollywood movie *Snowden* (directed by Oliver Stone), and a consultant to the 2015 season of the television series *Homeland*. He would be nominated for the Nobel Peace Prize in 2014. He would attract over one million followers to his tweets in 2015. "For me, in terms of personal satisfaction, the mission's already accomplished. I already won," he informed the *Post* in his first live interview in Moscow in December 2013. It was a mission that involved a very high-stakes enterprise: taking not only domestic surveillance documents but America's military and foreign intelligence secrets abroad.

Whistle-blowers do not ordinarily steal military secrets. Nor do they flee to the territory of America's principal adversaries. A fugitive, especially one lacking a Russian visa, does not wind up in Moscow by pure accident. It's hard to imagine that a Russian president with the KGB background of Putin would give his personal sanction for a high-profile exfiltration from Hong Kong without weighing the gain that might proceed from it. Whatever else may be said of Putin, his actions show him to be a calculating opportunist. Part of his calculus would be that the defector from American intelligence had taken possession of a great number of potentially valuable documents from the inner sanctum of the NSA and, aside from these documents, claimed to hold secrets of great importance in his head. To be sure, the practical value of this stolen archive would require a lengthy evaluation by Russia's other intelligence services. But it is hard to believe that a defector who put himself in the hands of the FSB, the successor to the KGB, and other Russian intelligence services wouldn't be expected to cooperate with them. Even if such a defector did not carry these files with him to Moscow, intelligence services have the means to recover digital files, even after they are erased from a computer or if they are sent to the cloud. Moreover, once secret documents are taken, they are compromised. Yet for much of the American public, Snowden remained a hero.

PART TWO

THE INTELLIGENCE CRISIS

What you've seen so far [in the Snowden theft of documents] is just the tip of the iceberg.

—RETIRED ADMIRAL MICHAEL MCCONNELL,
vice-chairman, Booz Allen Hamilton, 2013

CHAPTER 13

The Great Divide

That moral decision to tell the public about spying that affects all
of us has been costly, but it was the right thing to do and I have
no regrets.

—EDWARD SNOWDEN, Moscow, 2013

I N THE TWELVE-MINUTE VIDEO on *The Guardian*'s website,
Snowden correctly identified himself as an infrastructure analyst
at a regional base of the National Security Agency in Oahu, Hawaii.
He also revealed in a calm, unemotional voice that he had been the
source for the stories in both *The Guardian* and *The Washington
Post*. He said that he had supplied the secret, classified documents
that the two newspapers had used in their scoops about domestic
surveillance being conducted by the NSA, America's enormous electronic surveillance agency. These sensational revelations had been,
literally, the talk of the world, and now, in another major news event,
the boyish-looking Snowden took responsibility for what would
turn out to be the largest theft of top secret documents in the history of U.S. intelligence.

In the video, it will be recalled, Glenn Greenwald, who had broken the NSA story in *The Guardian*, questioned Snowden. What
was his motive? Greenwald asked. Why did he do it? Snowden
replied that he had become horrified by the NSA's secret operations,

which, to him, represented a kind of distillation of the excesses of the American national security state, and he had therefore made it his mission to blow the whistle. He believed that the public needed to be informed of the existence of a vast, secret surveillance operation directed against tens of millions of Americans that flagrantly violated U.S. laws and was a grave threat to their privacy and their freedoms. Within hours of the release of that video on the *Guardian* website, Snowden was known throughout the world as a courageous whistle-blower.

In Laura Poitras's remarks in accepting her Academy Award for *Citizenfour* on February 22, 2015, she said that Snowden acted as a whistle-blower not only to "expose a threat to our privacy but to our democracy itself." She received a standing ovation.

A large part of the public who viewed this powerful film, including many of my colleagues in journalism whose writing I greatly respect, came to accept Snowden's whistle-blowing narrative. The film so convincingly depicted Snowden as an altruistic young man willing to risk his own personal freedom and face years of imprisonment for the sake of others that editorial writers asked that he be given clemency from prosecution.

"Sitting on his unmade bed—white sheets and covers, white headboard, white bathrobe, white skin—Snowden seems like a figure in some obscure ritual, being readied for sacrifice," George Packer wrote about the film in a widely read article in *The New Yorker*.

This powerful narrative, as lucidly articulated by Poitras, Greenwald, and other Snowden supporters, described the NSA activities exposed by Snowden as part of a vast criminal conspiracy involving, among others, President Obama, James Clapper, the director of national intelligence, and both Democratic and Republican members of the congressional oversight committees. It further derided any claims that there was evidence that Snowden's theft of NSA secrets went beyond simply exposing government misdeeds. For example, this narrative asserted, as if it were established fact, that U.S. government officials had deliberately "trapped" Snowden in Russia. According to Snowden, the purpose of this government ploy was to "demonize" him. "There was no question that I was going to be subject to a demonization campaign," Snowden said in an interview from Moscow, "They [Greenwald and Poitras] actually recorded me on camera saying this before I revealed my identity." The purpose of this demonization was to divert attention from the government's own crimes.

To be sure, it is not unprecedented for the government to release defamatory information about individuals who have embarrassed U.S. intelligence by defecting. When two NSA analysts, William Martin and Bernon Mitchell, defected to Russia in the 1960s and accused the NSA of violating international law after arriving in Moscow, U.S. government officials responded by putting out the story that they were homosexual lovers, which was both untrue and irrelevant to the intelligence secrets that they had compromised. It is certainly possible that the government put out information to intentionally defame Snowden. Secretary of State John Kerry characterized him as a coward who should "man up" by returning to the United States.

While one can discount such characterizations against Snowden by government officials as demonization, as I do, one cannot as easily dismiss the independent evidence that undermines Snowden's assertion that his sole motive was blowing the whistle on illicit surveillance in the United States. For example, in 2014, the Lawfare Institute, a nonprofit organization that publishes a blog on national security concerns, in cooperation with the Brookings Institution, did an independent analysis of all the published documents that Snowden provided to the media. It concluded that with some notable exceptions, such as the two documents initially published by *The Guardian* and the *Post*, the now-famous FISA Verizon warrant and the PRISM slides, few of the other documents that Snowden had given Poitras and Greenwald for publication had anything to do with either domestic surveillance or infringements on the privacy of Americans. By the Lawfare Institute's count, 32 of Snowden's leaks to these journalists concerned the NSA's overseas sources and methods, 9 identified overseas locations of the NSA's intelligence bases, 25 revealed the identities of foreign officials of interest to U.S. intelligence agencies, 14 disclosed information about Internet companies legally cooperating with the NSA, and 19 concerned technology products that the NSA had been using or researching.

Some secret methods that Snowden made public compromised the NSA's state-of-the-art technology of which adversaries had been unaware. For example, the NSA had devised an ingenious technology in 2008 for tapping into computers abroad that had been "air-gapped," or intentionally isolated from any network to protect highly sensitive information, such as missile telemetry, nuclear bomb development, and cyber-warfare capabilities. The secret method that the NSA used involved surreptitiously implanting speck-sized circuit boards into air-gapped computers. These devices then covertly transmitted the data back in bursts of radio waves. Once Snowden exposed this technology, and the radio frequency transmission it used, America lost this intelligence capability.

In addition, a considerable number of the published documents did not even belong to the NSA but were copies of reports sent to the NSA by its allies, including the British, Australian, Canadian, French, Norwegian, and Israeli intelligence services. Snowden provided journalists with secret documents from the British cyber service GCHQ, describing its plans to obtain a legal warrant to penetrate the Russian computer security firm Kaspersky to expand its "computer network exploitation capability." What the GCHQ was revealing in this secret document was its own capabilities to monitor a Russian target of interest to British intelligence. While the release of these foreign documents might have embarrassed allies of the United States, they exposed no violations of U.S. law by the NSA. It was a legitimate part of the NSA's job to share information with its allies. This raises the question: What constitutes whistle-blowing?

To the general public no doubt, a whistle-blower is simply a person who exposes government misdeeds from inside that government. But in the eyes of the law, someone who discloses classified information to an unauthorized person, even as an act of personal conscience, is not exempt from the punitive consequences of this act. Indeed, if a person deliberately reveals secret U.S. operations, especially ones that compromise the sources and methods of U.S. intelligence services, he or she may run afoul of American espionage laws.

In the past, when government employees have disclosed highly classified information to journalists to redress perceived government misconduct, they were almost always prosecuted. During

Barack Obama's presidency, there were six government employees who, as a matter of personal conscience, shared classified information they obtained from the FBI, the CIA, the State Department, and the U.S. Army with journalists. They were all convicted: Shamai Leibowitz in 2010, Chelsea Manning in 2013, John Kiriakou in 2013, Donald Sachtleben in 2013, Stephen Kim in 2014, and Jeffrey Sterling in 2014. Like Snowden, they claimed to be whistle-blowers informing the public of government abuses. But because they disclosed classified documents, they were dealt with as lawbreakers. All six were indicted, tried, convicted, and sentenced to prison. Sterling, a CIA officer who allegedly turned over a document to James Risen, a Pulitzer Prize–winning reporter for the *Times,* was sentenced to forty-two months. The most severe sentence was meted out to Private Manning, whom an army court sentenced to thirty-five years in a military stockade, as noted earlier.

The prison time that others received did not go unnoticed by Snowden. He had been following the Manning case since 2012. In fact, he posted about it shortly before he began stealing far more damaging documents than Manning had. He would therefore likely have been aware that by revealing state secrets he had sworn to protect, he would be risking imprisonment unless, unlike Manning, he fled the country. His motives, no matter how noble they might be, would not spare him—any more than they spared the other six—from determined federal prosecution.

The view of those on the Snowden side of the divide is grounded not in legal definitions but in a broader notion of morality. Snowden's supporters do not accept that the law should be applied to Snowden in this fashion. A writer for *The New Yorker* termed it "an act of civil disobedience." His supporters argue that Snowden had a moral imperative to act, even if it meant breaking the law. They fully accept his view that he had a higher duty to protect citizens of all countries in the world from, as he put it, "secret pervasive surveillance." That higher duty transcended any narrower legal definitions of lawbreaking. Ben Wizner, a lawyer from the American Civil Liberties Union who has represented Snowden since October 2013, argues that Snowden's taking of classified documents was an "act of conscience" that overrode any legal constraints because it "revitalized democratic oversight in the U.S." and, without question, caused a much-needed debate on government surveillance.

In this ends-justify-the-means view, any person with access to government secrets can authorize him- or herself to reveal those secrets to the world if she or he believes it serves the public good. Further, because doing so would be an "act of conscience," he or she should be immune from legal prosecution.

For Snowden's supporters, his "act of conscience" justifies his claim to being a whistle-blower, even though the preponderance of the secrets he disclosed had to do with the NSA's authorized activity of using its multibillion-dollar global arrays of sensors to intercept data in foreign countries. For example, one of the thirty allied intelligence services that the NSA cooperated with in 2013 was the cyber service of Israel. Because Snowden deemed this cooperation to infringe on privacy rights, he revealed documents bearing on the NSA's data exchange with Israel. He subsequently told James Bamford, in an interview in *Wired* magazine in August 2014, that supplying such intelligence to Israel was "one of the biggest abuses we've seen." Snowden therefore believed he was justified in revealing information concerning Arab communications in Gaza, the West Bank, and Lebanon that the NSA had provided the Israeli cyber service, known as Unit 8200. In doing so, he compromised an Israeli source. But how could this act qualify as whistle-blowing? Providing Israel with such data was not some NSA rogue operation. It was part of a policy that had been approved by every American president— and every Congress—since 1948. Snowden had every right to personally disagree with this established U.S. policy of aiding Israel with intelligence, but it is another matter to release secret documents to support his view. If the concept of whistle-blowing were expanded to cover intelligence workers who steal secrets because they disagree with their government's foreign policy, it would also have to include many notorious spies, such as Kim Philby.

Snowden's concept of whistle-blowing also applied to the NSA's spying on adversary nations. "We've crossed lines," Snowden said in regard to China. "We're hacking universities and hospitals and wholly civilian infrastructure." The NSA's operations against China were such "a real concern" for Snowden that he targeted lists of the NSA's penetrations in China. Putin echoed this expansion of the whistle-blowing concept to adversaries. He complimented Snowden for having "uncovered illegal acts by the United States around the globe." Putin's defense of Snowden not only implied a global concept of whistle-blowing that justifies breaking U.S. laws but also pointed to America's double standard in publicly complaining about Russian and Chinese cyber espionage.

Snowden's whistle-blower interpretation gained immense public resonance. Even after President Obama and leaders of both houses of Congress roundly denounced Snowden for betraying American secrets, the majority of the public, according to a Quinnipiac poll taken in July 2013, still considered "Snowden a whistleblower who did a service revealing government domestic spying programs." Moreover, Snowden's revelations helped stoke a growing distrust of the American government itself. According to polls conducted by the Pew Research Center after Snowden came forward, just 19 percent of the public said that "they can trust the government always or most of the time." The support for Snowden was not limited to America. On October 29, 2015, a majority of the European Parliament voted to award Snowden the official status of a "human rights defender."

The former congressman Ron Paul went even further. He organized a clemency petition in February 2014 for Snowden, stating, "Thanks to one man's courageous actions, Americans know about the truly egregious ways their government is spying on them," and his son Senator Rand Paul, who was a candidate for the Republican presidential nomination in 2016, called for a pardon for Snowden.

Senator Paul's concern fitted with the growing public apprehension over increasing intrusion on privacy. Snowden was correct, in my opinion, in describing the threat of a surveillance state and the loss of privacy as a legitimate public concern. "We actually buy cell phones that are the equivalent of a network microphone that we carry around in our pockets voluntarily," he pointed out from Moscow.

The very technology involved in the electronic equipment we all use in the twenty-first century has made mass surveillance part of our daily life. There can be little doubt that our privacy has been largely eroded, if not entirely negated, by the widespread use of cell phones, credit cards, social media, and the search engines of the Internet. When we use smart phones, our location is relayed to our telephone service provider every three seconds. The phone companies collect and archive our phone usage "metadata," which includes whom we called and how long we spoke. When we use Google to search for anyone or anything on the Internet, that activity is captured by Google, a company whose profits mainly come from making available to advertisers the results of its surveillance and collection of its users' searches. When we use Gmail, Google's e-mail service, used by nearly one billion senders and recipients, we agree to allow Google to read the actual contents of our correspondence to find keywords of interest to advertisers.

When we use a credit card, the credit card company also retains data about what we buy and where we go. When we travel in automobiles equipped with GPS, every turn and stop is tracked and recorded. And when we are in public places with CCTV (closed-circuit television) cameras, our image is recorded and archived. When we use Facebook, Twitter, and other so-called social media, as over two billion people do today, we allow these companies to collect, retain, and exploit their surveillance of our movements, associations with other people, and stated preferences. When we use Amazon and other online stores, we allow them to track and archive a great deal of our commercial activity. For Internet companies such as Facebook, Twitter, and Yahoo!, like Google, collecting private data on hundreds of millions of their members provides them with vast searchable databases that are easily marketable. The exploitation of these databases is a fundamental aspect of their business plans. Without such surveillance of their users, social media companies would not be able to turn a profit. Indeed, they may be more aptly called surveillance media than social media. For those of us who use them to post pictures and communicate, any notion of personal privacy is largely illusory.

To be sure, there is a distinction to be made between the surveillance of our activities to which we voluntarily agree in exchange for the benefits and conveniences that we gain from social media, search engines, and other Internet companies and the surveillance done by the government, which we do not voluntarily invite—or want. We willingly waive our privacy for corporations but not for governments.

What the public might not fully realize, however, is that the government can access all the personal information in the databases of private companies if it issues a subpoena or search warrant, which it does often. As Snowden himself pointed out, "If Facebook is going to hand over all of your messages, all of your wall posts, all of your private photos, all of your private details from their server, the government has no need to intercept all of the communications that constitute those private records." These Internet companies, even if they are only interested in exploiting the data for their own profit, cannot refuse to share this information with the NSA, the FBI, and other government agencies if they have a subpoena or search warrant.

That reality became evident to me in my investigation of the rape charges brought (and subsequently dropped) against Dominique Strauss-Kahn, the managing director of the International Monetary Fund, in 2011. Immediately after his arrest, Cyrus Vance Jr., the district attorney of New York County, issued a subpoena for Strauss-Kahn's cell phone records, credit card records, hotel room electronic key records, e-mails, room service bills, and the CCTV videos of his activities (some of which I published in my article about the case in *The New York Review of Books*). Nor is this access uncommon. According to Vance in 2016, his office issues thousands of such subpoenas every year. Even though Apple made headlines by refusing to comply with a court order to help the FBI unlock the iPhone of a dead mass murderer in 2016, it had complied with many previous subpoenas. In fact, in 2015 alone, it quietly provided the backed-up data of some seventy-one hundred iPhone customers to government authorities.

If anyone doubts the pervasiveness of government data collection, consider a little-known government agency called the Consumer Financial Protection Bureau. Created in 2010 by Congress, it mines data on a monthly basis from some 600 million personal credit card accounts, targeting about 95 percent of the credit card users in the United States. In addition, through eleven other data-mining programs, it gathers data on everything from private home mortgages and student loans to credit scores and overdrafts in personal bank accounts. This ubiquitous surveillance of virtually every non-cash transaction came about because of advances in computer technology that made it economically feasible to mine such data.

Snowden's concern about NSA domestic surveillance is certainly not misplaced. Ever since the 9/11 attacks, the NSA has increasingly played a role in this surveillance state, not by its own choice, but because Congress mandated it. In 2001, it empowered the NSA to obtain and archive data on American citizens. Accordingly, the NSA obtained the billing records of customers from phone and Internet companies and archived these records. The bulk collection of these billing records was intended to build a searchable database for the government that could be used to trace the history of the telephone and Internet activities in the United States of FBI-designated foreign terrorists and spies abroad. The government's rationale for keeping these anti-terrorist programs secret from the public was that it did not want the foreign suspects to realize their communications in America were being monitored.

The public only learned that the phone company was routinely turning over its billing records on June 6, 2013, when Snowden disclosed it to *The Guardian* and *The Washington Post*. The documents he provided the journalists showed that the NSA had been obtaining phone records collected by Verizon every three months. While this revelation might have shocked the American public, the NSA had not acted on its own. It had acted under a warrant issued by a secret court established by Congress in 1978 as part of the Foreign Intelligence Surveillance Act for each request for records. Congress empowered the FISA court, whose judges are appointed by the president, to hear cases and authorize search warrants in secret in cases involving national security.

As its name implies, the FISA court was meant to deal with matters bearing on foreign intelligence activities in the United States. That restriction changed after the terrorist attacks of September 11, 2001. A month after the attacks, Congress expanded the purview of the FISA court by passing the USA Patriot Act (an acronym that stands for Uniting and Strengthening America by Providing Appropriate Tools Required to Intercept and Obstruct Terrorism). Part of the act, Section 215, euphemistically referred to as the "library records" provision, permitted the FISA court to issue warrants authorizing searches of records by the NSA and other federal agencies to investigate international terrorism or clandestine intelligence activities. Through these FISA authorizations, the NSA could obtain "tangible things" such as "books, records, papers, documents, and other items." Under the interpretation of this section of the law by both the Bush and the Obama administrations, the FISA court was enabled by Congress to issue warrants to telephone companies demanding that they turn over to the NSA the bulk billing records of all calls made in America. The FISA court need only deem these records to be "relevant" to the FBI's investigations of terrorists and spies.

Essentially, the NSA, to create a searchable database of telephone billing records, used the FISA court's controversial interpretation of the word "relevant" in Section 215. Such a "haystack," as the NSA called the national collection of billing records, could allow the FBI to instantly find missing "needles," as this tracking was supposed to work, even if the connections were made years earlier. For example, if the FBI had a lead on a foreign suspect, it could search the database for any telephone calls made by the foreign suspect to telephone numbers in America and then who those people called. The FBI always had this power, if it obtained a warrant, but it did not previously have the "haystack" of records in a single database. General Keith Alexander, who headed the NSA between 2005 and 2014, believed that maintaining such a haystack database made sense. "His approach was, 'Let's collect the whole haystack,'" according to one former senior U.S. intelligence official quoted by *The Washington Post*.

According to critics of NSA domestic surveillance, including the ACLU, the results provided by this vast database did not justify its immense potential for abuse. In early May 2015, just three weeks before this part of the Patriot Act was set to expire, a three-judge panel of the Second U.S. Circuit Court of Appeals in New York agreed with the ACLU position, overturning a lower court decision that said it was legal. The panel found that the word "relevant" in the act was not intended by Congress to justify the acquisition and storing of the bulk records of telephone companies for possible future use. Soon afterward, Congress replaced the Patriot Act with the USA Freedom Act, which effectively transferred bulk storage of billing records from the NSA to the phone companies themselves. Despite the change in venue, the records of individuals were still not completely private. Under the new law, the FBI via a FISA warrant could still search the phone company's databases.

The core of Snowden's charge in the media was that the FISA court overreached its authority by issuing sweeping warrants that allowed the NSA to obtain data collected by private phone and Internet companies. In the initial story published in *The Guardian* on June 6, Snowden disclosed one such FISA warrant to support his charge. It was issued by Judge Roger Vinson of the FISA court on April 25, 2013, and ordered Verizon to turn over to the FBI all its billing records of landline customers for the next ninety days. The FBI presented this FISA authorization to the NSA, which acts as a service organization for the FBI and the CIA in collecting communications data. The NSA, with the FISA warrant in hand, then obtained the Verizon billing records.

Snowden also provided the *Post* and *The Guardian* with another secret document: a PowerPoint presentation on twenty slides, sent by the NSA to other intelligence agencies. It described a program it was using for monitoring the Internet. Its code name was the aforementioned PRISM. It was authorized under Section 702 of the Foreign Intelligence Surveillance Act and was designed to collect messages sent over the Internet from foreigners. Such information was in fact obtained with the knowledge of the service providers. It also required a written directive from both the attorney general and the director of national intelligence and a review by the Department of Justice every three months for each and every case. After obtaining this data, the NSA ran programs, as required by law, to "minimize" all non-foreign names that had been picked up "incidentally," such as, for example, communications targeted terrorists in Pakistan had with Americans. But, as Snowden correctly pointed out, many of these American names stayed in the database. In addition, whenever the Justice Department actually opened an investigation against Americans in contact with foreign suspects, as it did in 170 cases in

2013, it could obtain warrants from the FISA court to search these Americans' Internet activities.

These two documents raised legitimate questions for many Americans, including members of Congress, about the proper role of the FISA court, including whether it should conduct its business in secret. If Snowden had released only these two documents that related to unwarranted domestic surveillance and other possible violations of the law by the NSA, it would be difficult for any reasonable person not to see his actions as a potentially valuable public service. Indeed, additional safeguards were necessary in an age in which new technologies enabled mass surveillance of the public. As the three-judge panel of the Second U.S. Circuit Court of Appeals would later find, Congress had not intended Section 215 of the Patriot Act to be used to justify the bulk collection of American records. If he had limited his illegal downloading to the few documents about bulk collection, it would be more difficult to argue that he was not a whistle-blower in the spirit if not the letter of the law, and even a hero in the struggle to preserve our civil liberties. But in fact, Snowden took a great many other secret documents that did not bear on the civil liberties of Americans. He claimed he was acting on behalf of citizens in foreign countries by exposing the NSA's and the CIA's spying operations abroad, but that same claim could also be made by any espionage agent stealing U.S. secrets to benefit the people of another country.

As a result, the Snowden case produced a great divide in the American appreciation of him. On one hand, he has been almost universally lauded and lionized by what might be seen as the mainstream media, by numerous academics, and even, as we have seen, by members of Congress. The journalists who assisted him, Greenwald, Poitras, and Gellman, have been celebrated for the roles they played in bringing Snowden's revelations to the public and received the 2014 Polk Award for national security reporting. The *Post* and *The Guardian*, the newspapers that initially published the purloined documents, won the 2014 Pulitzer Prize for public service.

In other circles, the reaction has been very different. American and British intelligence officials, senior members of the Obama administration, and members of the oversight committees of Congress do not view Snowden as a hero or even an authentic whistleblower. Instead, they see him as a betrayer of secrets who willfully brought damage to the United States and benefits to its adversaries. The holders of this darker view of Snowden base it on classified reports of the full extent of the theft of classified data. Those officials believe that only a handful of the tens of thousands of documents he stole involved domestic surveillance and that those few documents served as a cover for a much larger theft.

Admiral Michael Rogers, who replaced General Alexander as head of the NSA in March 2014, said at a public forum at Princeton University, "Edward Snowden is not the 'whistleblower' some have labeled him to be." He further explained to Congress, "Snowden stole from the United States government a large amount of classified information, a small portion of which is germane to his apparent central argument regarding NSA and privacy issues."

General Martin Dempsey, the chairman of the Joint Chiefs of Staff, went even further. In testifying before the House Armed Services Committee on March 6, 2014, after estimating that the Snowden breach could cost the military "billions" to repair, he added, "The vast majority of the electronic documents that Snowden exfiltrated from our highest levels of security had nothing to do with exposing government oversight of domestic activities." Dempsey based this assessment on a then still-secret Defense Intelligence Agency report on the breach. The classified DIA report showed that Snowden took "over 900,000" military files from the Department of Defense in addition to the NSA files he had taken. The Defense Department loss in terms of the number of files stolen actually exceeded the loss—in sheer numbers—of NSA documents. Lieutenant General Mike Flynn, the DIA director who directed the study, testified to the Senate Select Committee on Intelligence that the breach "has caused grave damage to our national security."

To be sure, this was not the first time that the cryptological branches of the military had been compromised. The spy ring of John Walker had provided thousands of the navy's reports on breaking Russian ciphers to the KGB during the Cold War. But the Snowden breach exposing military sources was an order of magnitude greater than any past breach.

The CIA's assessment was no less grim. Morell, the deputy director of the CIA in 2013, wrote that Snowden's action went beyond taking the handful of documents, such as the FISA order, "that addressed the privacy issue." Instead, as Morell put it, "he backed up a virtual tractor trailer and emptied a warehouse full of documents—the vast majority of which he could not possibly have read and few of which he would likely understand—[and] he delivered the documents to a variety of news organizations and God knows who else." As a result, Morell concluded, "Snowden's disclosures will go down in history as the greatest compromise of classified information ever." General Alexander, the head of the NSA at the time of the theft, asserted that Snowden did "the greatest damage to our combined nations' intelligence systems that we have ever suffered." Obviously, military intelligence officers would not be on Snowden's side of the divide (and the Snowden breach ended the careers of many of them, including Alexander). But political leaders in both parties could also be found on the anti-Snowden side of the divide. "I don't look at this as being a whistle-blower," the Democratic senator Dianne Feinstein of California, the head of the Senate Intelligence Committee, said after she was briefed on Snowden's theft. "I think it's an act of treason." The Republican representative Mike Rogers of Michigan, her counterpart on the House Intelligence Committee, said on the NBC program *Meet the Press* that Snowden might be working for a foreign intelligence service. And a former prominent member of President Obama's cabinet went even further, suggesting to me off the record in March 2016 that there are only three possible explanations for the Snowden heist: (1) it was a Russian espionage operation; (2) it was a Chinese espionage operation; (3) it was a joint Sino-Russian operation. These severe accusations generated much heat but little light. They were not accompanied by any evidence showing that Snowden had acted in concert with any foreign power in stealing the files or, for that matter, that he was not acting out of his own personal convictions, no matter how misguided they might have been.

On this side of the divide, Snowden's critics regard the whistle-blowing narrative as at best incomplete and at worst fodder for the naive. They point out that the FISA document that gave him credentials as a whistle-blower was only issued in the last week of April 2013, which was four months *after* he first contacted Greenwald and almost nine months after he began illegally copying secret documents. They further believe that the evidence contradicts Snowden's claims that he stole only documents that exposed NSA transgressions into domestic surveillance, that he turned over all the stolen documents to journalists, and that he was forced to remain in Moscow by the actions of the U.S. government. They also find that the unprecedented size and complexity of the penetration of NSA files, compromising hundreds of thousands of secret documents pertaining to U.S. operations against adversary nations, according to the NSA's and the Pentagon's estimates, is not easily explained given Snowden's avowed purpose for his theft.

The deep split in how Snowden is perceived brings to mind the famous drawing of a duck-rabbit cartoon first published in 1900 in the book *Fact and Fable in Psychology*. The figure is perceived either as a duck or as a rabbit, but it cannot be seen as both simultaneously. Whether a person sees a rabbit or a duck in this test may depend on the information available to that person. Similarly, what may account for the sharp divide between the pro-Snowden and the anti-Snowden camps is a disparity in their available information.

The pro-Snowden camp's view is largely informed by Snowden himself. Snowden supporters prefer to believe his words rather than his actions. In the anti-Snowden camp are administration officials and the members of the House and Senate intelligence oversight committees who have been at least partially briefed on the continuing investigations of the Snowden affair. The members of the Senate Intelligence Committee, for example, were told by David Leatherwood, the director of operations for the Defense Intelligence Agency, that the military files compromised by Snowden included documents bearing on military plans and weapons systems; foreign governments' intelligence activities (including special activities); intelligence sources, or methods of cryptology; scientific and technological matters relating to national security; and vulnerable systems, installations, infrastructures, projects, plans, and protection services related to national security and the development, production, or use of weapons of mass destruction. The members of the House and Senate Intelligence Committees, but not the public, have also been privy to an NSA investigation that established the chronology of Snowden's actions, including changing jobs, removing 1.5 million classified files from the NSA base in Hawaii, and flying to Russia.

Additional information does not necessarily change the minds of people who already have a firm view. In the field of social psychology, the testing of "confirmation theory" consistently shows that people tend to more readily reject new information that contradicts their pre-existing beliefs. For example, when Lee Harvey Oswald was arrested in the Texas Theater on November 22, 1963, he said famously, "I haven't shot anybody." Ten months later, the Warren Commission presented evidence, including ballistic tests, that it claimed showed that Oswald had shot three people, including President John F. Kennedy, less than an hour before making his statement. Yet many of those who believed Oswald's public proclamation of his innocence chose to believe that the government had falsified all the incriminating evidence to tarnish Oswald (who had been killed on November 24, 1963) rather than accept that they had been wrong in believing Oswald.

The charges, countercharges, and defamatory name-calling in the Snowden case therefore only deepened the great divide. Those who saw Snowden as a democratic hero exposing the abuses of power of an out-of-control national security state tended to dismiss anything that depicted Snowden in a negative light as a fabrication, while those who saw Snowden as a "traitor" tended to dismiss anything that depicted him in a more positive light.

When it comes to the murky universe of spy agencies, the problem in deciding where the truth lies is further heightened by the possibility of deliberate deception. Spy masters are, after all, in the business of concealing their most sensitive operations. It is often considered essential that important secrets be protected by what Winston Churchill famously termed "a bodyguard of lies." Top intelligence officials are not exempt from this practice. Consider, for example, the response to a question concerning the NSA's operations made by James Clapper, the director of national intelligence, to the Senate Intelligence Committee on March 12, 2013. The Democratic senator Ron Wyden of Oregon, who was on the committee, asked the spymaster if the NSA collected data on Americans. Clapper answered that the NSA did not knowingly "collect any type of data" on millions of Americans. Clapper's answer was clearly untrue, but it did not mislead Senator Wyden or any other members of the Senate Intelligence Committee; Clapper had truthfully testified in a classified session of the committee earlier that week that the NSA did collect Americans' telephone records. It was the American people who were being misled. Yet none of the senators on the committee corrected this obviously false answer. When Clapper realized he had misspoken, he could not publicly correct the record of the public session, because to do so would be revealing classified information he had sworn to protect. No doubt other intelligence officers find themselves in a similar bind in discussing secret matters. This suggests that there is a risk in accepting statements made by the intelligence chiefs at face value.

But Snowden also has a credibility problem. He has told numerous untruths, including some calculated to help him insinuate himself into the key positions from which he stole secrets and some calculated to cover up the nature of his theft. For example, Snowden got access in the spring of 2013 to the NSA's super-secret computers that stored these electronic files by working at Booz Allen Hamilton. On his application to Booz Allen in March 2013, as we've seen, Snowden claimed to be in the process of completing a master's degree at the University of Liverpool in computer security sciences. Snowden had not completed a single course there and purposely lied to get access to classified documents and then to get safely away with them.

He was also not entirely truthful with the journalists whose trust he sought when it suited his purpose of protecting himself. For example, as we have seen, in contacting Laura Poitras under the alias Citizen Four in January 2013, he told her that he was currently a "government employee," although in fact he was working for a private contractor at the time.

Snowden had little concern about misleading journalists when it suited his purpose. For example, he told Alan Rusbridger of *The Guardian*, Brian Williams of NBC News, James Bamford of *Wired*,

Katrina vanden Heuvel of *The Nation*, Barton Gellman, and Jane Mayer of *The New Yorker* that the U.S. government intentionally acted to "trap" him in Moscow by revoking his passport while he was already on a plane to Moscow on the afternoon of June 23. None of these journalists asked Snowden what the basis for his oft-repeated allegation was. If they had, they would have discovered that he had no independent basis for his assertion. When asked about it during the Q&A following his July 12 press conference in Moscow, he indeed said that the only knowledge he had about the suspension of his passport was what he had "read" in the news reports. But all the news stories prior to his statement reported that his passport had been revoked on June 22, while he was still in Hong Kong. ABC News, for example, reported that the U.S. "Consul General–Hong Kong confirmed Hong Kong authorities were notified that Mr. Snowden's passport was revoked June 22." By advancing that date to when his plane was in "midair" on June 23, Snowden provided to unsuspecting journalists an untrue alibi for his presence in Russia.

The credibility problem with Snowden assumed a more sinister dimension once he put himself and his fate in the hands of the Russian authorities in Moscow. Even though the Obama administration decided against revealing the extent of the Russian intelligence service's participation in Snowden's move from Hong Kong to Moscow, or what intelligence services call an "exfiltration," I was told by a presidential national security staff adviser that the government acted to protect the intelligence sources used by the CIA, the NSA, and the FBI to track Snowden's movements in the latter part of June in Hong Kong. The CIA's deputy director, Morell, would go no further than to state that during that period he had no doubt that the intelligence services of Russia and China "had an enormous interest in him and the information he [Snowden] had stolen." Presumably, the last thing these adversary services would want would be to make this "interest" transparent to the United States.

The role of concealment must be taken into account when assessing information bearing on the work of espionage services. When I was interviewing James Jesus Angleton—the CIA's legendary ex-counterintelligence chief, active in the 1970s—for a book on deception, I learned that intelligence services play by a different set of rules from historians when it comes to their espionage successes. Angleton, a famously baroque thinker himself, impressed on me the complexity of espionage. He said, "It's not enough just to steal a secret. It must be done in a way that the theft remains undetected."

Deception is employed to obscure the nature and the extent of the espionage theft. One of the most famous examples of this principle was the deception used by British intelligence in World War II to conceal its success in breaking the German ciphers generated by the Enigma machines. If German naval intelligence had discovered Britain was able to read the ciphers it used to communicate with its U-boats, it would have stopped using them. So British intelligence hid its coup by supplying false information to known German spies to account for the sinking of U-boats, including the canard that British aerial cameras could detect one ingredient in the paint used to camouflage the U-boats.

That same hoary principle of deception applies to modern-day communications intelligence. If the Russian, Chinese, or any other adversary intelligence service got its hands on the documents stolen by Snowden from the NSA's repositories in Hawaii in 2013, it would likely employ deception, including well-crafted lies, to create as much ambiguity as possible as to the missing documents. From this counterintelligence perspective, the intelligence issue that spawned the great divide cannot be resolved by accepting the uncorroborated statements made by a source, such as Snowden, who may be in the hands of the Russian security services in Moscow.

By the same token, the calculations made by NSA officials about the extent of the theft are also suspect. After all, the NSA is an intelligence service that often engages in secret machinations. We know that its top officials reported to the House and Senate Intelligence Committees, as well as the president's national security adviser, that Snowden compromised over one million documents. But if this was disinformation, it is difficult to see its purpose. Inflating the extent of the damage of the Snowden breach to the president, Congress, and the secretary of defense obviously reflected poorly on their own management of the NSA, and their own careers. Yet such a possibility cannot be precluded in the arcane world of intelligence.

As in any case involving the loss of state secrets, uncontested facts remain in extremely short supply. The opinion-laden appellatives such as "patriot" and "traitor" that have tended to fill the gap in the great divide do little to address the important mystery of how many thousands of state secrets were taken from the United States. How did Snowden breach the supposedly formidable defenses of the NSA? Did he have any assistance? How did he escape to Moscow? And what was the final destination of the stolen documents? How Snowden succeeded in this coup cannot simply be pieced together from his own statements and interviews. The story also requires a visit into the wilderness of mirrors of a counterintelligence investigation. For this endeavor, it is necessary to return to the crime scene: the NSA's base in Hawaii.

CHAPTER 14

The Crime Scene Investigation

Any private contractor, not even an employee of the government, could walk into the NSA building, take whatever they wanted, and walk out with it and they would never know.

—EDWARD SNOWDEN, Moscow, 2014

FIFTEEN MILES NORTHWEST of Honolulu on the island of Oahu, adjacent to the sprawling Wheeler Air Force Base, is a 250,000-square-foot, man-made mound of earth and reinforced concrete surrounded by an electrified fence. Inside the mound is a three-story structure originally built by the air force in World War II as a bomb-proof aircraft repair facility. In the Cold War, it was modernized to withstand enemy chemical, biological, radiological, or electromagnetic pulse attacks and was used by the navy's operation center for its Pacific fleet. After the Cold War, the huge edifice was turned over to the NSA, which, as stated earlier, had been created as an intelligence service to intercept the communications and signals of foreign countries after World War II, a mission that included vacuuming into its giant computer arrays telephone messages, missile telemetry, submarine signals, and virtually everything on the electromagnetic spectrum of interest to the U.S. Defense Department and U.S. intelligence agencies. As the NSA developed it, this Hawaiian base became one of its primary regional bases for gathering Asian communications intelligence. It provided a valuable window on the activities of adversary nations in the Pacific region and was able to monitor the ballistic missile tests and submarine activities of China, North Korea, and Russia. By 2013, the Kunia base had a vast array of state-of-the-art technology, including ninety Cray supercomputers arranged in a horseshoe configuration, used to decipher and make sense of the intercepted signals from China, Russia, and North Korea. At the heart of the Hawaiian complex was a unit with both military and civilian employees. A large share of the civilians who ran the computers worked under two-year contracts with the NSA's leading civilian contractor, Booz Allen Hamilton.

General Alexander, who, as I said, headed the NSA in 2013, first learned about an impending story in *The Guardian* on June 4, while he was in Germany meeting with its top intelligence officials, from Janine Gibson, *The Guardian*'s American website editor. She had notified the NSA it intended to break a story focusing on the organization. It took NSA counterintelligence less than forty-eight hours to determine that a civilian employee at the base from which documents were stolen had not reported back to work on May 22. His civilian supervisor had delayed reporting the absence to the NSA until May 28. It also determined that the missing civilian employee, Snowden, had lied on his application for a medical leave and had flown to Hong Kong. Personal records showed he was being trained as an analyst at the Threat Operations Center and had worked there for less than six weeks. He had taken the medical leave on May 18 and left the country by plane. By June 6, he had become the NSA's main suspect.

Alexander flew to Washington, D.C., after assigning the sensitive job of investigating the breach to a team headed by Richard "Rick" Ledgett, who was then director of the NSA's Threat Operations Center at the NSA's headquarters in Fort Meade, Maryland. Ledgett was the logical choice to head the damage assessment investigation because the center's regional branch in Hawaii was under his command. Ledgett flew to Hawaii, where his first task was to reconstruct the chronology of Snowden's moves, or, as the tactic is called in counterintelligence parlance, "walking the cat back."

The NSA had also notified the FBI of Snowden's possible involvement in the theft of state secrets in the first week of June. The FBI is in charge of criminal investigations of civilian U.S. intelligence workers, even if the alleged crime occurs on an NSA base. The FBI immediately dispatched a task force of agents to investigate a potential espionage case in Hawaii. When questioned, Lindsay Mills said Snowden was away on a business trip. After determining from airline and hotel data that he was in Hong Kong, the FBI realized Snowden was a possible intelligence defector. It froze his credit and bank cards. It also notified the passport office in the State Department and the legal attachés at the Hong Kong consulate. The legal attachés, who were actually FBI field agents posted in Hong Kong, located Snowden at the Mira hotel on June 8. On the evening of June 9, Snowden revealed in his twelve-minute video posted on the *Guardian* website that he was the source of the stolen NSA documents. Because Hong Kong is part of China, U.S. law enforcement did not have the means to recover them.

At that point, determining the magnitude of the theft of documents became a critical concern of the investigation. Aside from the few dozen documents published by *The Guardian* and *The Washington Post*, what else had Snowden stolen?

Within the next few days, a small army of forensic investigators from the FBI, the Defense Department, and the "Q" counterintelligence division of the NSA swarmed onto the NSA base in Hawaii. The proximate crime scene for their investigation was the National Threat Operations Center. They examined the cubicle where Snowden had last worked and then began retracing all his activities at the NSA from 2009 to 2013. To begin with, they needed to find out how many documents from the center had been copied and taken by Snowden.

Meanwhile, the Defense Intelligence Agency (the Pentagon's own intelligence service) was kept partially in the dark. Although the NSA is officially part of the Department of Defense, it operated with a high degree of autonomy with its own inspector general, investigative staff, and reporting channels. The DIA did not learn from the NSA that Snowden had stolen military documents concerning the joint Cyber Command until July 10. The number of stolen military documents from the Department of Defense was staggering.

The DIA found from its forensic examination that Snowden had copied "over 900,000" military files. Many of these non-NSA files came from the Cyber Command, which had been set up in 2011 by the NSA and the army, navy, marine, and air force cryptological services to combat the threat of warfare in cyberspace. The loss was considered of such importance that between 200 and 250 military intelligence officers worked day and night for the next four months, according to the DIA's classified report, to "triage, analyze, and assess Department of Defense impacts related to the Snowden compromise." The job of this unit, called the Joint Staff Mitigation Oversight Task Force, was to attempt to contain the damage caused by the Snowden breach. In many cases, containment meant shutting down NSA operations in China, Russia, North Korea, and Iran so they could not be used to confuse and distract the U.S. military.

The NSA and the Defense Department were not the only government agencies concerned with determining the extent of the breach. The NSA acted as a service organization for the CIA through handling most if not all of its requests for communications intelligence to support both its international espionage and its analytic operations. Although the CIA and the NSA were both part of the so-called intelligence community, the NSA did not immediately share with the CIA details of the Snowden breach. Despite the immense potential damage of the theft, it was not until June 10 that the CIA's director, John Owen Brennan, and his deputy, Michael Morell, were briefed by the NSA. When Morell realized how much data Snowden had taken, he was astounded.

"You might have thought of all the government entities on the planet, the one least vulnerable to such grand theft would have been the NSA," he wrote. "But it turned out that the NSA had left itself vulnerable." According to Morell, he bluntly told the NSA briefer that it was urgent for the CIA to be brought in on the case. After all, the CIA had employed Snowden only four years earlier. Specifically, Morell said, the CIA needed to find out three things: Had CIA documents been part of Snowden's haul? How long had Snowden been stealing documents? Had Snowden been working "with any foreign intelligence service, either wittingly or not"?

According to Morell, the effort to get a direct answer from NSA officials to these three key questions "proved maddeningly difficult." He found that in mid-June NSA officials with whom he dealt were so "distraught at the massive security breach" that initially they refused to allow even CIA officers to participate in the ongoing security review. A former NSA executive told me there was "near panic" at the NSA. Finally, Morell called Chris Inglis, a former professor of computer science who had risen to be the NSA's deputy director at the time of the breach. Inglis, who headed operations for the NSA, told him "the news was not good." Among the data copied by Snowden were a large number of CIA secrets. By the time the CIA learned that its secrets had been compromised, Snowden was headed to Russia.

The investigation of a crime involving potential espionage is no easy task. In this case, it required attempting to solve a jigsaw puzzle in which not only were key pieces missing but also, because it involved adversary intelligence services, some of the found pieces might deliberately have been twisted to mislead the U.S. investigators.

By late July, NSA investigators had made their initial assessment. They determined that most of the material had been taken from sealed-off areas known in intelligence speak as "compartments," which in this case were files stored on computers that were isolated from any network. Each compartment electronically tracks all the activities that occur in it on its logs, including the password identity of any person who has gained entry to any compartment. From a forensic examination of these logs, NSA investigators were quickly able to reconstruct the timeline of the theft. The logs showed that an unauthorized party without proper passwords had begun copying files in mid-April, which was just days after Snowden began his job at the center. The illicit activity ended just before Snowden's last day of work there. So this piece fit in with Snowden's guilt.

The size of the theft was another matter. Ledgett was certainly in a position to know (in the shake-up that followed, he would replace Inglis as deputy director of the NSA). According to Ledgett, the perpetrator had "touched" 1.7 million documents, moving from compartment to compartment. Of these "touched" documents, according to the analysis of the logs, more than one million of them had been moved by the unauthorized party in mid-May to an auxiliary computer intended to be used for temporary storage by authorized service personnel. Finally, the data was transferred off this auxiliary computer presumably to thumb drives or other external storage devices. This download occurred just days before Snowden left the NSA on May 17, 2013, having told the agency that he needed a medical leave of absence.

The quantity of stolen documents, 1.7 million, does not necessarily reveal the damage and can itself be misleading. Many documents do not reveal current or known sources or methods, and others may have little value to an enemy. And a large portion of the documents might have been duplications. The quality of some of these documents is another matter. Just one document that exposed a source or method of which enemies are unaware can be of immense value. One such document taken by Snowden provided what Ledgett called "a roadmap" to the NSA's current secret operations, revealing to an adversary such as Russia, China, or Iran "what we know, what we don't know, and, implicitly, a way to protect themselves." There were many documents in the Snowden breach that met these criteria, according to a national security official at the Obama White House.

General Alexander closely followed the investigation as it developed over the summer of 2013. By then, of course, the whole world knew that Snowden had stolen a vast trove of NSA documents. Alexander saw major inconsistencies developing between Snowden's personal account of the theft and what had actually happened. The timeline established by the government's investigators did not match Snowden's story line. "Something is not right," Alexander said in an interview.

For one thing, Snowden had made the claim to journalists, four months after he was in Russia, that he had turned over all the documents he took from the NSA's compartments to Poitras and Greenwald in Hong Kong. On August 18, the investigators had the opportunity to examine the files that Snowden had given to Poitras and Greenwald. This discovery came when British authorities, under Schedule 7 of Britain's Terrorism Act, detained David Miranda, Greenwald's romantic partner, at Heathrow Airport. Miranda was suspected of acting as a courier for Greenwald and Poitras. According to Greenwald's account, Snowden had given both him and Poitras identical copies of the NSA documents in Hong Kong. When Greenwald returned home to Rio de Janeiro, he found his copy was corrupted. But Poitras still had her digital copy of whatever stolen documents Snowden had distributed to them. So Greenwald dispatched Miranda from Rio to Berlin to get a copy of Poitras's thumb drive. On the return trip, Miranda's plane stopped at Heathrow, where British authorities detained him and temporarily took the thumb drive from him. Poitras had written out the password for Greenwald, and Miranda kept it with the thumb drive. The British copied the contents and shared them with the NSA. As a result, the NSA discovered that Snowden had only given Poitras fifty-eight thousand documents. The damage assessment team under Ledgett determined that some of these documents had been edited out of much larger documents that the NSA logs showed Snowden had copied. By the count of both the NSA and the Defense Department teams, almost one million documents were unaccounted for. What happened to the missing documents?

The NSA investigation found that the chronology of the theft of documents did not support Snowden's claim to journalists that he had only been seeking whistle-blowing documents. Most of the documents he took first did not concern the domestic activities of the NSA. Only toward the end of the theft did he copy documents that would qualify as whistle-blowing. The court order to Verizon that was the basis of the initial *Guardian* exposé was only issued by the FISA court on April 27, 2013. The other main whistle-blowing document he revealed, the PowerPoint presentation about PRISM, was only issued in April 2013. Yet Snowden had been downloading documents for at least nine months before he copied these documents.

When I discussed the chronology of the copied documents with a former government official briefed on the investigation, he suggested that Snowden's purpose might have changed between 2012 and 2013. When I asked him what might have induced the change, he replied, "That is one of the unanswered questions." That Snowden only took these two whistle-blowing documents at the tail end of his nine-month operation, and after he had contacted Poitras and Greenwald, suggests he might have had another motive prior to contacting journalists. In light of this chronology, the investigation had to consider the possibility that his whistle-blowing was, partly if not wholly, a cover for another enterprise.

Snowden told journalists he had access to "millions of records that [he] could walk out the door with at any time with no accountability, no oversight, no auditing, the government didn't even know they were gone." However, he was not among the limited number of individuals at the center who had access to these documents. Both the NSA's and Booz Allen's employment records showed that Snowden had not yet completed his requisite on-the-job training when he carried out the theft. Consequently, he had not yet been provided with the passwords he needed to get the documents. Even if he had remained at the NSA long enough to finish his training, he would only have been provided with the password to the particular compartment relevant to his work, not to all compartments. The tight control over these passwords was, according to a former top NSA official, a critical part of the NSA's security framework. He told me that Snowden, at least during the period of the thefts in April and May 2013, had no more legitimate access to the compartments than the cleaning personnel. Somehow, though, Snowden converted his proximity to access.

If a hundred top-quality diamonds were stolen from locked vaults at Tiffany by a recently hired trainee who, it turned out, did not have the combination to open these vaults, the police would be expected to consider that the trainee might have had help from a current or former insider at the company who knew the combinations. Snowden, who had accomplished a similarly inexplicable feat, said in his video confession that he was solely responsible. However, it is perfectly logical to assume, given the circumstances, that he might have had help, unwitting or witting.

The FBI could assume either that the NSA's security regime was so badly flawed that Snowden could trick his fellow workers into providing him with access or that there was another individual at the center who might have assisted or directed Snowden. When the investigation came to this fork in the road in the summer of 2013, according to a source on the House Intelligence Committee, it chose the former route.

Finally, there was the question of whether Snowden had gone to

Russia by design or by accident. Whenever an intelligence worker steals sensitive compartmented information of interest to a foreign adversary and then defects to that adversary, it raises at least the specter of state-sponsored espionage. It is a commonly accepted presumption in counterintelligence that a spy, fearing arrest, flees to a country that has some reason to offer him protection. When the British spies Guy Burgess, Donald Maclean, and Kim Philby fled to Moscow during the Cold War, the presumption was that they had a prior intelligence connection with Russia. Philby confirmed that in his 1968 memoir, *My Silent War*. So in the case of Snowden, counterintelligence had to consider the possibility that his theft of state secrets and his arrival in Moscow might not be totally coincidental.

Snowden blamed high officials in the U.S. government who purposely "trapped him" in Russia. He told the editor of *The Nation*, "I'm in exile. My government revoked my passport intentionally to leave me exiled" and "chose to keep me in Russia." He repeated that assertion over a dozen times, but as we've seen, it had no basis in fact. Whenever criminal charges are lodged against a U.S. citizen by the Department of Justice, the State Department, in accordance with the U.S. code of justice, marks in the electronic passport validation advisory system that that person's passport is valid only for return to the United States. After criminal charges were publicly filed against Snowden on June 21, it advised foreign governments that because Snowden was wanted on felony charges, he "should not be allowed to proceed in any further international travel, other than is necessary to return him to the United States." Rather than "exiling" Snowden, the government acted to facilitate his return home. With his passport, he could have flown home from either Hong Kong or Moscow, where he, like any other person accused of a felony, would face the charges against him. Snowden's unfounded claims suggested to investigators that he had something to hide about his arrival in Russia.

The counterintelligence investigation had access to State Department records showing that its representatives in Hong Kong had informed authorities there on June 16 that there were criminal charges against Snowden. Only a typographical error in spelling out Snowden's middle name—James instead of Joseph—in the criminal

charges prevented the Hong Kong police from immediately ordering his detention. His Hong Kong lawyers were certainly advised of
these pending charges no later than June 21, when they were published on the front page of the *South China Morning Post* in Hong
Kong. Presumably, Snowden knew that actions by the U.S. government were already in progress and that one of these actions would
include restricting his passport. One of his lawyers, Jonathan Man,
even accompanied Snowden to the airport out of his concern that he
would not be allowed by Hong Kong authorities to go through passport control. Ordinarily, Hong Kong passport control scans passports
when tourists exit but does not check them against a computerized
database.

In any case, when Snowden arrived in Russia on June 23, any
future international travel decisions for him would be up to the government of Russia, not that of the United States. It could have sent
him back to Hong Kong, as is normally done when someone arrives
without a proper visa, or to the United States. The only government with the actual means to "trap" him in Russia was the Russian
government.

Senior intelligence officials also knew that the U.S. government,
rather than conspiring to keep Snowden in Moscow, had met nearly
every day while he was in Hong Kong with Lisa Monaco, President
Obama's homeland security adviser, in the White House Situation
Room to find a way to prevent Snowden and his cache of secrets
from falling into Russian hands. Robert S. Mueller III, then the FBI
director, reportedly even directly appealed to the FSB head, Alexander Bortnikov, to return Snowden to the United States.

U.S. intelligence also knew that it was no accident that Snowden
wound up in the hands of Russia. He had been in contact with Russian officials in Hong Kong. It will be recalled that Putin admitted to
this liaison on September 3, in a press briefing on state-owned Channel One television; he also divulged that he had advance knowledge
of Snowden's plan.

"I will tell you something I have never said before," Putin said.
Snowden "first went to Hong Kong and got in touch with our diplomatic representatives." Putin was told then that an American "agent
of special services" was seeking to come to Russia. Putin added that

he declared that this agent would be "welcome, provided, however, that he stops any kind of activity that could damage Russian-US relations."

Even before that public confirmation of the Russian role in Hong Kong, the White House was well aware of it. On June 23, the Democratic senator Charles Schumer of New York correctly said, based on a White House briefing, that "Vladimir Putin had personally approved Snowden's flight" to Moscow. The NSA had the means to monitor Russian communication between Moscow and Hong Kong. The NSA also reportedly intercepted contacts between these Russian officials and Russian representatives of Aeroflot, the Russian state-owned airline that had flights between Hong Kong and Moscow. Aeroflot (like most other international carriers) ordinarily requires international passengers to have both a valid passport and, if necessary, a visa to the country of their destination. Those rules had to be waived for Snowden's exfiltration from Hong Kong. Snowden's defection to Moscow was not a haphazard result of unexpected circumstances. Russia obviously knew he was coming. This raised new questions for the investigation. What led Snowden to defect to Russia? Was his arrival in Moscow planned by Russian intelligence in advance of his going public in Hong Kong? Was any other party, such as China, privy to the plan? Was there a quid pro quo?

Putin's authorization could certainly account for Aeroflot's waiving its usual passport and visa check to allow Snowden to board its plane, as well as the dispatch with which Russian officials whisked Snowden off the plane after it landed at the Moscow airport. It could also account for Snowden's vanishing from public view for the next three weeks and the promulgation of the cover story that Snowden was unwillingly trapped at the airport by the U.S. government. The reasons behind Putin's move were less clear.

By September 2013, the investigation was looking into a veritable abyss. Snowden's culpability was no longer an issue. What was lacking from Snowden's video, or the two-hour film made by Laura Poitras, was any specific information on how many documents he had copied, how he had obtained the passwords to the computers on which they were stored, the period of time involved in the theft, or how he had breached all the security measures of the NSA in

m money raised on the Internet. In 2015, for instance,
ffered $100,000 bounties to any whistle-blowers who
e site with secret documents exposing details of the
Trade Agreement.

ng alone necessarily a line that divides whistle-blowers
In many cases, whistle-blowers have accomplices who
arry out their mission. For example, in 1969, the cel-
stle-blower Daniel Ellsberg, a military analyst at the
ation, had an accomplice, Anthony Russo, who had also
and. (Both were indicted by the government.) Acting in
copied secret documents that became known famously
on Papers.

lowers can also, like conventional spies, enter into elabo-
cies to carry out an operation. On the night of March 8,
whistle-blowers working together with burglary tools
e FBI office in Media, Pennsylvania, and stole almost all
here. The conspirators escaped and kept their identities
er forty-two years.

tions also do not necessarily produce a distinction
stle-blowers and conventional spies. Consider Philip
ft the CIA in 1969 for what he described as "reasons
." Specifically, he said he objected to the CIA's covert
atin American dictators. After contacting the Soviet
Mexico City, he defected to Cuba, where he leaked infor-
xposed CIA operations. Although Agee insisted he was
wer, and he adamantly denied offering any secrets to the
, the KGB viewed him as a conventional spy. Accord-
alugin, the top Soviet counterintelligence officer in the
cow, who defected to the United States, Agee offered
irst to the KGB residency in Mexico City in 1973 and
uban intelligence service. Agee provided the KGB with
rove" of U.S. secrets, Kalugin revealed. "I then sat in
Moscow reading the growing list of revelations coming
Despite this disparity, Agee still defined himself to the
histle-blower because he also had exposed CIA opera-
ublic.

len case blurs the demarcation line even further. Unlike

Hawaii. Nor would that data be forthcoming from Snowden, who may be the only witness to the crime. By June 23, he was in a safe haven in Moscow. Even though the grand jury case against Snowden was cut and dry, it was also irrelevant because the United States does not have an extradition treaty with Russia.

The purpose of the intelligence investigation went far beyond determining Snowden's guilt or innocence, however. Its job was to find out how such a massive theft of documents could occur, how the perpetrator escaped, and, perhaps most urgent, who had obtained the unaccounted-for stolen documents from Snowden.

In his interviews with journalists in Moscow, Snowden studiously avoided describing the means by which he breached the security aperture of America's most secret intelligence service. He only told the journalists who came to Moscow to interview him, with a bit of pseudo-modesty, that he was not "an angel" who descended from heaven to carry out the theft. But the question of how Snowden stole these documents may be the most important part of the story. The NSA, after all, furnishes communications intelligence to the president, his national security advisers, and the Department of Defense, intelligence that is supposedly derived from secret sources in adversary nations. If these adversary nations learn about the NSA's sources, then the information, if not worthless, cannot be fully trusted. The most basic responsibility of the NSA is to protect its sources. Yet Snowden walked away with long lists of them. In doing so, he amply demonstrated that a single civilian employee working for an outside contractor, even one not having the necessary passwords and other access privileges, could steal documents that betrayed these vital sources. He also demonstrated that such a massive theft could go undetected for at least two weeks.

If Snowden managed this feat on his own, as he claims in his Hong Kong video, it suggests that any other civilian employee with a perceived grievance against NSA practices or American foreign policy could also walk away with some of the most precious secrets held by U.S. intelligence. Such vulnerability extends to tens of thousands of civilian contract employees in positions similar to the one held by Snowden. The lone disgruntled employee explanation is therefore hardly reassuring. If true, it calls into question the entire multibillion-dollar enterprise of outsourcing the management of the NSA's computer networks and other technical work to outside contractors. It also casts doubts on the post-9/11 decision by the intelligence community to strip away much of the NSA's "stovepiping" that previously insulated its most sensitive computers. Without such stovepiping, any rogue civilian employee could bring down the entire edifice of shared intelligence.

A finding that Snowden had acted in concert with others in breaching compartments at the NSA would hardly be any more reassuring. Such collaboration among intelligence workers would reflect gravely on the mind-set of the NSA. Snowden described an atmosphere in which intelligence workers exchanged lewd photographs of foreign suspects. Some NSA employees met to protest the NSA policies. Did this violation of the NSA's rules also involve abetting the theft of documents? If so, the NSA would have to evaluate further vulnerabilities that might arise when it entrusts its secrets to technicians who do not share its values. A collaborative breach would signal an immense failure of the present concept of the counterintelligence regime in the NSA.

From what I gathered from government officials who were familiar with the investigation, there was a concern that answering the "how" question would rouse serious doubts about the very ability of the NSA to carry out its core mission of protecting the government's intelligence secrets. However it was organized, it was clear that Snowden had played a major role in what amounted to a brilliant intelligence coup.

Did Snowden

When you look at the totality of S
hypothesis that jumps out at you,
ity to do all these things, is that h
somebody who was very competen
—GENERAL MICHAEL HAYDEI

A WHISTLE-BLOWER enters th
secrets for reasons of conscier
conscience-driven spies are called,
agents." For instance, the British
of the most important Russian spie
ological recruit. He stole immensel
for the Russian intelligence service w
compensation.

The acceptance of money is not
tinction when it comes to espionag
paid, but some whistle-blowers also
work. Indeed, under federal laws, w
multimillion-dollar bounties for expo
whistle-blower Bradley Birkenfeld,
was paroled from prison in 2012, rec
for providing data that exposed illicit
bank. Assange also offered political v

bounties fi
WikiLeaks
provided
Trans-Paci
Nor is a
from spie
help them
ebrated w
Rand Cor
worked at
concert, t
as the Per
Whistl
rate cons
1971, eig
broke int
the FBI fi
secret for
Self-d
between
Agee, w
of consci
support
embassy
mation t
a whistle
Soviet U
ing to O
KGB in
CIA sec
then to
a "treas
my offic
from A
public a
tions to
The

In a stunning video in Hong Kong on June 9, 2013, Edward Snowden admitted he stole NSA documents published earlier that week by *The Guardian* and *The Washington Post*. Snowden, a twenty-nine-year-old employee of an outside contractor for the NSA, said that he took the documents to expose the NSA's surveillance of U.S. citizens.

Twenty-two days before Snowden's video confession, the largest theft of American secrets in history had taken place at the pastoral-looking NSA base on the island of Oahu, Hawaii. When I viewed it from the outside (above left, behind parking lot), it looked like little more than a grassy hillock, but it contained some of the nation's most sensitive secrets, including a road map to all its intelligence targets. Snowden copied hundreds of thousands of documents, including this road map, before he fled to Hong Kong.

Snowden, using an alias, sent Barton Gellman secret NSA documents from Hong Kong fifteen days before he went public. He asked Gellman to write a story for the *Post* and put in it a cipher key to help prove his bona fides to an unnamed foreign mission. Gellman refused the request and did not go to Hong Kong but published the story.

Snowden, using another alias, also sent the filmmaker Laura Poitras, right, and the blogger Glenn Greenwald NSA documents after Snowden arrived in Hong Kong on May 20. Poitras and Greenwald flew to Hong Kong to meet their anonymous source, who they discovered was Snowden.

Snowden moved into the Mira hotel on the Kowloon side of Hong Kong on June 1 after spending eleven days in an undisclosed location arranged by a "carer." He would later falsely tell Poitras and Gellman that he had been at the Mira since he arrived on May 20. It was not the only untruth he would tell them.

Snowden took Poitras and Greenwald to room 1014 at the Mira on June 3. The glass partition separates the bedroom from the bath. Even though Snowden said he didn't want "to be the story," he allowed Poitras to film him for twenty hours during the next six days. In this cramped space, he let her film him revealing the contents of stolen NSA documents to her colleague Greenwald. This footage became the centerpiece of Poitras's full-length documentary *Citizenfour*.

General Keith Alexander, the director of the NSA, flew to the crime scene in Hawaii soon after the story by Poitras and Greenwald appeared. The damage assessment would take over a year to complete because more than one million documents from the NSA, the CIA, and the Department of Defense had been compromised by Snowden. Alexander resigned seven months later, concluding Snowden's theft had done "irreversible and significant damage" to the United States and that "the [NSA] system did not work as it should have."

ABOVE Vladimir Putin personally authorized Snowden's flight from Hong Kong to Moscow, bragging about ordering Snowden's exfiltration. Putin not only gave Snowden a safe haven in Russia but invited him to participate in one of his press conferences on Russian television.

RIGHT Snowden called Julian Assange of WikiLeaks for assistance from Hong Kong. Assange booked false flights for Snowden to divert Western intelligence.

The Russian airline Aeroflot allowed Snowden to board its flight on June 23 without the necessary visa. When the flight landed in Moscow, he was taken off the plane by security officials in what was termed a "special operation." From that moment on, he was in Russian hands.

General Michael Hayden was CIA director when Snowden, then twenty-three, began his intelligence career. In 2007, Snowden was sent to Geneva as a junior CIA communications officer. His CIA career ended less than two years later, when he was caught tampering with a CIA computer system. After the general was briefed on the extent of Snowden's theft, Hayden said, "I would lose all respect for the Russian and Chinese security services if they haven't fully exploited everything Snowden had to give."

After leaving the CIA, Snowden was hired by Dell, an outside contractor for the NSA, and sent to work on computer issues at the Yokota base in Japan. While working as a system administrator there in 2010, he spotted a hole in the security system that would allow a disgruntled employee or spy to steal classified information. It was the same flaw he would use three years later to steal documents.

Still working for Dell, Snowden moved to Hawaii, where he rented this house. It was no more than a ten-minute drive to the NSA base where he worked in a windowless structure eight hours a day with eighteen-year-old military employees of the NSA. It was here that he maneuvered to get greater access to secret documents.

Snowden lived in Hawaii with twenty-seven-year-old Lindsay Mills, his girlfriend for six years. She described her life with him as an "emotional roller coaster." Soon after arriving, she began pole dancing at a local bar.

U.S. CYBER COMMAND NATIONAL SECURITY AGENCY CENTRAL SECURITY SERVICE

NSA headquarters at Fort Meade, Maryland, had a position that Snowden sought in 2012. After three years in dead-end jobs at Dell in Japan and Hawaii, Snowden sought to advance himself by getting an executive position at the NSA itself. In the summer of 2012, he stole the answers to the NSA entrance exam and, with the answers, easily aced it. Even so, he didn't get the NSA executive position. He continued working at Dell in Hawaii but grew progressively more disgruntled about the NSA.

Jacob Appelbaum, called by *Rolling Stone* the "most dangerous man in cyberspace," shared an interest with Snowden in promoting Tor software, which allowed hacktivists and others to hide their identities on the Internet. Aside from working at the NSA, Snowden was "moonlighting" by operating the largest server in Hawaii for this software. Snowden allowed Appelbaum to question him about NSA activities, along with Poitras, in mid-May 2013 while he was still at the NSA.

Runa Sandvik was Appelbaum's associate in promoting Tor software. She went to Hawaii in December 2012 to co-host with Snowden an anti-surveillance hackers' gathering, an event called by hacktivists a CryptoParty. Although Snowden revealed to her his true identity, Sandvik did not disclose that she knew Snowden prior to his going public until nine months after he went to Russia.

Snowden held his CryptoParty in BoxJelly in downtown Honolulu in December 2012. Here, he advocated measures designed to defeat NSA surveillance while working for the agency. He even invited selected NSA co-workers to attend, and some did. Whether or not any helped him, he couldn't have committed his thefts in May 2013 without help, witting or unwitting. The owner of BoxJelly told me he had not been questioned by the FBI or anyone else about the CryptoParty.

Anatoly Kucherena was appointed Snowden's "legal representative" in Russia at Sheremetyevo International Airport outside Moscow on July 12, 2013. A man with connections in high places, Kucherena effectively blocked access to Snowden to all but a few foreigners. Because he served as the liaison between Snowden and Russian security services, he was in a unique position to answer a key outstanding question of the case: Did Snowden bring American secrets to Russia? The answer, as he confirmed to me, is yes.

Snowden's first appearance in Russia was in a cordoned-off lounge at the Moscow airport on July 12, 2013. Seated to his right is Sarah Harrison, the "ninja" Assange had sent to Hong Kong to help him get to Russia; a government-supplied translator is on his left. No press was allowed into this Russian-style "press conference." Snowden officially requested asylum.

Anna Chapman, one of the "sleeper agents" planted by Russian intelligence in America after the Cold War ended, jokingly offered to marry Snowden. One objective of her sleeper network in America was to service a possible recruit in the NSA. The FBI arrested her in 2010 and sent her back to Russia.

Left to right, the director Laura Poitras, the journalist-author Glenn Greenwald, and Snowden's longtime girlfriend, Lindsay Mills, accept the best documentary feature Oscar for *Citizenfour* during the eighty-seventh Academy Awards. Capturing on film a true crime in progress, the transfer of state secrets, as Poitras did, is truly an extraordinary achievement. But the documentary, based on Snowden's self-serving narrative, reinforced the myth that Snowden stole only documents that revealed the crimes of the U.S. government so as to give them to journalists. It neglects the reality that the vast majority of the documents he took, including military secrets, had nothing to do with the misdeeds of the government and were not given to journalists.

other whistle-blowers who uncovered what they considered government malfeasance by virtue of their jobs, Snowden, by his own admission, took a new job in 2013 specifically to get access to the SCI files concerning NSA sources that he stole from the Threat Operations Center. Switching jobs in order to widen one's access to state secrets is an activity usually associated with penetration agents, not whistle-blowers. While the technical distinction between a whistle-blower and a spy may still serve the media in the case of Snowden, it does not help in solving the counterintelligence conundrum. A complex theft of state secrets had been successfully carried out in a supposedly secure site. The only known witness, Snowden, had escaped to Russia, where he could be of no help in reconstructing the crime for American intelligence agencies. The stolen data was kept in the equivalent of sealed "vaults"—actually computer drives that were not connected to the NSA network. If ever there was a locked-room mystery, this was it.

According to the FBI investigation, Snowden pierced these barriers by using passwords that belonged to other people and using credentials that allowed him to masquerade as a system administrator. It was a feat that must have required meticulous planning.

To address such a mystery, a counterintelligence investigation starts with a tabula rasa, stripping away all the previous assumptions, including that Snowden was the lone perpetrator. It builds alternative scenarios to test against the known facts. To be sure, scenario building differs from that of a conventional forensic investigation aimed at finding pieces of evidence that can be used to persuade a jury in a courtroom. Unlike a judicial investigation concerned with guilt and innocence, scenario building looks to develop a story that is, concurrently, intrinsically consistent and humanly plausible, and in the process it also identifies and explores the possible holes in the case.

"Scenarios deal with two worlds: the world of facts and the world of perceptions. They explore for facts but they aim at perceptions inside the heads of decision makers. Their purpose is to gather and transform information of strategic significance into fresh perceptions," wrote Pierre Wack in the *Harvard Business Review* in 1985. Such scenarios must aim at constituting a limited set of mutually exclusive alternatives. The point is to assure that any alternative that fits the relevant facts, no matter how implausible it may initially seem to be, is not neglected.

One of the most vexing problems that had to be explained by these scenarios is how Snowden got the passwords to up to twenty-four of these vaults. He could not have obtained these passwords during his previous employment at Dell, because Dell technicians did not have access to the Level 3 documents stored in these compartments. Nor, as noted earlier, was he given access to them when he transferred to Booz Allen, because he had not completed the requisite training.

Snowden had also, it will be recalled, relinquished his privileges as a system administrator when he transferred to Booz Allen, so he did not have the privilege to override password protection. In short, his new position as an infrastructure analyst did not give him the ability to enter compartments that he had not yet been read into.

As I've said, there are two possible ways he could have gotten these passwords: either he had assistance from a party who had access to them, or he found flaws in the NSA's security procedures that left the supposedly closed vaults effectively unlocked.

The Unwitting Accomplice Possibility

It is possible that if Snowden received assistance, it was entirely unwitting. He might have obtained some passwords through deception, such as tricking co-workers into typing their passwords into a device that captured them. As the NSA informed Congress in 2014, three of his fellow workers told the FBI that Snowden might have deceived them to gain access to their passwords. He could have simply asked other analysts at the center who had been read into compartments for their passwords. Such an approach would be extremely risky for the analyst, who could lose his job and security clearance by cooperating. It could also be risky for Snowden because any analyst he approached was supposed to report any request for a password to a security officer. Making such requests even more suspicious, Snowden had been working at the Threat Operations Center for just a few weeks as a trainee and was not well known to other analysts there. "It is inconceivable to me that his co-workers would divulge their passwords to him," a former Booz Allen executive, who had also worked at the Defense Intelligence Agency, told me. "If he was a system administrator, he might trick a threat analyst into entering his password into his computer under the pretext that he needed it to deal with an urgent hardware issue." But, it will be recalled, Snowden was not a system administrator at the center. Snowden therefore "had no plausible reason for requesting passwords to compartments he had not been read into," the former executive said. He said that NSA executives might have been read into all twenty-four of the compartments, but he deemed it inconceivable they would illicitly share their passwords with Snowden. I asked him what the chance was of his voluntarily obtaining some twenty-four passwords from co-workers in five weeks. "In my opinion, near zero," he said.

It is possible of course that Snowden could have simply observed others typing in their passwords, one by one, but that would take time and possibly attract attention. I asked the former Booz Allen contractor whether it was possible that Snowden could have used a device for intercepting another computer's electronic signals, called by hackers a "key logger." Such a device, which is obtainable over the Internet, could be used to steal the passwords of the analysts who had been read into the compartments. My source said that while it was possible that Snowden smuggled in a key logger in his backpack, it could not be operated unless it was hardwired to a computer inside the center, because, like those at all other NSA facilities, the computers had been insulated to block any form of wireless transmission. This precaution was taken to guard against an EMP, or electromagnetic pulse, attack by an enemy. The only way Snowden could intercept keystrokes was to attach a cable from his key logger to each of his fellow workers' computers. In this scenario, he would have had to surreptitiously build his own wired network connecting his hidden key logger to twenty-four separate computers. Moreover, he would have to do this wiring in an open-plan office where he could not count on these additional wires, even if rigged one by one, not being noticed by either other analysts in the room or the "geek squad" of system administrators who regularly checked connections. Making the task even more risky, according to my Booz Allen source, there were closed-circuit cameras. The only way he could mitigate the risk of detection was by having someone help him build this network.

Even if Snowden had managed to obtain all the necessary passwords from colleagues, he would have had to transfer the files to an external storage device. This was not a matter of simply attaching a thumb drive or other external device to a port, because, unlike in movies such as *Mission: Impossible,* the ports on the computers at the NSA were ordinarily sealed shut. This measure was taken specifically to prevent any unauthorized downloading by NSA workers. The only people at the center who had the authorization, and the means, to open these ports and transfer data were system administrators, according to the former Booz Allen executive. System administrators needed to have this privilege to deal with glitches in the computers. Snowden was no longer a system administrator and had no such privileges. So again, he would have needed help. He would have needed to either borrow a system administrator's credential or forge his own.

The credential he would need is called a public key infrastructure, or PKI, card with its authentication code embedded in a magnetic strip. When I asked the former Booz Allen executive if Snowden possessed the skill set to forge such a card, he said that he strongly doubted any NSA employee would be capable of such a forgery without special equipment. Just asking such a favor could "set off alarms," my source said.

The unwitting accomplice scenario had another stumbling block: time. We know from Poitras that Snowden told her in early April 2013 that he planned to deliver documents to her in six to eight weeks (which he in fact did). But he had not yet started working for Booz Allen at the center until that same month. It does not seem plausible that in making such a commitment he was merely counting on his ingenuity in the face of strangers to fulfill it. The only way he could have known for certain that he would be able to borrow a PKI card and obtain the passwords, whether by trickery, by observation, or by a key router, before he had begun working at the center was that he already knew someone there who would help him.

The Witting Accomplice Possibility

The witting accomplice scenario better fits with the principle in logic called Occam's razor, which suggests that when one is choosing between alternative explanations, the one that requires the fewest assumptions should be given priority. It would be relatively easy to gain access to passwords if Snowden had the cooperation of an insider at the center who had been read into the compartments or, even better, if he had the cooperation of a system administrator with the necessary PKI cards and shell keys to bypass the password protection. Such an accomplice could also help explain how Snowden was able to get the job at the center in the first place, how he knew in advance that he could find there the "lists" of the NSA sources in foreign countries, and how he knew that there were security traps at the center. Such a witting accomplice might even have prepared in advance the "spiders" that Snowden used to index the files.

The witting accomplice scenario of course requires an unsettling expansion of the plot. It means Snowden collaborated with one or more insiders at the center to steal secret documents. It is not difficult to imagine, in light of the lax background checks for outside contractors servicing the NSA, that there were others in the "geek squad" who shared Snowden's antipathy to NSA surveillance. Certainly, we know that Snowden found other NSA workers who were willing to attend his anti-surveillance CryptoParty in December 2012. Some might be willing to offer Snowden help if he was willing to go public. Indeed, if the geek culture produced one Snowden, why wouldn't it produce others? If such an accomplice lacked Snowden's willingness to flee to another country, he might have limited his participation to supplying technical assistance. For his part, Snowden might have agreed to divert suspicion from his accomplice by taking sole responsibility for the crime when he went public.

All of this is theoretically possible, but no witting accomplice was ever identified. The FBI, which was in charge of the domestic part of the investigation of the Snowden case, questioned all of Snowden's co-workers at the center over the course of six months and failed to find anyone who knowingly helped Snowden. If the accomplice was an idealistic amateur, it is likely the FBI would have found him.

Three co-workers did admit to the FBI, as noted earlier, that they might have inadvertently given Snowden their passwords, but these three slips would not account for Snowden's breach of all the other compartments. Of course, there might have also been less forthcoming co-workers who hid their slips in divulging their passwords to Snowden.

This raises the more sinister possibility that the accomplice was not an amateur co-worker but a spy who was already in place when Snowden arrived. Such a penetration agent could have been recruited by an adversary intelligence service before Snowden came on the scene. After Snowden expressed a desire to expose the NSA's domestic surveillance, it could then have used him as an "umbrella" to hide its own activities. Finding such a means to protect a source while exploiting his or her information is not uncommon in espionage operations, and because Snowden was willing to flee America and go public, he could serve as a near-perfect umbrella. "Snowden may have carried out of the NSA many more documents than he knew about," Tyler Drumheller, the former CIA station chief, said. It could also account for the disparity between the claims of Snowden and the NSA damage assessment as to the number of documents that were compromised.

As far-fetched as this scenario may seem, less than three years before the Snowden breach the NSA had received a warning from a CIA mole (to be discussed in greater detail later) that the Russian intelligence service might have recruited a KGB mole at the Fort Meade headquarters of the NSA. No mole was found in 2010, and if one existed, it could not have been Snowden, who was working for the NSA in Japan in 2010. Such a putative mole could conceivably have acquired enough information to later facilitate Snowden's operation.

As Snowden acknowledges, he was not a happy worker at the NSA. He complained in his posts over the Internet between 2010 and 2013 about superiors and what he considered NSA abuses to co-workers. If someone assumed the guise of a reluctant whistle-blower, he would have little difficulty in approaching Snowden. Snowden might not even know his true affiliation beyond that he shared Snowden's anti-surveillance views. If Snowden then voiced an interest in exposing the NSA's secrets, this person could supply him with the necessary guidance, steering a still-unsuspecting Snowden first to the Booz Allen position and afterward to his associates in Hong Kong. By taking sole credit for the coup in the video that he made with Poitras and Greenwald in Hong Kong, he acted, as he told Greenwald, to divert suspicion from anyone else. This move could also give any collaborator he might have had in Hawaii time to cover his or her tracks.

The astronomer Carl Sagan famously said in regard to searching the universe for signals from other civilizations that the "absence of evidence is not evidence of absence." That injunction also applies to the spooky universe of espionage. The fact that a mole hunt fails to find a hidden collaborator at the NSA does not necessarily mean such a mole does not exist. Historically, we have many notable cases in which Russian moles eluded long, intensive investigations. Robert Hanssen penetrated the FBI for over twenty years for the KGB without being caught. Similarly, Aldrich Ames acted as a KGB mole in the CIA for more than ten years and passed all the CIA's sophisticated lie detector tests. Both Hanssen and Ames eluded intensive FBI and CIA investigations that lasted over a decade. According to Victor Cherkashin, their KGB case officer, whom I interviewed in Moscow in 2015, the KGB was able to hide their existence from investigators for such a long period partly because of the widespread belief in U.S. intelligence that moles were fictional creatures that sprang from the "paranoid mind" of James Jesus Angleton. When I then cited the signature line from the movie *The Usual Suspects,* "The greatest trick the devil ever pulled was convincing the world he didn't exist," Cherkashin thinly smiled and said, "CIA denial [of moles] certainly helped."

In view of such past successes of the Russian intelligence services, it cannot be precluded that there was another person in the NSA working with the enthusiastic Snowden as cover to prevent any light from falling on his own surreptitious spying. While it may seem extremely unlikely that Snowden had such assistance, the alternative scenario, that Snowden broke into the sealed compartments and

CHAPTER 16

The Question of When

The NSA was actually concerned back in the time of the crypto-wars with improving American security. Nowadays, we see that their priority is weakening our security.

—EDWARD SNOWDEN, Moscow, 2015

IN HIS 1974 NOVEL, *Tinker, Tailor, Soldier, Spy,* John Le Carré helped establish the concept in the public imagination of a mole burrowing into a rival intelligence service. Le Carré's now-classic mole, code-named Gerald by the KGB, managed in the novel to gain access to the inner sanctum of the British intelligence service MI6. Aided and guided by his controllers in Moscow, he systematically stole British intelligence secrets. As Le Carré wove the plot, the brilliantly orchestrated operation involved spotting, compromising, and recruiting others to gradually advance Gerald the mole to a position of power. Such well-organized penetrations are not limited to fiction. The career of the KGB mole Heinz Felfe, who was advanced through the ranks of West German intelligence by an elaborate series of sacrifices by his controllers in Moscow until he actually headed West German counterintelligence in 1961, could have served as the nonfiction inspiration for Le Carré's 1963 novel, *The Spy Who Came in from the Cold.* As U.S. intelligence only found out after the Cold War ended, the KGB also had the ability to sustain moles for decades.

The CIA also had its share of long-term successes, such as Alexander Poteyev, who fed the CIA secrets for over ten years while burrowing into Russian intelligence. In the choreography of these operations, as in Le Carré's fiction, rival intelligence services ensnared and sacrificed recruits, as if playing a chess game, to advance their moles. Despite notable successes such as Felfe and Poteyev, a great number of these elaborate conspiracies fail to insinuate a mole into their adversaries' confidence. Intelligence services therefore also take advantage of a more prosaic source: the self-generated spy, or, as they are called in the trade, a "walk-in."

Although they are largely unsung in novels, these walk-ins are an important part of espionage. A counterespionage review done for the Presidential Foreign Intelligence Advisory Board (PFIAB) in 1990 found that most U.S. spies in the Cold War had taken documents on their own volition and only afterward offered them to an adversary service. Self-generated spies have diverse motives. Some intelligence workers steal secrets for financial gain. Others take them to further an ideological interest. As opportunistic enterprises, intelligence services do not turn walk-ins away if they have valuable intelligence. Indeed, some of the most successful moles were not recruited, or even controlled, by spy agencies. They were self-generated penetrations, or "espionage sources," as the KGB preferred to call them, who first stole secrets and later voluntarily delivered them to an adversary.

Hanssen, who successfully penetrated the FBI for the Russian intelligence services from 1979 to 2001, according to the assessment of a 2002 presidential commission, had caused "the worst intelligence disaster in US history." Eleven years later, George Ellard, a former NSA inspector general who had been a member of that commission, compared Hanssen with Snowden "in that they both used very well-honed IT abilities to steal and disclose classified information vital to our national security."

It is also possible to exploit a walk-in even after he has left his service. For example, the KGB major Anatoliy Golitsyn was an ideological self-generated spy who walked into the U.S. embassy in Helsinki on December 15, 1961. He asked to see the CIA officer on duty and announced to him that he had collected a trove of KGB secrets, including information that could identify its key spies in the West.

He offered to defect to the United States. The CIA accepted his offer, and through this archive of secrets he had previously compiled, he became one of the CIA's most productive sources in the Cold War.

The job of an intelligence service is to take advantage of whatever opportunities come its way in the form of self-generated spies. If a Russian walk-in had not yet burned his bridges to his own service, U.S. intelligence officers were under instructions to attempt to persuade the walk-in to return to his post in Russia and serve as a "defector-in-place," or mole. "While defectors can and do provide critical information," a CIA memorandum on walk-ins during the Cold War noted, "there are very few cases in which the same individual may not have been of greater value if he had returned to his post." Of course, if a walk-in believed he was already compromised, as Golitsyn did, a decision would have to be made whether the value of his intelligence merited exfiltrating him to the United States.

This required evaluating the bona fides of the walk-in. Not all walk-ins are accepted as defectors. Some walk-ins are deemed "dangles," or agents dispatched by the KGB to test and confuse the CIA. Others are rejected as political liabilities, as happened to Wang Lijun, a well-connected police chief in China. In February 2012, Wang walked into the U.S. consulate in Chengdu asking for asylum. The State Department decided against it. After Wang left U.S. protection, he was arrested for corruption and received a fifteen-year prison sentence. Such decisions about walk-ins are not made without due consideration, often at the highest level of a government, because exfiltrating a defector can result in diplomatic ruptures and political embarrassments.

Conversely, it raises espionage concerns when an adversary government authorizes the exfiltration of a rogue employee of an intelligence service. At minimum, it suggests that a rival government placed value on what the defector could provide it. The Snowden case is no exception. Whatever Snowden's prior relations might have been with Russia, it can be assumed that after he fled to Moscow, in light of the intelligence value of the stolen documents, he would wind up in the hands of the Russian security services. That assumption was reinforced by subsequent countermeasures that were implemented by adversaries moved to block secret sources of NSA surveillance, as the CIA deputy director later revealed. Such moves could indicate that at least part of the U.S. communications intelligence that Snowden had stolen was in enemy hands. The CIA and NSA's monitoring of these countermeasures was itself extremely delicate, because revealing what they learned about Russian and Chinese countermeasures risked compromising even more U.S. communications sources than had Snowden.

General Alexander said in his interview with *The Australian Financial Review,* "We absolutely need to know what Russia's involvement is with Snowden." He further said, "I think Snowden is now being manipulated by Russian intelligence. I just don't know when that exactly started." At what point did Snowden first come in contact with the Russians? The counterintelligence issue was not *if* this U.S. intelligence defector in Moscow was under Russian control but *when* he came under it.

There were three possible time periods when Snowden might have been brought under control by the Russian intelligence service: while he was still working for the NSA; after he arrived in Hong Kong on May 20, 2013; or after he arrived in Russia on June 23, 2013.

The NSA Scenario

The first scenario could stretch as far back as when Snowden was forced out of the CIA in 2009. It will be recalled that the CIA had planned to launch a security investigation of Snowden, but it was aborted when he resigned. He had also incurred large losses speculating in the financial markets in Geneva, which is the kind of activity that had in the past attracted the interest of foreign intelligence services. So it has to be considered in this scenario that Snowden had been recruited by the Russians after he left the CIA and directed to take jobs at civilian contractors servicing the NSA.

Such "career management," as it is called by the CIA, could explain why Snowden had switched jobs in March 2013 to Booz Allen Hamilton, which, unlike his previous employer, Dell, allowed him to gain proximity to the super-secret lists of the telecommunications systems that the NSA had penetrated in Russia and China. This could account for how he managed to acquire the necessary passwords to accrue privileged information. It could also account for why the documents he copied that pertained to NSA operations in Russia were not among those he gave to Poitras, Greenwald, and other journalists. Because Russia has had an active intelligence-sharing treaty with China since 1996, it could further explain why his first stop was Hong Kong, a part of China. It was a safe venue for debriefing Snowden, as well as establishing his credentials among journalists as a whistle-blower, before a decision was made to allow him to proceed to Russia.

The nearly fatal problem with this early recruitment scenario is Snowden's contacts with journalists. Snowden, it will be recalled, had contacted Greenwald in December 2012. Greenwald was a high-profile blogger in Brazil who did not use encryption or any security safeguards. Next, he contacted Poitras in January 2013 in Berlin; she was a magnet for NSA dissidents. Both of these contacts put Snowden's clandestine downloading at grave risk. As known opponents of U.S. intelligence agencies, these journalists might be, as they themselves suspected they were, under surveillance by American, British, Brazilian, or German intelligence services. Greenwald and Poitras might also tell others who were either under surveillance or informers. So no matter what precautions Snowden took, his secret enterprise, or just the fact he was in contact with anti-government activists, might be detected. At minimum, he could lose his access to secrets and be of no further use as a source at the NSA. He could also be interrogated and reveal the way he was brought under control. If Snowden had actually been under the control of the Russian intelligence service, the last thing it would allow was for him to take such a risk—or even to contact a single journalist. After all, the purpose of an espionage operation is to steal secrets without alerting anyone to the theft.

A former CIA officer told me that while anything could "go haywire" in an intelligence operation, it would be "unthinkable" that the Russian intelligence service would permit an undercover source it controlled in the NSA to expose himself by contacting journalists. Snowden's continued interactions with Poitras and Greenwald make it implausible that he was under Russian control *before* he went to Hong Kong.

The Hong Kong Scenario

The most compelling support for the scenario that Snowden was brought under Russian control while he was in Hong Kong comes, it will be recalled, from Vladimir Putin. His disclosure about the case leaves little doubt that Russian officials had engaged Snowden in Hong Kong, that Putin had authorized his trip to Moscow, and that the Russian government allowed him to fly to Moscow without a Russian visa. We know that Putin's version is supported by U.S. surveillance of Snowden's activities in Hong Kong. We also know that the Russians went to some lengths not only to facilitate his trip to Moscow but to arrange to keep him in Russia. This supports the possibility that the Russian intelligence service managed to bring Snowden under its sway during his thirty-four days in Hong Kong.

The Russian intelligence service might even have been aware of Snowden and his anti-NSA activities before his arrival on May 20. Snowden was anything but discreet in his contacts with strangers in the anti-surveillance movement, including such well-known activists as Runa Sandvik (to whom he revealed his true name and address via e-mail), Micah Lee, Jacob Appelbaum, Parker Higgins, and Laura Poitras. "It is not statistically improbable that members of this circle were being watched by a hostile service," a former NSA counterintelligence officer told me in 2015. When I told him that Poitras and others in her circle had used PGP encryption, aliases, and Tor software in their exchanges with Snowden, he said, arching his eyebrows, "That might work against amateurs, but it wouldn't stop the Russians if they thought they might have a defector in the NSA." He explained that both the NSA and hostile services have the "means" to bypass such safeguards.

I asked what the Russian intelligence service would have done if it had indeed spotted Snowden in late 2012 or early 2013. "Maybe just research him," he replied. As we know now, he pointed out, Russia and China probably had access to the 127-page standard form in his personnel file that he updated in 2011. They also had the capability to track his air travel to Hong Kong. "Could someone have steered him to Hong Kong?" I asked. He answered, with a shrug, "That depends on whether Snowden had a confidante who could have influenced him."

Whenever adversaries became aware of Snowden in this scenario, it was not until after he copied the NSA secrets and took them with him to Hong Kong that Russian intelligence officers offered him a deal. So from the Russian point of view, Snowden had already burned his bridges. Because he had used other people's passwords and access privileges to get into computers that he was not authorized to use, illegally moved documents, and given a false reason for his medical leave, it was only a matter of time, as he told Greenwald in his interview in Hong Kong, before NSA investigators would identify him as a possible spy. He could be of no further use at the NSA to an adversary. His intelligence value now lay in the documents he had taken with him or stored in the cloud as well as his ability to help clarify them in debriefing sessions. He could also inflict damage on the morale and public standing of the NSA by denouncing its spying in the media.

Once Snowden was in Hong Kong, the Russians would have no reason to restrain him from holding a press event or releasing a video. In fact, the KGB had organized press conferences for all the previous NSA defectors to Moscow. Hong Kong was a perfect venue for a well-staged media event because all the major newspapers in the world had bureaus there. Snowden's disclosures about NSA spying could serve to weaken the NSA's relations with its allies.

It is also possible that Russian or Chinese intelligence did not become aware of Snowden until after he went public in June by having *The Guardian* release his video. The video would have convinced the Russians or the Chinese of how dissatisfied Snowden was with the NSA. Because dissatisfaction is one of the classic means of recruitment in the intelligence business, he would certainly become a prime target for recruitment after he went public.

The CIA also considered the possibility that Snowden might

have been reeled in unwittingly. Morell suggested in his book that Snowden might not himself have fully realized "when and how he would be used."

It can be safely assumed that the decision made by Putin's intelligence service to allow Snowden to travel to Russia proceeded from something other than softhearted sentiment about his welfare. After Putin learned that there was an American in Hong Kong from the "special services" seeking to come to Russia, he also learned from Snowden's own disclosure on the video released that Snowden had taken a large number of NSA documents to Hong Kong: indeed, some were shown on the video. After that self-outing by Snowden, Putin had plenty of time to calculate the advantages and disadvantages of allowing him to come to Moscow.

Putin could offer him not only freedom from arrest but also a platform to express his views. The exploitation of an intelligence defector, even after he yields his secrets, can be the final stage of a successful intelligence operation. The CIA considered one of its greatest coups of the Cold War its release of the espionage-acquired secret speech of Nikita Khrushchev to the Communist Party of the Soviet Union in 1956 exposing the transgressions of the previous regime of Joseph Stalin. Making public these deeds was meant by the CIA to sow discord both inside the Soviet Union and to disrupt its relations with its allies. General Alexander suggested that Putin might similarly be "looking to capitalize on the fact that [Snowden's] actions are enormously disruptive and damaging to US interests." This potential gain, if Alexander's assessment is correct, provided Putin with an additional reason to have his representatives in Hong Kong offer Snowden exfiltration.

Snowden was in no position to refuse. After the release of the video, there was no going back to America without his facing a determined criminal prosecution. He would have known that in almost every prior case intelligence workers who had intentionally released even a single classified document had gone to prison. As his Internet postings show, he had closely followed the ordeal of Bradley Manning, whose trial was coming to its conclusion while Snowden was in Hong Kong. Manning had been kept in solitary confinement under horrific conditions for over a year while awaiting his trial and was facing a long prison sentence. There was no reason for Snowden to expect a better outcome for himself if he returned to the United States or was arrested anywhere else that had an extradition treaty with the United States. As the Russian officials in Hong Kong would have informed him, Russia had no extradition treaty with the United States. It was also one of the few places in the world that he could reach from Hong Kong without flying through airspace in which he might be intercepted by a U.S. ally. Snowden was told he could take the direct Aeroflot flight to Moscow without a valid passport or visa.

That Snowden's alternative to going to Russia was going to prison gave the Russians considerable leverage in Hong Kong. The Russian "diplomats" could have used this leverage to extract a quid pro quo. The price of admission might have meant putting himself in the hands of Russian intelligence and telling it all he knew.

The Moscow Scenario

The final possibility is that Snowden did not come under Russian control until after he arrived in Moscow. After assessing the negative attitude that Snowden expressed toward government authority on the video that was released by *The Guardian*, the Russian "diplomats" in Hong Kong might have concluded that Snowden could bolt if too much pressure was exerted on him there. The Russians could afford to be patient. They knew that Interpol and the United States would be pursuing Snowden throughout the world and that he had no valid travel documents and that his credit cards had been frozen. They would likely know that Sarah Harrison had arranged his flight to Moscow on June 23. So they had no urgent need to apply pressure on him before his plane landed in Russia.

After the Russians took him in a "special operation" from the plane at the airport, he was informed by Russian authorities that he would not be allowed to go to Cuba, Venezuela, Iceland, Ecuador, or any other country without the permission of Russian officials, which would not be immediately forthcoming. He was now at the mercy of the Russian authorities. There was good reason for keeping him in a virtual prison in Russia. "He can compromise thousands of intelligence and military officials," Sergei Alexandrovich Markov, the co-chairman of the National Strategic Council of Russia and an adviser to Putin, pointed out. "We can't send him back just because America demands it."

So Snowden was consigned to the transit zone of the airport, which is a twilight zone neither inside nor outside Russia, a netherworld that extends beyond the confines of the airport to include safe houses and other facilities maintained by the FSB for the purposes of interrogation and security. Stranded at the Moscow airport, no matter what he had believed earlier in Hong Kong, Snowden would quickly realize that he had only one viable option: seeking protection in Russia.

Even though the FSB is known by U.S. intelligence to strictly control the movements and contacts of former members of foreign intelligence services in Russia, Snowden might not have realized the full extent of the FSB's interest in him. He naively told *The Washington Post* in December 2013, in Moscow, "I am still working for the NSA right now. They are the only ones who don't realize it." Whatever he might have been thinking, a former U.S. communications intelligence worker who stole American state secrets, such as Snowden, would be under the FSB's scrutiny.

Andrei Soldatov, the co-author of the 2010 book *The New Nobility: The Restoration of Russia's Security State and the Enduring Legacy of the KGB*, who was personally knowledgeable about FSB procedures, explained the FSB would monitor "every facet of Snowden's communications, and his life." General Oleg Kalugin, who, as previously mentioned, defected from the KGB to the United States in 1995, added that the FSB (following the standard operating procedures of the KGB) would be "his hosts and they are taking care of him." Kalugin further said in 2014, "Whatever he had access to in his former days at NSA, I believe he shared all of it with the Russians, and they are very grateful." This assessment was backed by Frants Klintsevich. As the first deputy chairman of the Kremlin's defense and security committee at the time of Snowden's defection, he was in a position to know Snowden's contribution. "Let's be frank," he said in a taped interview with NPR (in Russian), "I think Snowden did share intelligence. This is what security services do. If there's a possibility to get information, they will get it."

Even without Klintsevich's comments, top American intelligence officers had little doubt that the Russian security services would do their job. Michael Hayden, for example, who in succession headed three American intelligence services, was certainly in a position to appreciate the capabilities of the Russian and Chinese intelligence services. He told me in 2014 that he saw no other possibility than that Snowden would be induced to cooperate in this situation, saying, "I would lose all respect for the Russian and Chinese security services if they haven't fully exploited everything Snowden had to give." They certainly had that opportunity when Snowden spent almost six weeks at Sheremetyevo International Airport. The FSB controlled his access to food, lodgings, the Internet, and whatever else he needed to survive there. If he did not cooperate, the FSB could also return him to the United States, where in the eyes of the Department of Justice he had betrayed the United States by stealing secrets and taking them abroad. What recourse did Snowden have? In a word, the FSB held all the cards but one—Snowden's help with the stolen documents. Even if Snowden disliked the tactics of the Russian security services, he now had a powerful inducement not to decline the requests of the Russian authorities.

Two weeks after his arrival, the Russian authorities provided him with a convenient path to full cooperation with Russia. He was put in contact with Anatoly Grigorievich Kucherena, a silver-haired, fifty-two-year-old lawyer who is known to be a personal friend of Putin's. Kucherena did tasks for Putin's party in the Russian parliament, or Duma. He had excellent connections in the Russian security apparatus because he served on the oversight committee of the FSB. Kucherena offered to serve as Snowden's pro bono lawyer. On July 12, Snowden officially retained him as his legal representative in Moscow. In explaining the relationship, Kucherena said, "Officially, he is my client, but at the same time, I provide a number of other services to him." According to Kucherena, Snowden turned down all requests to meet with any representative of the U.S. embassy in Moscow. From that point on, he would act as Snowden's go-between with the FSB and other Russian agencies.

At the outset, Kucherena made it clear to Snowden that he would have to play by Moscow's rules before the Kremlin would grant him permission to stay in Russia. To begin with, Snowden had to withdraw any applications he had made elsewhere for asylum. He had to put his fate entirely in the hands of Putin's Russia. He would also have to be fully candid with the Russian authorities on what was of great value to Putin: the secret documents he had acquired.

Eighteen days later, Snowden received Russian identification papers that allowed him to resettle in Moscow. He was provided with a residence and allowed to set up a broadcasting studio in it that he could use for Internet appearances at well-attended events around the world, such as South by Southwest and TED. Snowden was, according to Kucherena, also furnished with bodyguards. To help earn his keep, he was said by Kucherena to be employed at an unidentified Moscow cyber-security firm. To complete his resettlement, Lindsay Mills, whom he had left behind in Hawaii, was given a three-month visa and was allowed to temporarily live with him in Moscow. This afforded him a lifestyle that Snowden described in an interview as "great."

It would strain credibility that such privileges would be awarded to an intelligence defector who had refused to cooperate with Russian authorities. In Snowden's case, he was even allowed to participate in Putin's telethon on state-controlled television. On it, he was called on to ask Putin if the Russian government violated the privacy of Russian citizens in the same way that the American government violated the rights of its citizens. Putin, smiling at Snowden's presumably vetted question, answered in a single word: "No."

In the Moscow scenario, the Russians acted to advance their interests. They gave Snowden sanctuary, support, perks, and high-level treatment because he agreed to cooperate with them. If Snowden had not paid this basic price of admission, either in Russia or before his arrival, he would not have been accorded this privileged status.

CHAPTER 17

The Keys to the Kingdom
Are Missing

There's a zero percent chance the Russians or Chinese have
received any documents.

—EDWARD SNOWDEN, Moscow, 2013

A CRITICAL MISSING PIECE in the Snowden enigma is the whereabouts of the NSA documents. Greenwald told the Associated
Press that the documents that Snowden had taken from the NSA
constituted "the instruction manual for how the NSA is built" and
that they "would allow somebody who read them to know exactly
how the NSA does what it does, which would in turn allow them to
evade that surveillance or replicate it." Snowden, for his part, said on
camera in his Hong Kong interview in June 2013 that NSA investigators would have "a heart attack" when they discovered the extent
of the breach.

Ledgett, the NSA official who had conducted the damage assessment, while not having a heart attack, confirmed that Snowden had
taken a massive number of documents and among them was what
he deemed the NSA's "keys to the kingdom." These keys could presumably open up the mechanism through which the United States
learns about the secret activities of other nations and, by doing so,
bring down the American signals intelligence system that had for

sixty years monitored government communications. It had also kept track of adversaries' missile telemetry, submarine movements, and nuclear proliferation.

The Snowden breach was not without precedent at the NSA. There had been two Russian spies at the NSA during the Cold War, Jack Dunlap and David Sheldon Boone, who took a limited number of documents, but no one since the end of the Cold War is known to have taken a single NSA classified document. Now an insider had removed a vast number of the NSA's documents. Many of these documents were classified TS/SCI—"Top Secret, Sensitive Compartmented Information"—which, as NSA secrets went, were deemed the gold standard of espionage because they revealed the sources used in communications intelligence. Whatever the assessment of Snowden's motivation, the single question that needed to be answered was, what happened to these stolen files?

Recall the huge disparity between the number of documents that the NSA calculated that Snowden compromised and the number of documents he is known to have handed over to journalists in Hong Kong on a thumb drive. When the House and Senate Intelligence Committees asked the NSA how many documents Snowden took, the NSA could not come up with a definitive number despite having employed a world-class team of experts to reconstruct the crime. The NSA could say that 1.7 million documents had been selected in two dozen NSA computers during Snowden's brief tenure at Booz Allen in 2013, including documents from the Department of Defense, the NSA, and the CIA. Of these "touched" documents, some 1.3 million had been copied and moved to another computer.

There was evidence that Snowden had used preprogrammed spiders to find and index the documents. He had said that he took the job at Booz Allen to get access to data that he copied. So as far as the NSA was concerned, of course, the 1.3 million documents he copied and moved were considered compromised. On top of this haul, Snowden had copied files while working at Dell in 2012. As a system administrator there, he could download data without leaving a digital trail. As previously mentioned, more than half the documents actually published in newspapers had been taken during Snowden's time at Dell.

Snowden's supporters do not accept that he stole such a large number of documents. According to Greenwald, the NSA vastly exaggerated the magnitude of the theft in order to "demonize" Snowden. Snowden also disputed the magnitude of the 1.7 million number. He told James Bamford of *Wired* in early 2014 that he took far fewer than the 1.7 million documents that the NSA reported were compromised. He offered, however, no more specific details on the magnitude of his theft. Nor did he offer Bamford any way to verify his assertion other than to say that he had purposely left behind "a trail of digital bread crumbs" at the NSA base in Hawaii so that the NSA could determine which documents he "touched" but did not download. A government official familiar with the investigation said no such "bread crumbs" were found by the NSA.

It is possible that the NSA Damage Assessment team under Ledgett falsified its findings or otherwise inflated the number of documents that Snowden stole. NSA executives might have also lied to Congress to exaggerate the loss. But why would these officials engage in an orchestrated deception that made them look bad? Exaggerating the magnitude of the theft would only magnify Ledgett and the NSA's failure in its mission to protect U.S. secrets.

Officials had no reason to demonize Snowden for legal reasons. He already had been. Greenwald and Poitras had already revealed that Snowden had given them a vast number of NSA classified documents on a thumb drive that revealed, as Greenwald put it, the "blueprints" of the NSA. This drive contained, it will be recalled, no fewer than 58,000 highly classified documents. In the eyes of the law, that constituted an unprecedented breach of the laws passed to protect communications intelligence. In any case, in Russia Snowden was not in any jeopardy, no matter how many documents he was said to have stolen. Interestingly, the thirty-five-page Defense Intelligence Agency's damage assessment reports that 900,000 Pentagon documents compromised by Snowden were *not* made public. That was only disclosed via a *Vice* magazine Freedom of Information request in June 2015.

Many of the putative 1.3 million documents that the NSA says were copied and moved were duplicate copies. Others were outdated or otherwise useless routing data. So the quantity does not tell the whole story. Of far more importance is the quality of some of the data that Snowden had copied. Just a single one of these documents could cripple not just the NSA but America's entire multibillion-dollar apparatus for intercepting foreign intelligence. The previously cited road map, which was thirty-one thousand pages long, listed critical gaps in U.S. coverage of China, Russia, and other adversaries, including those cited by President Obama's national security team. It was not found among the files on the thumb drive given to Poitras and Greenwald. Nor were most of the missing Level 3 lists concerning NSA activities in Russia and China found on the thumb drive, even though Snowden said he had taken his final job at Booz Allen to get access to these lists. If Snowden had not given these documents to Poitras, Greenwald, or other journalists, where were they?

The compartment logs showed that Snowden copied and transferred these Level 3 documents in his final week at the NSA. He presumably had them in his possession in Hong Kong when he arrived on May 20. On June 3, according to Greenwald, Snowden had sorted through the documents to determine which ones were appropriate to give to journalists. On June 12, he told the reporter Lana Lam in Hong Kong that he was going through the documents, country by country, to determine which additional ones he should pass on to journalists. Eleven days later, he departed Hong Kong for Moscow carrying at least one laptop computer. After arriving in Moscow, he suggested he still had NSA secrets in his possession. "No intelligence service—not even our own—has the capacity to compromise the secrets I continue to protect," he wrote to the former senator Gordon Humphrey. "I cannot be coerced into revealing that information, even under torture." Much of the material he copied while working at Booz Allen remained, as far as the NSA could determine, missing. Had he brought these files under his "protection" to Russia?

An answer soon came from Snowden's Moscow lawyer. On September 23, Anatoly Kucherena was extensively interviewed on the RT channel in Russia. The interviewer, Sophie Shevardnadze, who had a show called *SophieCo*, was a well-admired journalist. She is the granddaughter of Eduard Shevardnadze, a former foreign minister and Politburo member of the Soviet Union and, after the Soviet Union broke up, the first president of Georgia. Even though she had interviewed many top political figures in Russia, obtaining an hour-long interview with Kucherena was a coup because, until then, he had not discussed Snowden in a television interview.

About halfway through the interview, Shevardnadze brought up the highly sensitive subject of the disposition of the NSA documents. If anyone was in a position to know about these documents, it was Kucherena. He had acted as an intermediary for Snowden in his negotiations with Russian authorities, including the FSB. As such, he would be privy to the status of the secret material that was of interest to the Russian intelligence services. When I interviewed Kucherena in Moscow in 2015, he told me that "all the reports" concerning Snowden had been turned over to him by "Russian authorities" in July 2013. "I had all of Snowden's statements," he said. If so, he presumably knew what Snowden had told the Russian security services.

Had Snowden come to Russia with empty hands or bearing gifts? Shevardnadze directly asked Kucherena if Snowden had given all the documents he had taken from the NSA to journalists in Hong Kong. Kucherena answered her question without any evasion, saying that Snowden had only given "some" of the NSA's documents in his possession to journalists in Hong Kong. He had kept the remaining documents in his possession. That confirmed what Snowden had told Greenwald, Poitras, and Lam in Hong Kong. Snowden told them that he had divided the stolen NSA documents into two separate sets of documents. One set he gave to Poitras and Greenwald on thumb drives. The other set, which he told them he considered too sensitive for these journalists, he retained for himself. U.S. investigators at the NSA, the CIA, and the Department of Defense would like to know what Snowden did with the set of documents he had retained for himself and had not shared with the journalists in Hong Kong.

Shevardnadze, who makes it a point to drill her interviewees, pressed Kucherena as to whether Snowden still had these NSA files, or "material," in Russia. The dialogue went as follows (from the transcript supplied to me by Shevardnadze).

SHEVARDNADZE: So he [Snowden] does have some materials that haven't been made public yet?

KUCHERENA: Certainly.

Shevardnadze asked the next logical question: "Why did Russia get involved in this whole thing if it got nothing out of it?"

Kucherena replied, "Snowden spent quite a few years working for the CIA. We haven't fully realized yet the importance of his revelations." Kucherena was on the FSB's public oversight board. He was clearly in the picture. Kucherena's answer was completely consistent with the statement Snowden made three weeks after arriving in Russia in his previously mentioned e-mail to Senator Humphrey.

It is certainly possible that Snowden transferred the NSA files from his own computers and thumb drives to storage on a remote server in the cloud before coming to Russia. According to the findings of House Permanent Select Committee on Intelligence, Snowden left "a number of encrypted computer hard drives" in Hong Kong from which data could have been transferred to the cloud. Anyone who is connected to the Internet can store and retrieve files by entering a user name and a password.

For Kucherena to be certain Snowden had access to the so-far-unrevealed data, Snowden must have demonstrated his access either to him or to the authorities. The Russians obviously knew Snowden had the means to retrieve this data one way or the other. Because the data concerned electronic espionage against Russia, the FSB would have been keen to obtain the documents, and the FSB is not known to take no for an answer in issues involving espionage.

Even if Snowden refused to furnish his key encryption, according to a former National Security Council staffer, the Russian cyber service in 2013 had the means, the time, and the incentive to break the encryption. It is unlikely it would have had to go through the trouble. It doesn't take a great stretch of the imagination to conclude that, willingly or under duress, Snowden shared his access to his treasure trove of documents with the agencies that were literally in control of his life in Russia.

Kucherena's answer on the television program may also help to explain Putin's decision to allow Snowden to come to Moscow. It was not a minor sacrifice for Putin. His foreign minister, Sergei Lavrov, had spent almost six months negotiating with Hillary Clinton's State Department a one-on-one summit between President Obama and President Putin. Not only would this summit be a diplomatic coup for Russia, but also it would add to Putin's personal credibility in advance of the Olympic Games in Russia. In mid-June, after U.S. intelligence reported to Obama's national security adviser that Snowden was in contact with Russian officials in Hong Kong, the State Department explicitly told Lavrov that allowing Snowden to defect to Russia would be viewed by President Obama as a blatantly unfriendly act. As such, it could (and did) lead to the cancellation of the planned summit. Putin knew the downside of admitting Snowden.

But if Snowden had a large archive of files containing the sources of the NSA's electronic interceptions, as Snowden claimed he had in Hong Kong, there was an enormous potential intelligence upside. Putin had to choose between the loss of an Obama summit and an intelligence coup. Would Putin have made the choice he did if Snowden had destroyed, or refused to share, the stolen data?

"No country, not even the United States, would grant sanctuary to an intelligence defector who refused to be cooperative," answered a former CIA officer who had spent a decade dealing with Russian intelligence defectors. "That's not how it works." If so, it seems plausible to believe that, as Kucherena said, the documents Snowden brought to Russia explain why Russia exfiltrated him from Hong Kong and provided him with a safe haven.

The Quickly Changing Narrative

Three weeks after Kucherena's appearance on Shevardnadze's show, on October 17, Snowden had his first interview exchange with a journalist since his arrival in Russia. It was over the Internet with James Risen of *The New York Times,* as noted earlier. Snowden now asserted a very different narrative. The subsequent front-page story, which carried the headline "Snowden Says He Took No Secret Files to Russia," reported that Snowden claimed he gave all his documents to journalists in Hong Kong and brought none of them to Russia. He also said that he was "100 percent" certain that no foreign intelligence service had had access to them at any point during his journey from Honolulu to Moscow. When I later asked Kucherena in Moscow why Snowden changed his story in direct contradiction of what Kucherena had stated, he said, "Wizner."

He was referring to Ben Wizner, Snowden's ACLU lawyer in Washington, D.C. Wizner had joined the ACLU in August 2001 after graduating from NYU Law School and clerking for a federal judge. At the ACLU, he became an effective foe of NSA surveillance. "I had spent ten years before this [Snowden leak] trying to bring lawsuits against the intelligence community," he explained in an interview with *Forbes* in 2014. Prior to the Snowden leak, he had frequently been consulted by Poitras on government surveillance issues (and appeared in Poitras's 2010 documentary, *The Oath*). He had also been engaged in a lawsuit aimed at exposing the NSA's subpoenas for Verizon records.

He had first learned about Snowden from Poitras in January 2013 while Snowden was still working for Dell at the NSA base in Hawaii. At that time, Poitras did not know Snowden's real name, but she informed Wizner that she was in touch with a person identifying himself as a senior officer in U.S. intelligence. (Poitras did not know at that time that her source, Snowden, was lying to her about his position.) Wizner also was shown e-mails by Poitras in which Snowden said he had information about the government's secret domestic surveillance program. Wizner, according to Poitras, advised her to stay in touch with this source.

On July 13, 2013, after Snowden asked for asylum in Russia, Kucherena arranged an encrypted chat between Snowden and Wizner. According to Wizner, Snowden asked him at the outset, "Do you have standing now?" It was a question that suggested that Snowden was aware that the ACLU needed to gain standing in federal court to challenge the government's alleged domestic surveillance. Up until now, it was unsuccessful because it had no way to show it was a victim of surveillance. The FISA order to Verizon, which Snowden had taken had provided that standing to Wizner and the ACLU.

Aside from the opportunity Snowden offered the ACLU, Wizner no doubt believed in the salutary benefit of Snowden's revelations. When they discussed Snowden's legal situation in America, Snowden expressed an interest in obtaining some form of amnesty from prosecution. Wizner was willing to attempt to explore making a possible deal with the Department of Justice, but it would not be an easy task, especially if Snowden had turned over NSA documents to a foreign power.

Even to argue that Snowden was merely an NSA whistle-blower presented a serious challenge for Wizner. The ACLU had been involved with previous NSA whistle-blowers, but Snowden's case differed from those cases in important ways. Those whistle-blowers had not intentionally taken any NSA documents. Snowden, on the other hand, had not only taken a large number of NSA documents but also released tens of thousands of these top secret files to journalists based in Germany and Brazil, as well as to other unauthorized recipients. In addition, the Whistleblower Protection Act, passed by Congress in 1989, does not exempt an insider, such as Snowden, who signs a secrecy oath from the legal consequences of disclosing classified documents to journalists or other unauthorized people. Consequently, getting some form of amnesty for Snowden required bolstering his image as a person taking personal risks to fight for America. But if Snowden had taken even a single top secret document to Russia, it would strengthen the case in the court of public opinion that he had stolen communications intelligence secrets with the intent to damage the United States, which under the provisions of federal law could be considered espionage. In this regard, Kucherena's disclosure was extremely damaging to Snowden's position, and Snowden had, after all, already found refuge in Russia. Snowden had two options, according to Wizner, the "first is to be where he is in Russia. And the second is to be in a maximum security prison cell, cut off from the world." These, of course, would be the options of any espionage defector who fled to Russia.

One way to mitigate the damage was for Snowden to substitute a new narrative. Wizner took it upon himself to screen potential journalists and other outlets for Snowden. He told a reporter for *The New York Times* that, except for Oliver Stone, all individuals who have "met with Snowden have just gone through me, and we've hooked it up." Nor did he limit his extraordinary control to interviews. In the case of Stone's movie *Snowden,* Wizner asked for the right to veto any shots featuring Snowden in the film. In it, he would tell handpicked journalists that he had given all his documents to Poitras and Greenwald in Hong Kong and took none of them to Russia. Wizner could then argue that documents such as the FISA court order were improperly classified secret and that disclosing them served the public good. The government might not be able to contest his claim without further revealing NSA sources. Under these circumstances, it might be induced to agree to a plea bargain for Snowden. Changing the narrative would also help enhance his public image as a whistle-blower.

Snowden's new narrative that he had destroyed all the documents he had in his possession before coming to Moscow and had no access to any NSA documents, not even those that he had distributed to journalists, was reinforced in a series of interviews that Wizner helped arrange. "I went the first six months without giving an interview," Snowden later said. "It wasn't until December 2013 that I gave my first interview to Barton Gellman." (Snowden did not count his Internet exchange with Risen in October as an "interview.")

In late December 2013, Snowden met with Barton Gellman. It was his first face-to-face meeting with a journalist since he had arrived in Russia in June. Snowden turned his laptop toward Gellman and, as if proving his point, said to him, "There's nothing on it. . . . My hard drive is completely blank." That his computer had no files stored on it at that moment of course meant very little. Just six weeks earlier, Snowden had met with the former CIA officer Ray McGovern, who had been invited to meet him in Moscow along with three other American whistle-blowers. At that meeting, he told McGovern that he had stored all the NSA data he had taken on external hard drives. Gellman asked about the precise whereabouts of the files, but, as he reported, Snowden declined to answer that question. He would only say that he was "confident he did not expose them to Chinese intelligence in Hong Kong." That answer did not nail down the issue, so Wizner arranged for *Vanity Fair,* which was preparing an article on Snowden, to submit questions. In his reply to them, Snowden wrote that he destroyed all his files in Hong Kong because he didn't want to risk bringing them to Russia. He expanded on this claim in three more interviews. These interviews were all with three journalists who had opposed NSA surveillance: James Bamford, writing for *Wired* magazine; Alan Rusbridger, the editor of *The Guardian;* and Katrina vanden Heuvel, the editor of *The Nation.* He also gave a televised interview to Brian Williams of NBC News in which he explained that because he had no access to the NSA documents in Russia, he could not provide access to the Russians even if they "break my fingers."

Snowden did not specify where, when, or how the putative destruction of the files occurred and offered neither witnesses nor evidence, other than the meaningless blank laptop screen, to corroborate it. Still his new self-serving narrative was widely accepted by the media. The fact remains, though, that Snowden went to considerable risk to select, copy, and steal Level 3 documents before leaving Hawaii for Hong Kong. These secrets were his last potential bargaining chips. Why would he have destroyed them in June in Hong Kong?

It is also difficult for me to accept that Snowden would destroy these documents because he feared the Russians might get them. If he was so concerned about the possibility, he could have stayed in Hong Kong and fought extradition instead of flying to Russia. Surely he must have realized that even without the files on his computer, the Russian intelligence service could still obtain the NSA secrets he held in his head. Indeed, as he told the *Times,* the secrets he held in his head would have devastating consequences for NSA operations.

In light of Kucherena's statement that in Russia Snowden had access to NSA documents, it would require a serious suspension of disbelief to accept Snowden's new narrative. Even if one were willing to accept his new claim, it still would not mean that the NSA documents had not fallen into the hands of adversaries. If he had destroyed all of the electronic copies of the NSA's data before boarding his flight to Moscow, he still couldn't be "100 percent" certain, as he claimed, that the data had not been accessed by others prior to his departure from Hong Kong. His files could have been copied without his knowledge, just as he had copied them without the NSA's knowledge. As former U.S. intelligence officers pointed out to me, adversary services could not be expected to shirk from employing their full capabilities once they learned that an American "agent of special services," as Putin called him, had brought stolen NSA documents to Hong Kong.

The *Times* reported from Hong Kong that two sources, both of whom worked for major government intelligence agencies, "said they believed that the Chinese government had managed to drain the contents" of the laptop that Snowden brought to Hong Kong. That China had the capability to obtain Snowden's data was also the view of the former CIA deputy director Morell. He said, "Both the Chinese and the Russians would have used everything in their tool kit—from human approaches to technical attacks—to get at Snowden's stolen data."

Snowden would not have been a particularly difficult target for them, especially after he started disclosing secrets to journalists at the Mira hotel. Not only could the Chinese service approach the security staff at the Mira, but they could track him after he left the hotel and moved, along with his computers, in and out of several residences arranged by his carer. Snowden, after all, had put himself in the hands of people whom he had never met before, including three Hong Kong lawyers, a carer, and three *Guardian* journalists. It is likely that the efforts of these adversary intelligence services to find him, and the NSA data, would further intensify after Snowden revealed to the *South China Morning Post* on June 12 that he had access to NSA lists of computers in China and elsewhere that the NSA had penetrated.

It wouldn't be only the Chinese service on his trail. The Russian intelligence service would also likely be tasked to acquire these NSA documents after Snowden's meeting with Russian officials in Hong Kong. And while he could get away with giving coy and elusive answers to journalists who asked him about the whereabouts of the NSA data, the Russian and Chinese officials in Hong Kong who could offer him an escape route from prison would likely demand more specific answers about the whereabouts of data they had not already obtained by technical means.

The Post–Hong Kong Documents

The NSA concern about who had access to its missing files deepened further when NSA documents continued to surface in the press *after* Snowden went to Moscow. If U.S. intelligence needed any further evidence that someone had access to the documents, these additional revelations provided it.

The most sensational of them was a purported document attributed to Snowden concerning the NSA hacking of the cell phone of the German chancellor, Angela Merkel. The story was published on October 23 on the *Der Spiegel* website. Appelbaum was the co-author of the story. Even though Snowden had by now been in Russia for four months, he was cited in the story, along with unnamed "others," as the source for the NSA document. Snowden did not deny it. Indeed, he took a measure of credit for the revelation, saying on German TV, "What I can say is we know Angela Merkel was monitored by the National Security Agency." If Snowden had been involved in the release of this document, it would be consistent with Kucherena's assertion that he had access to the archive.

Adding to the intrigue, Poitras was apparently caught by surprise when the Merkel story broke in *Der Spiegel*. She urgently texted Snowden on what she called "background" (which ordinarily means that a journalist will not attribute information to a source). She asked him in the text to explain the NSA's actions. Snowden explained to her that Merkel was listed by her true name (and not by a code name) in the NSA document because the German chancellor was an NSA "target not an asset." Presumably, Poitras would have already known that distinction if she had the document referred to in *Der Spiegel*. If the Merkel document was not among the data given to Poitras in Hong Kong, how did it get to the authors of the *Der Spiegel* article?

Appelbaum, of course, had been in contact with Snowden before he went public. He had served as Poitras's co-interrogator of Snowden while he was still working at the NSA in May 2013. Appelbaum was also one of the leading supporters of WikiLeaks. Because he was famously an advocate of revealing government secrets, it seems unlikely that he would have delayed releasing such a bombshell about Merkel's phone if Snowden had given him this document *before* he left Hong Kong in June 2013. Why would Appelbaum keep it secret for more than four months? The same pressure to publish would also apply to the journalists Snowden had dealt with in Hong Kong. If Snowden had given Poitras, Greenwald, Lam, or MacAskill the Merkel document, or even told them about it in their interviews with him in Hong Kong, *The Guardian* would have certainly rushed out such a scoop.

According to a source with knowledge of the Snowden investigation, there was no document referencing any spying on Merkel's phone among the fifty-eight thousand documents on the thumb drive that Snowden had given to Poitras and Greenwald in Hong Kong. That absence would explain why Poitras had to send a text to Snowden in Moscow to ask for an explanation after the story broke.

Further confirmation of the absence of this document in the material Snowden provided journalists in Hong Kong comes from James Bamford, a well-respected expert on the NSA. In the course of researching his 2014 article on Snowden for *Wired,* he was given access to all the documents Snowden gave to Poitras, Greenwald, and Gellman. Bamford used a sophisticated indexing program to search through the database specifically for the Merkel material. He did not find any. He reported that no document given to journalists in Hong Kong even mentioned Merkel. It therefore appeared that the Merkel document was provided to *Der Spiegel* after Snowden went to Moscow. If so, some party had access to NSA documents after Snowden arrived in Russia and provided the *Der Spiegel* authors with the scoop. In that context, it might not be a pure coincidence that Kucherena disclosed that Snowden had access to documents that he had not given to journalists in Hong Kong shortly before just such a document was published in Germany.

Bamford explored the possibility that there might be another person in the NSA who was stealing documents. He wrote to Poitras and asked her whether the Merkel document could have come from another person in the NSA. She declined, via a letter from her lawyer, to answer that question. But because she had not been the author of the *Der Spiegel* article, and had not been given the document, there is no reason to believe that she would know its provenance.

Documents continued to emerge years after Snowden arrived in

Moscow that were more embarrassing to America. In June 2015, the WikiLeaks website released another putative Snowden document, two years after he had supposedly wiped his computer clean in Hong Kong. It revealed that the NSA had targeted the telephones of three consecutive presidents of France—Jacques Chirac, Nicolas Sarkozy, and François Hollande.

According to a former NSA official, this document, like the 2013 Merkel material, was not among the data on the thumb drive given to journalists in Hong Kong, which Greenwald confirmed. Greenwald suggested to *The New York Times* that it might have been stolen by another penetration in the NSA, presumably one who had access to the same secret compartments as Snowden in 2013. Since Greenwald and Poitras had no way of knowing about the documents that Snowden did *not* give them, it is equally possible that the Russian intelligence services obtained this document from Snowden and later gave it to WikiLeaks. The release on Assange's WikiLeaks site came in the midst of NATO war games held near the Russian border, which Putin had vehemently denounced. The accompanying article was co-authored by Assange, who now claimed to have access to Snowden's NSA material. Because Assange had been in telephonic contact with Snowden in Hong Kong, and his deputy, Sarah Harrison, had spent five months in Moscow with Snowden in 2013, it is certainly possible Snowden was his source. But it seems difficult to believe that Assange waited two years before publishing because he has made it part of his modus operandi to publish documents immediately. Because WikiLeaks receives documents anonymously via its Tor software, any party with access to the Snowden files could have sent it. Subsequently, in July 2016, Assange released via WikiLeaks a cache of politically disruptive documents from the files of the Democratic National Committee. U.S. intelligence strongly suspected they been stolen by the Russian intelligence services and sent to WikiLeaks. If so, Russia made use of Assange and WikiLeaks to exploit selected fruits of its espionage activities

Greenwald and Poitras also released belated documents. On July 15, 2015, their web publication, *The Intercept*, released a Snowden document that cited an NSA intercept of an Israeli military communication concerning an Israeli raid in Syria on August 1, 2008. It revealed that a group of Israeli commandos killed General Muham-mad Suleiman, a top aide to President Bashar al-Assad who had been working with North Korea to build a nuclear facility in Syria. Israel had destroyed that facility in Operation Orchard nearly a year ear-lier. Whatever the purpose of this new release of an NSA document (which had little if anything to do with any of the NSA's own opera-tions), it was not among the data that Snowden had given Poitras and Greenwald in Hong Kong in 2013, according to a source with access to the investigation. Next, on January 28, 2016, *The Inter-cept* published data taken from a GHCQ (the British cipher service) file furnished by Snowden revealing military intelligence activities abroad. Specifically, it disclosed that the United States and Britain were intercepting data from Israel's military drones in 2008. Brit-ish intelligence had determined in 2013 that the material sent to Greenwald via a courier did not contain such GCHQ documents. If that is the case, then Poitras and Greenwald, like Appelbaum and Assange, were still receiving NSA documents that Snowden had allegedly stolen a long time after he went to Russia and claimed he had destroyed all his files.

The NSA reportedly determined that these belated documents, most of which concerned American allies in Germany, France, and Israel, had been among the material copied during the Snowden breach. They provided further reason to believe that someone still had access to the documents that were not distributed to journal-ists in Hong Kong. Kucherena's disclosure, just before the first post–Hong Kong release, that Snowden still had access to the NSA files made it appear plausible that Snowden sent these documents to *Der Spiegel, WikiLeaks,* and *The Intercept.*

A former high-ranking KGB officer I interviewed had a very dif-ferent view. He told me that in his experience an intelligence defec-tor to Russia would not be allowed to distribute secret material to journalists without explicit approval by the security service tend-ing him. He added that this injunction would be especially true in the case of Snowden because Putin had publicly enjoined him from releasing U.S. intelligence data. The more plausible alternative was that this material was released at the behest of the Russian intel-ligence service.

The mystery of the post–Hong Kong documents also intrigued members of the U.S. intelligence community with whom I discussed it. When I asked a former intelligence executive about the ultimate source for the Merkel story, he responded, "If Snowden didn't give journalists this document in Hong Kong, we can assume an intermediary fed it to Appelbaum to publish in *Der Spiegel*." According to him, the NSA investigation had determined that Snowden indeed had copied an NSA list of the cell phone numbers of foreign leaders, including the number of Merkel. This list became the basis of the *Der Spiegel* story.

It was also clear that Snowden gave credence to the release in Moscow. He made a major point about the hacking of Merkel's phone in an interview with *Wired* in 2014. Just about two weeks before the leak, Kucherena said Snowden still had access to the documents. Clearly, *someone* had access. But whoever was behind it, the release of information about the alleged bugging of Merkel's phone resulted in badly fraying U.S. relations with Germany in the midst of developing troubles in Ukraine. As it later turned out, according to the investigation of the German federal prosecutor, which concluded in 2015, there was no evidence found in this document, or elsewhere, that Merkel's calls were ever actually intercepted. Although they revealed little if anything that the intelligence services of Germany, France, and Israel were not already aware of, they raised a public outcry in allies against NSA surveillance, and the outcry became the event itself.

While these post–Hong Kong documents had little if any intelligence value, they provided further evidence that at least part of the stolen NSA documents was in the hands of a party hostile to the United States. If so, it wasn't much of a leap to assume that this party also had access to the far more valuable Level 3 documents revealing the NSA's sources and methods, such as the one that Ledgett had described as a "roadmap" to U.S. electronic espionage against Russia and China.

Within the intelligence community, this concern was heightened by new countermeasures to this espionage employed by Russia and China after Snowden reached Moscow. For example, there were indications that the NSA had lost part of its capabilities to follow

Russian troop movements in the Crimea and eastern Ukraine. U.S. intelligence officials even went so far as to suggest, according to a report in *The Wall Street Journal*, that "Russian planners might have gotten a jump on the West by evading U.S. eavesdropping."

Britain also discovered that some of its secret operations had been compromised after Snowden went to Moscow. According to a 2015 story in the *Sunday Times* of London, British intelligence had determined that Britain's intelligence-gathering sources had been exposed to adversary services by documents that Snowden had stolen from the NSA in 2013. These documents had been provided to the NSA by the GCHQ. Unless such intelligence disasters were freak aberrations, it appeared to confirm General Alexander's warning in 2014 that the NSA was "losing some of its capabilities, because they're being disclosed to our adversaries."

Snowden's supporters disputed this view. If only as an act of faith in Snowden's personal integrity, they continued to believe his avowal to Senator Humphrey that he had acted to protect U.S. secrets by shielding them from adversary intelligence services after he took them abroad. They also continued to take him at his word when he said he had destroyed all the NSA documents before going to Russia. Despite such protestations of patriotic loyalty, U.S. intelligence officials could not so easily dismiss the possibility that the missing documents still existed. After all, a U.S. intelligence worker who is dedicated to protecting America's secrets from its adversaries does not ordinarily steal them.

The NSA, the CIA, and the Department of Defense therefore had little choice but to assume the worst had happened: Russia and China had obtained access to the "keys to the kingdom." Whatever the extent of the actual damage, it was up to Alexander's replacement, Admiral Michael Rogers, both to restore morale and to rebuild the capabilities of America's electronic intelligence in the wake of the massive breach. According to a national security staff member in the Obama White House, that job would take more than a decade. The NSA had failed to protect vital assets. This intelligence failure did not happen out of the blue.

CHAPTER 18

The Unheeded Warning

The NSA—the world's most capable signals intelligence organization, an agency immensely skilled in stealing digital data—had had its pockets thoroughly picked.

—CIA DEPUTY DIRECTOR MICHAEL MORELL, 2015

IN APRIL 2010, the CIA received a stark reminder of the ongoing nature of Russian espionage. It came in the form of a message from one of its best-placed moles in the Russian intelligence service. This surreptitious source was Alexander Poteyev, a fifty-four-year-old colonel in the SVR, which was the successor agency to the first chief directorate of the KGB. While the FSB took over the KGB's domestic role in 1991, the SVR became Russia's foreign intelligence service. Its operation center was in the Yasenevo district of Moscow. The CIA had recruited Poteyev as a mole in the 1990s when he had been stationed at the Russian embassy in Washington, D.C. That it could sustain a mole in Moscow for over a decade attested to its capabilities in the espionage business. After he returned to Moscow, still secretly on the CIA's payroll, he became the deputy chief of the SVR's "American" section. This unit of Russian intelligence had the primary responsibility for establishing spies in the CIA, the FBI, the NSA, and other American intelligence agencies.

The SVR's last known (or caught) mole in U.S. intelligence was the CIA officer Harold Nicholson, in 1996. Before it could expand its espionage capabilities, it needed to build a network of Russian agents in the United States. For this network, it needed to groom so-called illegals, or agents who were not connected to the Russian embassy. This so-called illegals network was necessary because presumably all Russian diplomats, including the so-called legal members of Russian intelligence, were under constant surveillance by the FBI.

Advances in surveillance technology in the twenty-first century made it increasingly difficult to communicate with recruits through its diplomatic missions. To evade it, the "American" division of the SVR was given the task of placing individuals in the United States disguised as ordinary Americans. Their "legend," or operational cover, could be thin because they would not be applying for jobs in the government. Their job was simply to blend in with their community until they were called upon by the "American" department in Moscow to service a mole who had been planted in U.S. intelligence or other parts of the U.S. government. Until they were activated by such a call, they were classified as sleeper agents. Unlike the SVR's "legal" officers, who were attached to Russian embassies as diplomats and were protected from arrest by the Treaty of Vienna, the SVR's illegal agents lack diplomatic immunity. According to Pavel Sudoplatov, who served in the KGB in the Cold War, the sole job of such sleeper agents was to "live under cover in the West awaiting assignments for the Center." One assignment that justifies the expense of maintaining such agents is to service a penetration, after one is made, in the U.S. intelligence establishment. While waiting to be activated for such a job, sleeper agents were instructed to build every detail of their cover identity so as to perfectly blend in with Americans.

To build this American network of sleeper agents took the better part of a decade. In 2005, the SVR's "American" section in Moscow had begun methodically installing them in the United States. Almost all were Russian citizens who had assumed new identities to better blend into their communities.

The CIA learned of this sleeper program through Poteyev soon after it began. The issue was how to exploit this knowledge. When I was writing my book on international deception, James Jesus Angleton had pointed out to me that "the business of intelligence services requires understanding precisely the relationship of their opposition to them." His view, though his opponents inside the CIA would call it with some justification an obsession, was that an intelligence service had to focus on the moves of its rivals. To accomplish this "business" in the first decade of the twenty-first century, the CIA had to establish why its new opposition, the SVR, was laying the foundation for an espionage operation. What were its priorities in the resumption of the intelligence war? Its inside man in the SVR, Poteyev, provided it with a tremendous advantage in this relationship. He knew the links in a sleeper network that the SVR believed was safely hidden from surveillance. If they were followed, when they were activated, they could expose whatever recruits the SVR had in the American government. The CIA duly shared this information about the sleeper ring with the FBI, which had the responsibility for the surveillance of foreign agents in the United States. The FBI, for its part, kept the Russian sleeper agents under tight surveillance—an operation that grew in complexity and expense as more SVR agents arrived in the United States.

Meanwhile, in Moscow, Poteyev was following the unfolding operation. Part of his SVR job was to continue preparing these "Americans," as they were called by the SVR, for their assignments. Some had been sent as couples, others as singles. One of the singles that Poteyev personally handled was Anna Kushchyenko. She was a strikingly beautiful Russian student who changed her name to Anna Chapman by briefly marrying a British citizen she met at a rave party. After taking his name, she left him. After completing her training in Russia, she was sent by the SVR to New York City to establish herself as an international real estate specialist. Other "Americans" under Poteyev's watch became travel agents, students, and financial advisers. In all, Poteyev identified to the CIA twelve such sleeper agents. The cost of FBI surveillance of them over the years became sizable. According to a former FBI agent, around-the-clock surveillance on the movements and communications of a single individual can cost over $10,000 a day.

When the CIA received Poteyev's message in 2010 warning that Russian military intelligence had asked the SVR to activate some of its sleeper agents for a highly sensitive assignment, that suggested Russian intelligence had found a possible source who could supply it with valuable information. According to a former CIA intelligence official who later became involved in the case, the assignment involved preparing these agents to service a potential source in the NSA at Fort Meade, Maryland. If true, it suggested that Russian intelligence either had found or was working on a means of penetrating the NSA.

In 2010, the NSA division that handled such security and espionage threats reportedly initiated a counterespionage probe at the NSA's Fort Meade headquarters. According to a former NSA official, "They [were] looking for one or more Russian spies that NSA [was] convinced resided at Fort Meade and possibly other DoD Intel offices, like DIA." Because the NSA's cryptological service had in 2010 thirty-five thousand military and civilian contractor employees, the search for a possible leak was no easy matter. According to a subsequent note in the NSA's secret budget report to Congress, it would require "a minimum of 4,000 periodic investigations of employees in position to compromise sensitive information" to safely guard against "insider threats by trusted insiders who seek to exploit their authorized access to sensitive information to harm U.S. interests." According to a former executive in the intelligence community, that amount of investigation far exceeded the budgetary capabilities of the NSA. So while the investigation found no evidence of SVR recruitment, it remained possible that Russian intelligence had found a candidate in the NSA.

Meanwhile, in June 2010, to preempt such a leak in U.S. intelligence and avoid any potential embarrassment that could result, the FBI decided it could no longer engage in this sort of an intelligence game with the sleeper network. It arrested all twelve sleeper agents identified by Poteyev. After receiving a great deal of public attention (which led to their inspiring the FX series *The Americans*), the sleeper agents were deported to Russia. This move had both advantages and disadvantages. The main advantage was that it severed any communication link between the putative person of interest in the NSA and Russian intelligence via the sleeper agents. The main disadvantage was that it eliminated the possibility that FBI surveillance of the illegals might lead the FBI to a possible recruit in the NSA or elsewhere.

The preemptive arrests also had an unforeseen consequence. They resulted in accidently compromising Poteyev. When Chapman returned to Moscow after a spy exchange, she was taken to a well-publicized dinner with Putin. Afterward, she informed her debriefer at the SVR that only Poteyev had been in a position to know the password that an FBI agent had used to try to deceive her into believing she was speaking to an SVR officer. This brought Poteyev under immediate suspicion. Tipped off by the CIA to the FBI's error, Poteyev managed to escape by taking a train from Moscow to Belarus, where the CIA exfiltrated him to the United States. Poteyev had been saved from prison—or worse—but he was no longer useful to the CIA as a mole. Without the services of Poteyev in the SVR in Moscow, U.S. intelligence was unable to find out further details about the mission to which Poteyev's sleeper agents were to be assigned. All it had discovered was the history of the preparations for a major espionage revival. It now knew that the SVR had installed plumbing in America and that one or more agents in this network had been activated to handle a possible recruit in the NSA. But without anyone left in the sleeper network to follow and without an inside source in the SVR, it had no further avenues to fruitfully pursue. The revelation of the sleeper agents had little if any other intelligence value.

The NSA's own security investigation turned up no evidence of a leak at Fort Meade in 2010. That of course doesn't mean there hadn't been one. The Russian intelligence service had demonstrated in the past that it was well schooled in covering its tracks in operations against U.S. communications intelligence. For example, CIA counterintelligence had learned from a KGB defector in the early 1960s that Russian intelligence had penetrated the cipher room at the U.S. embassy in Moscow and, because of this operation, the KGB was able to decipher crucial communications. Even so, it failed to find either the perpetrator or any evidence of his existence for more than half a century. The operation was only definitively revealed by the Russian spymaster Sergey Kondrashev in 2007. Tennent Bagley, who headed the CIA's Soviet bloc counterintelligence at the time, lately wrote in his book that the ability of Russian intelligence to conceal this penetration for more than half a century "broke the record for secret keeping."

This Russian ability to penetrate U.S. intelligence was not entirely defeated by America's implementation of more sophisticated security procedures, such as the polygraph examination and extensive background checks. In 1995, eleven years before Snowden joined it, the CIA's inspector general completed a study of the KGB's use of false defectors to mislead the U.S. government from the end of the Cold War in the late 1980s through the mid-1990s. It found Russia had dispatched at least half a dozen double agents who provided misleading information to their CIA case officers.

Because the KGB operation went undetected for nearly a decade, the disinformation prepared in Moscow had been incorporated into reports (which had a distinctive blue stripe to signify their importance) that had been provided to Ronald Reagan, George H. W. Bush, and Bill Clinton. Even more shocking, in tracing the path of this disinformation, the inspector general found that the "senior CIA officers responsible for these reports had known that some of their sources for this information were controlled by Russian intelligence," yet they did not inform the president and officials receiving the blue-striped reports that they included Russian misinformation. What the CIA director John Deutch called "an inexcusable lapse" also reflected a form of institutional willful blindness in U.S. intelligence, borne out of a bureaucratic fear of career embarrassment so well described in Le Carré's spy novels. Detecting intelligence failures has, if anything, become even more difficult in the age of the anonymous Internet.

The Snowden breach demonstrated the NSA had few if any failsafe defenses against would-be leakers of communications intelligence. In the new domain of cyber warfare, conventional defensive rules do not apply. "There are no rivers or hills up here. It's all flat. All advantage goes to the attacker," General Hayden said in an interview in 2015 with the publisher of *The Wall Street Journal*. His point was that because there are no defensive positions, the United States in cyber warfare must rely on an aggressive offensive. If fully successful, such an offensive would so deeply penetrate the defenses of an adversary's intelligence organization that it could not mount any of its own surprise cyber attacks. It would also make it difficult if not impossible for adversary services to recruit a spy in the NSA. For example, the CIA penetration of the SVR in 2010 prevented it from using its sleeper network against U.S. targets. "The best defense in this game may be an overwhelming offensive," a former intelligence official said to me. "But that strategy only works if we can keep secret sensitive sources."

Central to this offensive strategy was the NSA's National Threat Operations Center in Oahu. It employed threat analysts to surreptitiously monitor the secret activities of potential enemies, mainly China, Russia, and North Korea. A large part of their job was to make transparent to the United States the hostile activities of the Russian and Chinese services so that they posed little if any intelligence threat to America. This strategy worked so long as the NSA guarded itself, but it also raised the issue, as the Roman Juvenal famously warned, "Quis custodiet ipsos custodes?" (Who will guard the guards themselves?)

Less than three years after the NSA had received the Poteyev warning, instead of guarding secrets, Snowden stole them. Despite all the measures the NSA had taken to protect its vital secrets, a lowly civilian employee had walked away with the lists of secret NSA sources in China and Russia and then gone first to China and then to Russia. In the hands of their intelligence services, these stolen lists had the potential to totally upend the NSA's offensive strategy. Because Russia and China have an intelligence treaty for sharing such spoils between them when it is to their mutual advantage, it had to be assumed that if either country had acquired the secrets from Snowden, they would be shared between them, altering the balance of power between the communications intelligence services of the United States and its adversaries.

Following the Snowden breach, both China and Russia had immense successes in breaking through the defenses of U.S. government networks, including the reported breaches in 2014 and 2015 of U.S. personnel files and background checks. When I asked General Hayden in June 2015 if these successes were made easier by those documents compromised by Snowden, he replied, "Even though I cannot make a direct correlation here, unarguably our adversaries know far more about how we collect signals intelligence than they ever did before [Snowden]."

If Snowden could cause such massive damage, so could other civilian trainees at the NSA. Someone in the chain of command had to take responsibility. General Alexander tendered his resignation on June 30, 2013. "I'm the director," he said, falling on his sword. "Ultimately, I'm accountable." Because President Obama did not want the head of the NSA resigning in the midst of the Snowden crisis, he asked him to stay on for another six months. He then appointed Rogers to be his replacement. Meanwhile, it had become undeniably clear to the review committee appointed by President Obama in 2013 that the NSA's own defenses had catastrophically failed. If so, this change was the equivalent of rearranging the deck chairs on the *Titanic* after it hit the iceberg.

PART THREE

THE GAME OF NATIONS

I learned that just beneath the surface there's another world, and still different worlds as you dig deeper.

—DAVID LYNCH, on his 1986 film, *Blue Velvet*

CHAPTER 19

The Rise of the NSA

There are many things we do in intelligence that, if revealed,
would have the potential for all kinds of blowback.
—JAMES CLAPPER, director of national intelligence, 2013

IN THE GAME OF NATIONS, which often is not visible to public
scrutiny, the great prize is state secrets that reveal the hidden
weaknesses of a nation's potential adversaries. The most important of these in peacetime is communication intercepts. It was just
such state secrets that Edward Snowden took from the NSA in the
spring of 2013. Before that breach, America's paramount advantage
in this subterranean competition was its undisputed dominance in
the business of obtaining and deciphering the communications of
other nations. The NSA was the instrument by which the United
States both protected its own secret communications and stole the
secrets of foreign nations. The NSA, however, has an Achilles's heel:
It is dependent on civilian computer technicians who do not necessarily share its values to operate its complex system. Because of this
dependence, it was not able in 2013, as it turned out, to protect its
crucial sources and methods.

Snowden exposed this vulnerability when he walked away with
the aforementioned descriptions of the gaps in America's coverage

of the communications of its adversaries. Even though the Cold War had been declared over after the collapse of the Soviet Union a quarter of a century earlier, the age-old enterprise of espionage did not end with it. Russia and China still sought to blunt the edge that the NSA gave the United States. The Snowden breach therefore needs to be considered in the context of the once and future intelligence war.

The modern enterprise of reading the communications of other nations traces back in the United States to military code-breaking efforts preceding America's entry into World War I. The invention of the radio at the end of the nineteenth century soon provided the means of rapidly sending and getting messages from ships, submarines, ground forces, spies, and embassies. These over-the-air messages could also be intercepted from the ether by adversaries. If they were to remain secret, they could not be sent in plain text. They had to be sent in either code, in which letters are substituted for one another, or, more effectively, a cipher, in which numbers are substituted for letters. Making and breaking codes and ciphers became a crucial enterprise for nations. By 1914, the U.S. Army and Navy had set up units, staffed by mathematicians, linguists, and crossword puzzle solvers, to intercept and decode enemy messages. After the war had ended in 1918, these units were fused into a cover corporation called the Code Compilation Company, which moved to new offices on Thirty-Seventh Street and Madison Avenue in New York City.

Under the supervision of the famous cryptographer Herbert O. Yardley, a team of twenty code breakers was employed in what was called the Black Chamber. Yardley arranged for Western Union, which had the telegraph monopoly in America, to provide the Black Chamber with all the telegrams coming into the United States. "Its far-seeking eyes penetrate the secret conference chambers at Washington, Tokyo, London, Paris, Geneva, Rome," Yardley wrote about the Black Chamber. "Its sensitive ears catch the faintest whispering in the foreign capitals of the world." But in 1929, at the instructions of President Herbert Hoover, Secretary of State Henry Stimson closed the Black Chamber, saying famously, "Gentlemen should not read each other's mail."

The moratorium did not last long. With war looming in Asia and

Europe, President Franklin D. Roosevelt reactivated the operation as the Signal Security Agency. It proved its value in breaking the Japanese machine-generated cipher "Purple." In June 1942, using deciphered Japanese messages to pinpoint the location of the Japanese fleet at Midway, America won a decisive naval victory in the Pacific. Germany's Enigma encoding machines, with three encoding wheels, proved more of a challenge. Initially, British cryptanalysts led by the brilliant mathematician Alan Turing succeeded in building a rudimentary computer to decipher Germany's messages to its submarines and bombers, but in 1942 Germany added a fourth set of encoding wheels, escalating what was essentially a battle of machine intelligence. The U.S. Navy then contracted with the National Cash Register Company to build a computing machine capable of breaking the improved Enigma, and in May 1943 it succeeded.

By the time the war ended in 1945, the United States had over one hundred giant decryption machines in operation. This unrivaled capability to read the communications of foreign nations, which remained one of America's most closely guarded secrets, was transferred to the Army Security Agency based at Fort Meade, Maryland. Then, on October 24, 1952, President Harry S. Truman greatly expanded its purview and changed its name to the National Security Agency.

The NSA was given two missions. The first one was protecting the communications of the U.S. government. The main risk was that the Soviets would find a way of breaching U.S. government channels of communications. The second mission was intercepting all the relevant communications and signals of foreign governments. This latter mandate included the governments of allies as well as enemies. The president, the other intelligence services, and the Department of Defense deemed what was relevant for national security. Even though the NSA remained part of the Department of Defense, its job went far beyond providing military intelligence. It also acted as a service agency to other American intelligence services. They prepared shopping lists of foreign communications intelligence targets for the NSA to pursue.

As the Cold War heated up in the 1960s, the NSA provided intelligence not only to the Pentagon but to the Department of State, the

Central Intelligence Agency, the Treasury Department, the Atomic Energy Commission, and the FBI. With a multibillion-dollar "black budget" hidden from public scrutiny, the NSA's technology director-ate invested in state-of-the-art equipment, including supercomputers that could break almost any cipher, antennas mounted on geosyn-chronous satellites that vacuumed in billions of foreign telephone calls, and other exotic capabilities. It also devised stealthy means of breaking into channels that its adversaries believed were secure. This enterprise required not only an army of technical specialists capable of remotely intercepting even the faintest traces of electromagnetic signals, hacking into computers, and eavesdropping on distant con-versations but also special units called "tailored access operations," to plant listening devices in embassies and diplomatic pouches. The NSA also organized elaborate expeditions to give access to or even penetrate physical cables in enemy territory. In 1971, for example, the NSA sent a specially equipped submarine into Russia's Sea of Okhotsk in Asia to tap through Arctic ice. The target was a Russian cable four hundred feet below the surface that connected the Rus-sian naval headquarters in Vladivostok with a missile testing range.

In 1980, President Ronald Reagan gave the NSA a clear mandate to expand its interception of foreign communications. In Executive Order 12333, he told the NSA that "all means, consistent with appli-cable Federal law and this [Executive] order, and with full consider-ation of the rights of United States persons, shall be used to obtain reliable intelligence information to protect the United States and its interests." It did not restrict any foreign country, either an adversary or an ally, from its surveillance.

The NSA's target soon became nothing short of the entire elec-tromagnetic spectrum. "We are approaching a time when we will be able to survey almost any point on the earth's surface with some sensor," Admiral Stansfield Turner, the former director of central intelligence, wrote in 1985. "We should soon be able to keep track of most of the activities on the surface of the earth." Bobby Ray Inman, a former director of the NSA and deputy director of the CIA, argued that the "vastness of the [American] intelligence 'take' from the Soviet Union, and the pattern of continuity going back years, even decades," greatly diminished the possibility of Soviet deception so long as the NSA kept secret its sources.

The NSA did not rely entirely on its own sensors for this global surveillance. It also formed intelligence-sharing alliances with key allies. The most important was with the British code-breaking service, GCHQ, which had achieved enormous success in World War II in using computers to crack the German Enigma cipher. This alliance expanded to include Canada, Australia, and New Zealand in the so-called Five Eyes Alliance. Because over 80 percent of international phone calls and Internet traffic passed through fiber-optic cables in these five countries, the alliance had the capability of monitoring almost all phone and Internet communications.

The NSA also established fruitful liaisons with the cyber services of Germany, France, Spain, Italy, the Netherlands, Portugal, Israel, Japan, and South Korea, which were often willing to provide the NSA with access to telecommunications links in their countries. These long-term allies greatly strengthened the NSA's hand in other ways in the intelligence war. For example, the so-called James Bond provision of the British Intelligence Services Act of 1994 allowed officers of the GCHQ to commit illegal acts outside Britain, including planting devices to intercept data from computer servers, cell phones, and other electronic targets. And, as Snowden's release of documents revealed in 2013 and 2014, these foreign allies fully shared their information with the NSA.

Of course, the liaison between the NSA and its allies was a two-way street. In 2013, none of these other countries had a global network of geosynchronous sensors in outer space and under the ocean that could monitor signals from missile launching, submarines, military deployments, nuclear tests, and other matters of strategic importance to them. Nor did these allies have the cipher-breaking capabilities of the array of NSA supercomputers. The NSA had assiduously built these means at a cost of over half a trillion dollars and employed tens of thousands of linguists who could translate almost any dialect or language of interest.

Even though these allies had their own cipher services and local capabilities, they depended on the NSA to provide them with a large share of their signals intelligence. From the perspective of defending themselves from potential threats, the deal that these allies had with the NSA was mutually advantageous.

The NSA's overseas intelligence gathering was not limited to adversary nations. With the exception of the Five Eyes allies, it gathered data that was deemed important by the president and the Defense Department in friendly countries. These operations had been approved by every American president and funded by every American Congress since 1941. After all, even in the realm of allies, activities take place that run counter to American interests. The 9/11 conspiracy, for example, was hatched in Hamburg, Germany, and financed in Dubai and Saudi Arabia.

Nor were American allies unaware of the reach of the NSA. "Yes, my continental European friends, we have spied on you. And it is true we use computers to sort through data by using keywords," the former CIA director James Woolsey wrote in *The Wall Street Journal* in 2000. "Have you stopped to ask yourselves what we are looking for?" Whether or not it was appreciated by other countries, the global harvesting of communications intelligence by the NSA was hardly a secret.

As the NSA expanded further, it delegated part of its work to regional bases, including ones in Utah, Texas, Hawaii, and Japan. The paramount task of the NSA remained monitoring the channels of communications that an adversary might use. The vast proliferation of these channels in cyberspace, which included e-mail, social media, document sharing, and other innovations of the Internet age, greatly complicated this task. Even so, this challenge was not insurmountable, because most of the Internet actually traveled through fiberglass landline cables that crossed the territories of the United States, Britain, and Australia. So the NSA found the technical means, including voluntarily gaining access to major Internet companies, to "harvest" vast amounts of this Internet data. America's other intelligence agencies quickly recognized the value of the communications intelligence gleaned from foreign telecommunications. John E. McLaughlin, who was the CIA's acting director in 2004, described the NSA as nothing less than the "very foundation of U.S. intelligence." It served as a "foundation" for the CIA because intercepted communications intelligence allowed the CIA (and other U.S. intelligence services) to test and verify the reports of their human sources in foreign countries. Moreover, because of the immense amount of foreign data that the NSA vacuumed in through its global sensors, it provided the CIA with an effective means for discovering new targets in adversary nations.

By the first decade of this century, the NSA's surreptitious efforts to render the Internet transparent to U.S. intelligence had earned it a new set of enemies. They were the previously mentioned hacktivists who were attempting to shield the activities of Internet users from the intrusions of government surveillance. They employed both encryption and Tor software to defeat that surveillance. But the NSA did not conceal that it was intent on countering any attempt to interfere with its surveillance of the Internet. It built back doors into encryption and worked to unravel the Tor scrambling of IP addresses. It made leading hacktivists targets. Brian Hale, the spokesman for the director of national intelligence, disclosed that the United States routinely intercepted the cyber signatures of parties suspected of hacking into U.S. government networks.

Following the 9/11 attacks on the Pentagon and the World Trade Center, the surveillance of the Internet became an integral part of the Bush administration's war on terrorism. In October 2001, Congress expanded the NSA's mandate by passing the USA Patriot Act. As I described earlier, Section 215 of the act directly authorized the NSA, with the approval of the FISA court, to collect and store domestic telephone billing records. The idea was to better coordinate domestic and foreign intelligence about al-Qaeda and other jihadist groups. This put the NSA directly in the anti-terrorist business. It also necessitated the NSA vastly increasing its coverage of the Internet.

The mantra in government in this post-9/11 intelligence world became "connect the dots." Congress through this act essentially demolished the wall between domestic and foreign intelligence when any NSA activity related to foreign-directed terrorism. It further made the NSA a partner with the FBI in tracking phone calls made from phones originating outside the United States by known foreign jihadists. If these calls were made to individuals inside, the NSA was now authorized to retrieve the billing records of the person called and those people whom he or she called. These traces were then supplied to the FBI. The new duties also increased the NSA's need to create new bureaucratic mechanisms to monitor its compliance with FISA court orders. Rajesh De, the NSA's general counsel at the time of the Snowden breach, described the NSA as becoming by 2013 "one of the most regulated enterprises in the world." Grafted onto its intelligence activities were layers of mandated reporting to oversight officials. Not only did the NSA have its own chief compliance officer, chief privacy and civil liberties officer, and independent inspector general, but the NSA also had to report to a different set of compliance officers at the Department of Defense, the Office of the Director of National Intelligence, and the Department of Justice. Additionally, the Department of Justice dispatched a team of lawyers every sixty days to review the results of "every single tasking decision" approved by the FISA court.

According to De, just assembling these reports involved thousands of hours of manpower. In addition, the president's Oversight Board required that the NSA's Office of the General Counsel and inspector general supply it every ninety days with a list of every single error and deviation from procedure made by every NSA employee anywhere in the world, including even minor typing errors. These requirements, according to De, inundated a large part of the NSA legal and executive staff in a sea of red tape. Yet this regulation could not undo surveillance programs such as the one Snowden revealed of Verizon's turning over the billing records of its customers to the NSA, because the NSA was in compliance with the FISA court order (even though, as it turned out in 2015, the FISA court might have erred in interpreting the law).

The NSA's focus on surveillance might have led to the neglect of its other mission: protecting the integrity of the channels through which the White House, government agencies, and military units send information. This task had been made vastly more difficult by the proliferation of computer networks, texting, and e-mails. To protect government networks from cyber attacks, the Pentagon belatedly created the U.S. Cyber Command in 2009. In it, the cyber-defense units of the army, navy, marines, and air force cyber forces were merged together and put under the command of the NSA director. General Keith Alexander became the first director of this new command. One problem for the Cyber Command was separating attacks by civilians, including criminals, hacktivists, and anarchists, from cyber warfare sponsored and supported by adversary states. Because foreign intelligence services often closely imitated the tools of civilian hackers, and were even known to provide them with hacking tools, it was not easy for the Cyber Command to unambiguously determine if the ultimate perpetrator of a cyber attack was state sponsored. For example, the identification of North Korea as the principal actor behind the attack on Sony in December 2014 appeared to be a rare success, but many cyber-security experts believed that it might be a false trail used to hide the real attacker. Clues could be fabricated in cyberspace to point to the wrong party.

The job of the Cyber Command was to prevent such an attack. To this end, it planted viruses on hundreds of thousands of computers in private hands to act as sentinels to spot other suspicious viruses that could mount such an attack. Private computers had become a new battleground in the cyber wars. It also built a capability to retaliate. Still, cyber attacks, which were launched through layers of other countries' computers, could not be unambiguously traced back to the true perpetrator.

This escalation by the Cyber Command set the stage for expanded forms of warfare in cyberspace. "The Chinese are viewed as the source of a great many attacks on western infrastructure and just recently, the U.S. electrical grid," General Alexander said in explaining the need for this consolidation. "If that is determined to be an organized attack, I would want to go and take down the source of those attacks." The same retaliation would presumably be used against Russia, Iran, or any other adversary. Dominance of cyberspace itself now became part of the NSA's mandate.

Even so, the most important job of the NSA remained intercepting secret information from Russia, China, Iran, and North Korea. To this end, it had an annual budget of $12.3 billion and some thirty-five thousand military and civilian employees. In 2013, James Clapper, director of national intelligence, justified the secret intelligence budget by saying in an open session of Congress, "We are bolstering our support for clandestine SIGINT [signals intelligence] capabilities to collect against high priority targets, including foreign leadership targets," and to develop "groundbreaking cryptanalytic capabilities to defeat adversarial cryptography and exploit Internet traffic." It was no secret to Congress, even before Snowden, that the NSA was attempting to monitor the Internet. What was a closely held secret before Snowden revealed it was that the NSA had found a way in 2007 to intercept Internet traffic before it was encrypted.

Through all this tumult, the heart of the NSA's activity remained its five-thousand-acre base at Fort Meade, Maryland. It commanded the most powerful mechanism for intercepting communications that the world had ever seen. No other country came close to its technology for intercepting information. The NSA not only was able to intercept secret information from potential adversaries but also—at least until the Snowden breach—managed to conceal these means from them. As long as these adversaries remained blind to the ways in which their communications were being intercepted, deciphered, and read by the NSA, they could not take effective countermeasures. Consequently, the NSA had the capability to provide the president and his advisers with continuous insights into the thinking and planning of potential enemies.

Keeping its sources and methods secret was no easy task. The NSA's technicians had to deal with continuous technical challenges to provide a seamless harvesting of data from a wide range of communication devices, including telephones, computers, and the Internet. It required continuous intra-agency communications between the NSA's own intelligence officers and a growing number of civilian technicians. It even had its own "Wiki-style" network through which they could discuss problems, called the NSANet. Because it could not tightly control access to this technical network, it expunged any mention of the sources and methods from the material circulated on the classified NSA network. Instead, it stored them in discrete computers, called compartments, which were disconnected from other computers at the NSA. These compartments could only be accessed by a limited number of analysts and NSA executives who had a need to know about the data they contained. These compartments were the final line of defense against an inside intruder.

In 2009, Snowden, as we know, found his way into the NSA through a temporary job with an outside contractor that was working for the NSA's Technology Directorate to repair and update its backup system. Four years later, by maneuvering to get hired by another outside contractor with access to the NSA's sources and methods, he was able to steal secrets stored in isolated computers bearing directly on the ongoing intelligence war. Snowden also copied from these compartments in a matter of weeks, as has been previously mentioned, the NSA's Level 3 sources and methods used against Russia, Iran, and China. The Snowden breach demonstrated that the NSA's envelope of secrecy was at best illusory.

After this immense loss, the NSA's sources inside these adversary countries were largely compromised, even if they were not closed down. Once these adversaries were in a position to know what channels the NSA was intercepting, they could use these same channels to mislead U.S. intelligence. A former top intelligence official told me, "The queen on our chessboard had been taken."

The NSA moved to mitigate the damage and find new ways of obtaining unexpected intelligence. In June 2014, the new NSA director, Rogers, had to confront flagging morale that, according to General Hayden, was near paralyzing the intelligence service. Rogers recognized that as a direct result of the Snowden breach, "the nation has lost capabilities against adversaries right now who are attempting to actively undermine us." But even with that loss, he observed, "the sky has not fallen."

As in the Chicken Little fable he cited, the world had not ended for the NSA. Nor had it ended for the multibillion-dollar outsourcing enterprise it superintended. The NSA might have lost many of its sources, or "capabilities," but Rogers held out hope that new sources could eventually be found to replace them. Compromised codes, after all, could be changed. New technological methods could be devised. New vulnerabilities could also be targeted in enemy territories. Although repairing the damage might take many "decades," according to Michael McConnell, the vice-chairman of Booz Allen, the new director had to get on with that task. McConnell, a former NSA director himself, pointed out that the NSA director's "first responsibility is to be the chief cheerleader." Rebuilding the NSA capabilities assumed, however, that there would not be another Snowden-sized breach.

The question remained: How could the NSA's vaunted secrecy have been so deeply penetrated by a mere analyst in training at a regional base in Oahu? The perpetrator himself could not be asked if he was in Moscow pointing to the "incompetence" of the NSA in his Moscow interviews. What was known, though, was that the young man who had taken the "queen" from the board had gained entry to the NSA's secret chambers through the back door, a portal opened to him by the NSA's reliance on outside contractors.

CHAPTER 20

The NSA's Back Door

You have private for-profit companies doing inherently governmental work like targeted espionage, surveillance, compromising
foreign systems. And there's very little oversight, there's very
little review.

—EDWARD SNOWDEN, Moscow, 2014

PRIOR TO SNOWDEN'S THEFT of NSA documents, the single most
shattering blow to the confidence of the U.S. intelligence community was the 1994 exposure of Aldrich Ames as a long-serving
Russian mole in the CIA. Ames, it will be recalled, had been a high-
ranking CIA officer, working at the CIA's Counterintelligence Center Analysis Group, before he was arrested by the FBI. He had also
worked as a mole for Russian intelligence.

In a plea bargain to avoid a death sentence (he was sentenced to
life imprisonment), he admitted that he had successfully burrowed
into the CIA and had worked there for over nine years on behalf of
the KGB. His description of his sub-rosa activities as a mole was part
of the plea bargain. This stunning revelation shook the CIA leadership to its core. Until then, CIA executives steadfastly denied that it
was possible that the KGB could sustain a mole in American intelligence. The Ames arrest also led the NSA to reassess its own vulnerability to penetration. Could there be an Ames inside the NSA?

The question was considered by the NSA's National Threat Operations Center, the same unit from which Edward Snowden later stole a huge trove of secret documents. According to a report in 1996 titled "Out of Control" (later released by the NSA), the danger of an Ames-type penetration could not be excluded. Even though the "threat officer" who wrote this report was not identified by name, his analysis proved incredibly prescient. He said that the NSA's drive to enhance its performance by networking its computers would result in the intelligence services' putting "all their classified information 'eggs' into one very precarious basket." The basket was the computer networks run by technicians called system administrators. He pointed out that the NSA was becoming increasingly dependent on such networked computer systems, and he predicted that the NSA's "Aldrich Ames," as he put it, would be a "system administrator," which was the position that Edward Snowden held nearly two decades later at Dell when he began stealing secrets.

The NSA's system administrators were, as the threat officer pointed out, very different from the traditional military employees at the NSA. They were usually civilians who effectively served as repairmen for complex computer systems. Moreover, many of them had not been directly hired by the NSA. Instead, their recruitment had been privatized to outside contractors.

This outsourcing had deep roots tracing back to World War II. Ed Booz and Jim Allen, the founders of Booz Allen Hamilton, obtained contracts to help manage ship construction from the U.S. Navy. After the war ended, they sought contracts for their firm in classified work. These contracts grew in size as the NSA needed more and more system administrators and other information technologists to manage the computer networks. These system administrators needed to be given special privileges to do their service job. One such privilege allowed them to bypass password protection. Another privilege allowed then to temporarily transfer data to an external storage device while they repaired computers. These two privileges greatly increased the risk of a massive breach. Seeing them as the weak link in the chain, the threat officer wrote in the report that "system administrators are likely to be increasingly targeted by foreign intelligence services because of their special access to information."

Before the computerization of the NSA, the threat officer noted, code clerks and other low-level NSA communicators had been the targets of adversary intelligence services. But the increasing reliance on computer technicians presented foreign intelligence services with much richer targets. He predicted that they would adapt their recruiting to this new reality. Specifically, he argued that adversary intelligence services would now focus their attention on system administrators. "With system administrators," he said, "the situation is potentially much worse than it has ever been with communicators." The reason, he explained, was that "system administrators can so easily, and quickly, steal vast quantities of information."

He further suggested that because system administrators are often drawn from the counterculture of hacking, they are more likely to be vulnerable to an adversary service using a fake identity for its approach, or a "false flag." A "false flag" was a term originally applied to a pirate ship that temporarily hoisted any flag that would allow it to gain proximity to its intended prey, but in modern times it describes a technique employed by espionage services to surreptitiously lure a prospect. False flags were a staple used by the KGB in espionage recruitment during the Cold War. They were usually employed when a target for recruitment was not ideologically disposed to assisting the intelligence service. To overcome that problem, recruiters hide their true identities and adopt a more sympathetic, bogus one.

In 1973, the KGB, working through one of its agents in the U.S. Navy, used the false flag of Israel to recruit Jerry Alfred Whitworth, who served as a communications officer with a top secret clearance for the navy. Like many other KGB recruits, Whitworth came from a broken family, dropped out of high school, took technical courses, and got a job as a communications officer. He was not disposed to working for Russia. But he was willing to steal enciphered and plain text cables to help in the defense of Israel. After he was thoroughly compromised by his espionage work, he was told by the KGB recruiter that he was actually working for Russia, but by this time he was too deeply compromised to quit. He continued his espionage work for another eight years. (Whitworth, who was arrested by the FBI in 1985, was convicted of espionage and sentenced to 365 years in prison.)

The Internet provided an almost ideal environment for false flags because its users commonly adopt aliases, screen names, and other avatars. The threat officer explained how easy it would be for the KGB to adapt such a false flag when dealing with a dissident system administrator working for U.S. intelligence. As the threat officer pointed out in his report, the KGB had used false flags in the late 1980s to surreptitiously recruit members of the "German Hanover Hackers," a community of anarchistic hackers who breached computer networks for fun and profit. Until then, these hacktivists stole corporate and private passwords, credit card information, and other privileged documents as a form of freelance espionage. Because of their fervent anti-authority ideology, the KGB disguised its recruiters as fellow hacktivists. The KGB succeeded in getting the Hanover hackers to steal log-in account identifications, source codes, and other information from U.S. government computer networks.

The weak link of system administrators became increasingly relevant as the NSA moved further into the digital age. By the beginning of this century, its growing networks of computers were largely operated by civilian technicians, including system administrators, infrastructure analysts, and information technologists, who were needed to keep the system running. Despite the warning by the threat officer, the NSA became more and more reliant on these outsiders as it reorganized to meet its new mandates for surveillance of the Internet in the war on terrorism.

The NSA had to compete with technology companies, such as Google, Apple, and Facebook, for the services of experienced IT workers. Though Booz Allen had been providing technically trained specialists to the government since the 1940s and '50s, congressionally imposed salary caps put the NSA at a disadvantage to private firms in its recruitment efforts. As a result, it increasingly contracted with private firms to find talent, especially in the rush for data-based intelligence following 9/11. Booz Allen, to meet increased demand, recruited civilian technicians from many unconventional areas, including the hacking culture. Ex-hackers who lacked (or shunned) employment opportunities in the corporate sector were suitable candidates for the system administrator jobs that these firms had contracted to supply the NSA. In the rush to expand, little heed was paid to the 1996 warning that this hacking culture might provide a portal to anti-government hacktivist groups. The NSA became so enamored with this new computer technology that it neglected the security implications of employing outsiders to service it. "All of us just fell in love with the ease and convenience and scale [of electronic storage]," General Hayden, who headed the NSA at the time, said to *The Wall Street Journal* in 2015. "So we decided to take things we used to keep if not in a safe, at least in our desk drawer, and put it up here [in a computer network], where it's by definition more vulnerable." Making matters even worse, as has previously been discussed, the NSA stripped away much of the so-called stove-piping that insulated highly sensitive data from the NSA's other computer networks. FBI Director Mueller, in his "Statement Before the Senate Committee on Homeland Security and Governmental Affairs," described a decade of post–9/11 intelligence reorganization thus: "One of the first steps was to centralize control and management of counterterrorism operations at headquarters to avoid the 'stove-piping' of information on terrorism cases in the 56 individual field offices across the country." Here the NSA was merely following the recommendations of the 9/11 Commission to make their data more accessible to other agencies concerned with potential terrorist attacks, but as a result, the inner sanctum of the NSA became more open to its new army of civilian technicians.

By 2013, much of the job of managing the NSA's classified computers had been handed over to a handful of private companies: Booz Allen Hamilton, which handled the most highly secret work; Dell SecureWorks; Microsoft; Raytheon; and IBM. In many respects, these five companies acted less like management consultants and more like temporary employment agencies in finding for the NSA the computer specialists who had the necessary security clearances.

The NSA found that the universe of independent contractors was governed by very different considerations from that of intelligence services. Unlike intelligence services, their fate depended on turning profits. Because the value of their contracts was largely limited by competitive bidding, their business plans were predicated on their ability to minimize the costs of fulfilling these contracts. Their principal cost was the salaries they paid their independent contractors. Their business plans therefore depended on finding large numbers of computer technicians in the private realm willing to work at an NSA base at relatively low wages. This task became more difficult as many potential recruits could find higher-paying employment with more of a future in the burgeoning private sphere. But the companies could also increase their revenue streams by getting additional contracts, which, in turn, meant recruiting even more workers.

Such a business plan could hardly afford to give the highest priority to the low probability of a security risk. In the private sector, there is usually an unambiguous external measure of failure. An automobile company such as General Motors can measure the performance of its executives by reckoning its change in net income. With secret intelligence work, the metrics for failure are far less clear. This curious aspect of secret work was part of the advice given to a White House lawyer in the Obama administration seeking a position with the NSA in 2012, who was told that among the advantages of working for a super-secret agency was that if one errs or has a failure, "it stays secret." The Snowden case showed that not all failures stay secret.

The NSA can certainly quantify the amount of data it is intercepting, but it obviously cannot count the intelligence that it misses. The a priori proposition in the intelligence game is that "what is successfully hidden is never found." But one failure that cannot be hidden is a security breach in which a perpetrator uses NSA data to publicly expose the NSA's sources.

Until the Snowden breach in 2013, the NSA had experienced only one such public failure. It was the capture by North Korea in 1968 of the USS *Pueblo*, which had been carrying out highly sensitive electronic communications interception for the NSA. The *Pueblo* crew failed to destroy the NSA's encoding machines, which were flown to Russia several days later. It was a horrible, costly breach. The Snowden breach was much worse because, among the thousands of documents he stole, he selected lists of the NSA's secret sources in adversary nations.

The Snowden breach was a failure that directly traced back to the NSA's largest and most trusted contractor, Booz Allen Hamilton, calling into question the vexing issue of privatizing secret intelligence. Booz Allen, like other private firms that did work for the government, was in the business to make money. Indeed, it had found government contracts so much more profitable than its work in the private sector that it sold its private sector unit to PricewaterhouseCoopers. The profitability of government work led the Carlyle Group's private equity fund to acquire a controlling stake in Booz Allen in July 2008. By 2013, it had increased its revenue by more than $1.3 billion by expanding its government contracts. Even more impressive, its operating profit on these contracts had doubled. It did not need to increase its core internal staff to achieve these profits; it just had to hire outside contractors. In 2008, Booz Allen claimed 20,000 employees on its internal staff; in 2013, it claimed fewer than 5,000. The resulting "reduced headcount," according to its January 30, 2013, quarterly report, greatly decreased its costs for incentive pay. It mainly accomplished this reduction by expanding the number of outside contractors it employed, 8,000 in these five years, by one Wall Street analyst's calculation. They were employed as system administrators, infrastructure analysts, computer security specialists, and other "geek squad" jobs at the NSA and other government agencies. Their main qualification was their prior security clearances (which as mentioned earlier saved Booz Allen the expense of vetting them and also the loss of income while waiting many months for a clearance).

Snowden therefore was highly desirable for Booz Allen from an economic point of view. Even though he had no prior experience as an infrastructure analyst, and he had been detected being untruthful about his degree in computer sciences, he not only had a SCI security clearance but was willing to take a cut in pay. In keeping with the Booz Allen business plan, such a recruit provided another cog in its profit machine.

Not only had the NSA outsourced much of its computer operations to private companies, but the Clinton administration in 1996 had privatized background checks for government employees requiring security clearances. The idea, backed by Vice President Al Gore, was to reduce the size of the federal government by outsourcing investigating the backgrounds of millions of government applicants for jobs. The task had previously been performed by the FBI, but it was assumed that a profit-making business could do it faster and more efficiently. The private company named U.S. Investigations Services was purchased in 2007 for $1.5 billion by Providence Equity Partners, a rapidly expanding investment firm founded in 1989 by graduates of Duke, Brown University, and the Harvard Business School. So like Booz Allen, USIS was backed by a hedge fund determined to make money by systematically cutting the cost of a service previously carried out by the government.

But such outsourcing had drawbacks. For one thing, unlike the FBI, USIS lacked the investigative clout to gain entry to certain government agencies. A Congressional review found that the privacy act permits disclosure of government agency records to the private firm if they are part of a "routine use of the records," but intelligence agencies did not consider all such requests to be "routine." For example, when it did the background check on Snowden in 2011, it could not get access to his CIA file. The "derog" in his file might have set off alarm bells, as might the fear that he had been threatened by an internal investigation over his alleged computer tampering in 2009. The FBI might have learned this about Snowden if it had done his background check.

The lack of adequate oversight was another problem. USIS closed cases and cleared applicants without completing an adequate investigation. According to a U.S. government suit filed in 2014, USIS had prematurely closed over 665,000 investigations in order to get paid for them more quickly. Because the more cases it completed each month, the more money it received from the government, the lawsuit alleged that USIS employees often "flushed" or ended cases before completing a full investigation to meet corporate-imposed quotas for getting bonuses. One employee, in an e-mail cited in the government's complaint, said they "flushed everything like a dead goldfish." As a result, some information specialists entering the NSA through the back door of outside contractors were not fully vetted. (On August 20, 2015, USIS agreed to forfeit $30 million in fees to settle the lawsuit.)

USIS was also open to sophisticated hacking attacks by outsiders. In August 2014, the Department of Homeland Security's counterintelligence unit discovered such a massive and persistent breach in USIS that it shut down its entire exchange of data with it. The intrusion into USIS records in this case was attributed to hackers in China most likely linked to the Chinese intelligence service. Such massive intrusions dated back to 2011. USIS's lack of security in its website left a gaping hole through which outside parties, including Chinese and Russian hackers, could learn both the identity and the background information of specialists applying for jobs at the NSA.

These private companies also did not sufficiently protect the personal data of their independent contractors working at the NSA. The hackers' group Anonymous took credit for the successful 2011 attack on the Booz Allen Hamilton servers. It also cracked the algorithms used to protect employees. It next injected so-called Trojan horse viruses and other malicious codes into Booz Allen servers that allowed it future entry. If amateur hackers such as Anonymous could break into the computers of the NSA's largest contractor, so could adversaries' state espionage services with far more advanced hacking tools. From these sites, China or Russia could obtain all the job applications and personal résumés submitted to contractors such as Booz Allen. It could then compile a list of the best candidates to do its bidding.

These deficiencies in the private sector were compounded by the failure of security in the government's own Office of Personnel Management. It used a computer system called e-QIP in which intelligence employees, including outside contractors, updated their computerized records to maintain or upgrade their security clearances. For example, Snowden updated his clearance in 2011. To do so, these employees constantly updated their financial and personal information. As it turned out, there was a major hole in the e-QIP system. It has repeatedly been hacked by unknown parties since 2010. In 2015, the U.S. government told Congress that China was most likely responsible, but Russia and other nations with sophisticated cyber services could have also participated in the hacking. In any case, the records of over nineteen million employees, including intelligence workers, became available to a hostile intelligence service. This breach would allow hostile services to obtain a great deal of information about independent contractors working at the NSA. They could then use this data to follow the movements of any of these intelligence workers they deemed of interest.

Despite all the potential flaws in it, the outsourcing system continued in place. It even featured a revolving door through which Booz Allen hired retiring executives from the intelligence services, such as the former NSA director Michael McConnell; James Woolsey, a former director of the CIA; and the retired general James Clapper, who later served as director of national intelligence.

The cozy relationship between the private firms and the NSA notwithstanding, the NSA leadership operated as if it were unaware that outsourcing could create a security problem. As far back as 2005 General Hayden, then the departing head of the NSA, had been warned of one such vulnerability in a memorandum written by a counterintelligence officer at the NSA. Like the earlier 1996 report by the threat officer, this memorandum noted the NSA had ceded responsibility for managing its secret systems to outsiders and warned that the NSA's reliance on them to manage its computers had opened a back door into the NSA. In addition, it warned that once an outside contractor managed to slip in through this back door, he could easily jump from one outsourcer to another. This was what Snowden did when he moved from Dell to Booz Allen Hamilton in 2013.

Despite its security flaws, outsourcing seemed to provide a number of advantages to the NSA. For one thing, it provided a means for circumventing the budget restrictions imposed by Congress on hiring new employees. In addition, because private companies had less rigid hiring standards, it greatly expanded the pool of young system administrators by tapping into computer cultures that would be antagonistic to working directly for the government. Finally, it drew less on NSA resources. Because these information technologists were only temporary employees, they were not entitled to military pensions, paid medical leave, and other benefits. It was a system that effectively replaced military careerists with freelancers.

The irony of the situation was that the NSA had surrounded its front doors with rings of barbed wire, closed-circuit cameras, and armed guards, but for reasons of economy, bureaucratic restrictions, and convenience it had left the back door of outsourcing open to temporary employees of private companies, even though it might take some time for them to gain entry to its inner sanctum.

"It was not a question of if but when one of the contractors would go rogue," the former NSA executive who wrote the 2015 memorandum told me. Snowden answered that question in 2013. Even more extraordinary than the theft itself was the reaction to it by the NSA. It turned out that there was no cost of failure levied against the outside contractor Booz Allen, which had employed Snowden when he bypassed its security regime to steal the keys to the kingdom. Booz Allen had not reported "red flags" concerning Snowden's attempt to get secrets to which he was not privy and his absence from work for six days. Nor was Snowden the last Booz Allen contractor to compromise NSA secrets. On August 27, 2016, the FBI arrested Harold Thomas Martin, who worked on a Booz Allen contract at an NSA facility, for stealing secret NSA documents. Even so, the NSA did not penalize Booz Allen. Instead, its revenues and profits from government contracts markedly increased between 2013 and 2016.

Despite these breaches the NSA did not alter its reliance on private contractors. The back door to the NSA remained wide open. Outsourcing to private companies has become an all but irreplaceable part of the intelligence system in America, Snowden's actions, and the risk of future similar actions, notwithstanding.

CHAPTER 21

The Russians Are Coming

The collapse of the Soviet Union was a major geopolitical disaster of the century.

—VLADIMIR PUTIN

IN THE FIRST INVASION of a European country since the end of the Cold War, Russian military forces moved into the Crimea and other parts of eastern Ukraine in February and March 2014. Unlike with previous Russian troop movements, such as those into Poland, Hungary, Czechoslovakia, and East Germany during the Cold War, the weeklong massing of Russian elite troops and sophisticated equipment for the move into Ukraine almost totally evaded detection by the NSA's surveillance. Never before had the NSA's multibillion-dollar armada of sensors and other apparatus for intercepting signals missed such a massive military operation. According to a report in *The Wall Street Journal* that cited Pentagon sources, Russian units had managed to hide all electronic traces of their elaborate preparations. If so, after more than half a century of attempted penetrations, Russia had apparently found a means of stymieing the interception capabilities of the NSA.

Putin had firm ideas about restoring Russia's power in the post–Cold War era. A formidable KGB officer before he became president of the Russian Federation in 2000, he made no secret that his goal was to prevent the United States from obtaining what he termed "global hegemony." His logic was clear. He judged the breakup of the Soviet Union in 1991 to be, as he put it, "a geopolitical disaster." He argued that the breakup had provided the United States with the means to become the singular dominant power in the world.

He sought to prevent that outcome by moving aggressively to redress this loss of Russian power. He upgraded Russia's nuclear force, modernized Russia's elite military units, and greatly strengthened Russia's relations with China. The last measure was essential because China was Russia's principal ally in opposing the extension of American dominance. Yet there was still an immense gap between them and the United States in communications intelligence.

Since the breakup of the Soviet Union, the NSA had continued to build up its technological capabilities, while Russia teetered on the edge of collapse in the early 1990s. But as previously mentioned, the NSA's legal mandate had been limited by Congress to foreign interceptions (at least prior to 9/11). As a result, it was required to separate out domestic from foreign surveillance, a massive process that not only was time-consuming but could generate dissidence within the ranks of American intelligence. It also could not legally use its surveillance machinery to monitor the telephones and Internet activities of the tens of thousands of civilian contractors who ran its computer networks—at least not unless the FBI began an investigation into them.

Here the Russian intelligence services had a clear advantage. They had a lawful mandate to intercept any and all domestic communications. In fact, a compulsory surveillance system called by its Russian acronym SORM had been incorporated into Russian law in 1995. It requires the FSB and seven other Russian security agencies to monitor all forms of domestic communications including telephones (SORM-1), e-mails and other Internet activity (SORM-2), and computer data storage of billing information (SORM-3). Not only did Russia run a nationwide system of Internet filtering in 2013, but it required its telecommunication companies to furnish it with worldwide data.

The NSA also had to deal with many peripheral issues other than the activities of Russia and China. It was charged with monitoring nuclear proliferation in Iran, Pakistan, and North Korea, potential jihadist threats everywhere in the world, and much else. The Russian foreign intelligence service, the SVR, could put its limited resources to work on redressing the gap with its main enemy: the United States.

Nevertheless, Putin had to reckon with the reality in 2013 that Russia could not compete with the NSA in the business of intercepting communications. And if the NSA could listen in on all the internal activities of its spy agencies and security regime, the ability of Putin to use covert means to achieve his other global ambitions would be impaired. In the cold peace that replaced the Cold War, Russia had little hope of realizing these ambitions unless it could weaken the NSA's iron-tight grip on global communications intelligence. One way to remedy the imbalance between Russian intelligence and the NSA was via espionage. Here the SVR would be the instrument, and the immediate objective would be to acquire the NSA's lists of its sources in Russia. If successful, it would be a game changer.

Such an ambitious penetration of the NSA, to be sure, was a tall order for Russian intelligence. Most of its moles recruited in the NSA by the KGB had been code clerks, guards, translators, and low-level analysts. They provided documents about the NSA's cipher breaking, but they lacked access to the lists of the NSA's sources and methods. These meager results did not inhibit Russian efforts. For six decades, ever since the inception of the NSA in 1952, the Russian intelligence service had engaged in a covert war with the NSA.

The Russian intelligence service is, as far as is known, the only intelligence service in the world that ever succeeded in penetrating the NSA. A number of NSA employees also defected to Moscow. The history of this venerable enterprise is instructive.

The first two defectors in the NSA's history were William Martin and Bernon Mitchell. They were mathematicians working on the NSA's decryption machines who went to Moscow via Cuba in 1960. The Russian intelligence service, then called the KGB, went to great lengths to get propaganda value from their defections. It even organized a ninety-minute press conference for them on September 6,

1960, at the Hall of Journalists and invited all the foreign correspondents in Moscow. Before television cameras, the defectors denounced the NSA's activities. Martin told how the NSA breached international laws by spying on Germany, Britain, and other NATO allies. Mitchell, for his part, suggested that the NSA's practice of breaking international laws could ignite a nuclear war. Indeed, he justified their joint defection to Russia in heroic whistle-blowing terms, saying, "We would attempt to crawl to the moon if we thought it would lessen the threat of an atomic war." The NSA review of the case, however, assessed that little damage had been done, because the NSA quickly changed the codes they had compromised. It noted, "The Communist spymasters would undoubtedly have preferred Martin and Mitchell to remain in place as moles, since their information was dated as of the moment they left NSA."

The next NSA defector was Victor Norris Hamilton, a translator and analyst at the NSA. He arrived in Moscow in 1962, and like Mitchell and Martin he claimed the status of a whistle-blower. This time, the KGB provided a newspaper platform. Writing in the Russian newspaper *Izvestia*, Hamilton revealed the extent of U.S. spying on its allies in the Middle East.

None of these three 1960s defectors revealed what, if any, NSA secret documents they had compromised. Nor did any of them ever return to the United States. Martin changed his name to Vladimir Sokolodsky, married a Russian woman, and died in Mexico City on January 17, 1987. Mitchell vanished from sight and was reported to have died in St. Petersburg on November 12, 2001. Hamilton, after telling Russian authorities stories about hearing voices in his head because of an NSA device implanted in his brain, was consigned to Special Psychiatric Hospital No. 5 outside Moscow.

There were also KGB spies in the NSA who were caught or died before they could defect. One of them was Sergeant Jack Dunlap. He was found dead of carbon monoxide poisoning in his garage on July 23, 1963. Although there was no suicide note, his death was ruled an apparent suicide. NSA classified documents were later discovered in his house. After that, NSA investigators unraveled his decade-long career as a KGB mole. Dunlap had been recruited by the KGB in Turkey in 1952. The standard KGB tool kit for recruitment was called MICE. It stood for Money, Ideology, Compromise, and Ego. The KGB used the first element, money, to compromise Dunlap. After he was compromised, it exploited him by getting him to steal NSA secrets. He had access to such secrets because he became the personal driver to Major General Garrison Coverdale, the chief of staff of the NSA. After Coverdale retired, he became the driver for his successor, General Thomas Watlington. These positions afforded him a security clearance and, even more important, a "no inspection" status for the commanding general's cars that he drove. This perk allowed him to leave the base with secret documents, have them photocopied by his KGB case officer, and then return them to the files at the NSA base before anyone else knew they were missing. He also used, likely at the suggestion of the KGB case officers, his "no inspection" perk to offer other NSA employees a way of earning money. He would smuggle off the base any items of government property that they took. Once he had compromised them through thefts, he was in a position to ask them for intelligence favors. This NSA ring could not be fully investigated because of his untimely death. Other than the packets of undelivered NSA documents found in his home, the investigation was never able to assess the total extent of the KGB penetration of NSA secrets. (Angleton suspected Dunlap was murdered by the KGB in what he termed a surreptitiously assisted death, to prevent Dunlap from talking to investigators.)

The Russian intelligence services continued recruiting mercenary spies in the NSA for the duration of the Cold War. The KGB successes included Robert Lipka, a clerk at the NSA in the mid-1960s, who was caught in a sting operation by the FBI and sentenced to eighteen years in a federal prison. Ronald Pelton, an NSA analyst, was recruited after he retired from the NSA. After he was betrayed by a KGB double agent in 1985, he was sentenced to life imprisonment. Finally, there was David Sheldon Boone, an NSA code clerk, who between 1988 and 1992 provided the KGB with NSA documents in return for $60,000. Boone, sentenced to twenty-four years in prison, was the last known KGB recruitment of the Cold War.

During the Cold War, Russian intelligence service officers operated mainly under the cover of the embassies, consulates, United Nations delegations, and other diplomatic missions of the Soviet

Union. As "diplomats," they were protected from arrest by the terms of the 1961 Treaty of Vienna Convention on Diplomatic Relations. Their diplomatic cover, however, greatly limited their field for finding potential recruits outside their universe of international meetings, diplomatic receptions, UN organizations, scientific conferences, and cultural exchanges. They therefore tended to recruit their counterparts in adversary services.

In this regard, the successful entrapment of Harold Nicholson in the 1990s is highly instructive. From his impressive record, he seemed an unlikely candidate for recruitment. He had been a superpatriotic American who had served as a captain in army intelligence before joining the CIA in 1980. In the CIA, he had an unblemished record as a career officer, serving as a station chief in Eastern Europe and then the deputy chief of operations in Malaysia in 1992. Even though his career was on the rise and he was a dedicated anti-Communist, he became a target for the SVR when he was assigned to the CIA's elite Russian division. Because the job of this division was to recruit Russian officials working abroad as diplomats, engineers, and military officers, its operations brought its officers in close contact with SVR officers. Nicholson therefore was required to meet with Russian intelligence officers in Manila, Bucharest, Tokyo, and Bangkok and "dangle" himself to the SVR by feigning disloyalty to the CIA.

As part of these deception operations, Nicholson supplied the Russians with tidbits of CIA secrets, or "chickenfeed," that had been approved by his superiors at the CIA. What his CIA superiors did not fully take into account in this spy-versus-spy game was the SVR's ability to manipulate, compromise, and convert a "dangle" to its own ends. As it turned out, Russian intelligence had been assembling a psychological profile on Nicholson since the late 1980s and found vulnerability: his resentment at the failure of his superiors to recognize his achievements in intelligence. The Russians played on this vulnerability to compromise him and then converted him to becoming its mole inside the CIA.

Nicholson worked for the SVR first in Asia; then he was given a management position at CIA headquarters, which is located in Langley, Virginia. Among other secret documents, he provided the SVR with the identities of CIA officers sent to the CIA's special training school at Fort Peary, Virginia, which opened the door for the SVR to make other potential recruitments. Meanwhile, it paid him $300,000 before he was finally arrested by the FBI in November 1996. (After his conviction for espionage, he was sentenced to twenty-three years in federal prison.) The CIA postmortem on Nicholson, who was the highest-ranking CIA officer ever recruited (as far as is known), made clear that even a loyal American, with no intention of betraying the United States, could be entrapped in the spy game.

When it comes to recruiting moles in a larger universe, intelligence services operate much like highly specialized corporate "headhunters," as James Jesus Angleton described the process to me during the Cold War era. He was referring to the similar approach that corporate human resource divisions had with espionage agencies. Both headhunt by searching through a database of candidates for possible recruits to fill specific positions. Both types of organizations have researchers at their disposal to draw up rosters of potential recruits. Both sort through available databases to determine which of the names on the list have attributes that might qualify or disqualify them for a recruitment pitch. Both also collect personal data on each qualified candidate, including any indication of his or her ideological leaning, political affiliations, financial standing, ambitions, and vanities, to help them make a tempting offer.

But there are two important differences. First, unlike their counterparts in the private sector, espionage headhunters ask their candidates not only to take on a new job but also to keep their employment secret from their present employer. Second, they ask them to surreptitiously steal documents from him. Because they are asking candidates to break the law, espionage services, unlike their corporate counterparts in headhunting, obviously need to initially hide from the candidates the dangerous nature of the work they will do. Depending on the targeted recruit, they might disguise the task as a heroic act, such as righting an injustice, exposing an illegal government activity, or countering a regime of tyranny. This disguise is called in the parlance of the trade a false flag, as mentioned earlier. By using such a false flag, the SVR did not need to find a candidate who was sympathetic to Russia or the Putin regime. In its long history dating back to the era of the czars, Russian intelligence had perfected the technique of false flag recruitment, through which it assumes an identity to fit the ideological bent of a potential recruit.

Russian intelligence was well experienced with false flags. It first used this technique following the Bolshevik revolution in 1917 to control dissidents both at home and abroad. The centerpiece, as later analyzed by the CIA, was known as the "Trust" deception. It began in August 1921 when a high-ranking official of the Communist regime in Russia named Aleksandr Yakushev slipped away from a Soviet trade delegation in Estonia and sought out a leading anti-Communist exile he had known before the revolution in Russia. He then told him that he represented a group of disillusioned officials in Russia that included key members of the secret police, the army, and the Interior Ministry. Yakushev said that they all had come to the same conclusion: the Communist experiment in Russia had totally failed and needed to be replaced. To effect this regime change, they had formed an underground organization code-named the Trust, because the cover for their conspiratorial activities was the Moscow headquarters of the Municipal Credit Association, which was a trust company. According to Yakushev's account, it had become the equivalent of a de facto government by 1921.

The exiled leader in Estonia reported this astonishing news to British intelligence, which, along with French and American intelligence, helped fund this newly emerged anti-Communist group. Initially, British intelligence had doubts about the bona fides of the Trust, as did other Western intelligence services sponsoring exile groups. But they gradually accepted it after they received intelligence reports confirming its operations from many other sources, including Russian officials, diplomats, and military officers who claimed to have defected from the Soviet government. Because these reports all dovetailed, they recognized the Trust as a legitimately underground organization.

Once the Trust had been established in the minds of the Western intelligence services, it offered them as well as exile groups the services of its network of collaborators. These services included smuggling out dissidents, stealing secret documents, and disbursing money inside Russia to sympathizers. Within a year, exile groups in

Paris, Berlin, Vienna, and Helsinki were using the Trust to deliver arms and supplies to their partisans inside Russia. The Trust also furnished spies' and exiled leaders' fake passports, which allowed them to sneak back into Russia to participate in clandestine missions. It even undertook sabotage and assassination missions paid for by Western intelligence services. As they learned of police stations being blown up and political prisoners escaped from prisons, these agents and dissidents came to further believe in the power of the Trust.

By the mid-1920s, no fewer than eleven Western intelligence services had become almost completely dependent on the Trust for information about Russia. They also sent millions of dollars into Russia via couriers to finance its activities.

But suddenly exiled leaders working in Russia under the aegis of the Trust began to vanish. Then top Western intelligence agents, including Sidney Reilly and Boris Savinkov, were arrested, and their networks were eliminated. Instead of the Communist regime collapsing, as the Trust had predicted, it consolidated its power and wiped out all the dissident groups. Finally, in 1929, the Trust was revealed by a defector to be a long-term false flag operation run by the Russian intelligence service. Even the Trust building, rather than being the cover for a subversive conspiracy, was the headquarters for the Russian secret police during this eight-year operation. The secret police had provided the documents fed to Western intelligence, briefed the agents who pretended to defect, published the dissident newspapers the Trust distributed, fabricated the passports it supplied exiles, blew up Russian buildings, and staged jail breaks to make the deception more credible. It also collected the money sent in by Western intelligence services, which more than paid for the entire deception. Because it was running the show, it could offer those lured into the trap an opportunity to work for it as double agents. The alternative, if they refused, was to face a firing squad.

Even after the Trust itself had been fully exposed, the Russian intelligence service continued to succeed with other false flag deceptions. During the Cold War, it set up a fake underground in Poland called WIN, modeled on the Trust. It set up false flag groups in Ukraine, Georgia, Lithuania, Albania, and Hungary. It also had agents masquerade as members of the security services of Israel, South Africa, Germany, France, and the United States to recruit unwitting agents. These deceptions became an integral part of the recruitments of the Russian intelligence services.

Penetrating the NSA and getting access to files from its stove-piped computers was a far more difficult challenge for the SVR. Approaching CIA officers, such as Nicholson, was relatively easy because it was part of the CIA officers' jobs to meet with their adversaries. NSA officers, on the other hand, did not engage in "dangles" or even attend diplomatic receptions. They had no reason, other than a sinister one, to meet with a member of the Russian intelligence service. Furthermore, unlike CIA officers, who, like Nicholson, are often posted in neutral countries where they can be approached in a social context, NSA officers work at well-guarded regional bases and are not part of the diplomatic life. Because a known employee of a foreign diplomatic mission could not even approach an NSA officer without arousing suspicion, the SVR would need to use an intermediary, called an access agent, whose affiliations were not known to the FBI. Such an operation would require establishing a network of illegals in America, as the SVR did after Putin became president. Even then, the intermediary would have to find a plausible pretext to approach the target without revealing his actual interest. Such complex operations at the NSA, as far as is known, only yielded a few low-level recruits.

The emergence of computer networks in the 1990s greatly expanded the SVR's recruiting horizon. It offered a new penetration opportunity at the NSA: civilian technologists working under contract for the U.S. government. Many of these civilians at the NSA, especially the younger ones, as we know, had been drawn from the hacking and game-playing culture; some had even taken courses on hacking techniques. They presented the SVR with inviting targets for recruitment. As was previously mentioned, Russian intelligence had considerable experience in Germany with hacktivists, who tended to be anarchists. There were also supporters of the libertarian movement. The common denominator was often their resentment, expressed in their postings, of the United States and its allies attempting to limit the downloading of copyrighted music, movies, and software on the Internet, all of which fell under the rubric of "freedom of the Internet." They also vocally objected to the NSA's using built-in back doors in its software to read their encrypted messages. Such people were not difficult to find on the Internet. The donors to Ron Paul's libertarian election campaign (including Snowden) were a matter of public record.

Even if there was no shortage of hacktivists who believed the surveillance of the Internet by the NSA was an evil worth fighting, the SVR still had to find a plausible way of approaching members of this counterculture without offending them. Clearly, the SVR could no longer use out-of-date Communist and anti-capitalist ideology as a lure. Russia was far more authoritarian than the United States when it came to the Internet. One viable alternative for the SVR was custom-tailoring false flags to appeal to hacktivists.

For this purpose, the Internet provided a near-perfect realm. Because it is a place where true identities cannot easily be verified, intelligence services could employ a protean kit of disguises to assume false identities to entice potential dissidents into communicating with them. The KGB's earlier efforts to use hacktivist groups in Germany had produced little if any intelligence about the NSA because of the stovepiping it used to isolate its computers from networks that could be hacked into from the outside. It will be recalled that the NSA threat officer had cited these failures in his 1996 report on NSA vulnerability. He also said that efforts of the Russian intelligence services to use false flag recruitments provided the KGB with "a learning experience." The KGB had learned that hacking by itself could not breach the NSA's protective stovepiping. He predicted that its next logical move would be to "target insider computer personnel." This false flag recruitment would aim at, in his view, system administrators, computer engineers, and cyber-service workers who either were already inside the NSA or had a security clearance that would facilitate getting jobs with NSA contractors.

Even with an appropriate false flag, the task of finding such a "Prometheus" required obtaining a database of those working at the NSA. There were some five thousand civilian technicians at the NSA of all political stripes. Hacking into the personnel records of the intelligence workers seeking to renew their security clearance was a place to begin. The Internet provided the SVR with just this opportunity. As you will recall, holes in the security of the computer networks of the U.S. Office of Personnel Management and USIS and the websites of the companies supplying the NSA with independent contractors had made the background checks on American intelligence workers available to the Chinese, and presumably other adversary intelligence service hackers, since 2011. If the SVR had access to this personnel data, the research for a candidate would be greatly facilitated. From the 127-page Standard Form 86, which each applicant for a security clearance submits, the SVR could filter out intelligence workers employed by the NSA by their educational background, employment history, affiliations, and foreign contacts. It could then search this data for candidates with a possible hacktivist profile.

This data could next be crossed with a list of individuals the SVR knew were in contact with high-profile activists who were part of the anti-surveillance movements. This would include core participants in the Tor Project, WikiLeaks, Noisebridge, CryptoParties, the Freedom of the Press Foundation, and the Electronic Frontier Foundation. (Snowden, for example, had been in touch with members of all these groups in 2012 and 2013.)

The SVR would have little problem monitoring even encrypted communications with leading figures in the anti-surveillance world. These activists, despite secrecy rituals such as putting their cell phones in refrigerators, remain visible to a sophisticated intelligence service such as the SVR. All the defensive tactics of Laura Poitras, including PGP encryption, Tor software, and air-gapped computers (computers that have never been connected to the Internet), did not keep secrets about her sources entirely to herself. Snowden, at a time when he was stealing NSA secrets in February 2013, went to great lengths to impress on Poitras the need for operational security about his contacts with her, but that injunction did not prevent her from telling at least five people about her source, including Micah Lee, the Berkeley-based technology operative for the Freedom of the Press Foundation; Jacob Appelbaum, the Tor proselytizer; Ben Wizner, the ACLU lawyer; Barton Gellman; and Glenn Greenwald. "It is not me that can't keep a secret," Abraham Lincoln joked. "It's the people I tell it to that can't." In the same vein, Poitras could hardly rely on these five confidants not to tell her secrets (and Snowden's) to others. Hours after he was told, Greenwald told his lover, David Miranda, about the source in great detail. He even asked him to evaluate the source's bona fides for him. Gellman, for his part, raised the matter with a former high official at the Justice Department.

Moreover, as the intelligence world knew, Poitras was herself a veritable lightning rod for attracting ex-NSA employees who objected to some of its surveillance programs. In 2012, her previously mentioned filming in Berlin of NSA insiders could make her communications of interest to intelligence services that wanted to keep tabs on possible NSA dissidents.

Nor was Snowden himself overly discreet. It will be recalled that he had also advertised his Tor-sponsored CryptoParty activities over the Internet and supplied Runa Sandvik, who worked with Appelbaum, his true name and address in Hawaii. Sandvik had no reason not to share the identity of her co-presenter with others in the Tor movement. Snowden, of course, had his girlfriend make a video of his presentation as well. He also bragged about operating the largest Tor outlets in Hawaii. Even if his Tor software provided him with a measure of anonymity, it was not beyond the ability of the world-class cyber services to crack it.

Under Putin, Russia had built one of the leading cyber-espionage services in the world. According to a 2009 NSA analysis of Russian capabilities, which was obtained by *The New York Times* in 2013, Russia's highly sophisticated tools for cyber espionage were superior to those of China or any other adversary nation. For example, investigators from FireEye, a well-regarded Silicon Valley security firm, found that in 2007 Russian hackers had developed a highly sophisticated virus that could bypass the security measures of the servers of both the U.S. government and its private contractors. According to one computer security expert, the virus had made protected Internet websites "sitting ducks" for these sophisticated Russian hackers. The cryptographer Bruce Schneier, a leading specialist in computer security, explained, "It is next to impossible to maintain privacy and anonymity against a well-funded government adversary."

Nor has the Russian cyber service made a secret out of the fact that it targets Tor software. It even offered a cash prize to anyone in the hacking community who could break Tor. Prior to 2013, according to cyber-security experts, it spent over a decade building cyber tools aimed at unraveling the Tor networks used by hacktivists, criminal enterprises, political dissidents, and rival intelligence operatives. To this end, it reportedly attempted to map out computers that served as major Tor exit nodes (such as the one Snowden operated in 2012 near an NSA regional base in Hawaii). It also reportedly attached the equivalent of "electronic ink" to messages, which would allow it to trace the path of messages that passed through them. Through this technology, it could tag and follow Tor users as their communications traveled across the Internet. It could even borrow their Internet identities. To be sure, the NSA also had such a capability. The Silk Road founder, Ross Ulbricht, discovered to his distress that his Tor software did not make his computer server in Iceland invisible. According to a former top official in the Justice Department, the NSA was able to locate it by cracking the Tor software (Ulbricht is currently serving a life sentence for his activities). Unlike adversary services, however, the NSA needs a warrant to investigate U.S. citizens who use Tor.

The NSA is hardly immune from an attack on its own computers. As the former CIA deputy director Morell wrote in his 2015 book, *The Great War of Our Time,* many financial institutions have "better cyber security than the NSA." The Internet certainly helped make the activities of U.S. intelligence workers visible to the SVR.

But to achieve its goals, the SVR still had to find at least one disgruntled civilian contractor inside the NSA who had access to the sealed-off computer networks. Did it find its man? If so, was it before or after Snowden arrived in Hong Kong with the Level 3 NSA files?

CHAPTER 22

The Chinese Puzzle

The first [false assumption] is that China is an enemy of the
United States. It's not.

——EDWARD SNOWDEN, Hong Kong, 2013

ON AUGUST 11, 2014, in the Atlantic Ocean, an event took place
of enormous concern to U.S. intelligence. A Chinese Jin-class
submarine launched an intercontinental ballistic missile. The missile
released twelve independently targeted reentry vehicles, each simu-
lating a nuclear warhead. Some forty-four hundred miles away, in
China's test range in the Xinjiang desert, each of the twelve simu-
lated nuclear warheads hit its target within a twelve-inch radius.

The test firing, which was closely monitored by the NSA, was a
strategic game changer. It meant that a single Jin-class submarine,
which carried twelve such missiles and 144 nuclear warheads, could
destroy every city of strategic importance in the United States. U.S.
intelligence further reported that China would soon use stealth
technology to make it more difficult to detect newer submarines and
give "China its first credible sea-based nuclear deterrent" against an
American attack.

By 2015, as its test in the Atlantic had foreshadowed, China had
armed its land-based as well as sea-based missiles with multiple

independently targeted warheads. Combined with the state-of-the-art technology it had licensed from Russia, its systematic use of espionage even made it possible for China to build its own stealth fighters.

Unlike the United States, China did not achieve this remarkable capability to launch independently targeted miniaturized nuclear weapons and stealth them by investing hundreds of billions of dollars in developing them. It obtained this technology mainly through espionage. The Chinese intelligence service stole a large part, if not all, of America's secret technology for weaponizing nuclear bombs during the 1980s and 1990s. The theft was so massive that in 1998 the House of Representatives set up a special bipartisan investigative unit called the Select Committee on U.S. National Security and Military/Commercial Concerns with the People's Republic of China. Based on the intelligence amassed by the NSA, the CIA, and other intelligence services, it concluded in its report that the Chinese intelligence service had obtained both by electronic and by conventional spying the warhead design of America's seven most advanced thermonuclear weapons. Moreover, it found that espionage successes allowed China to so accelerate the design, development, and testing of its own nuclear weapons that the new generation of Chinese weapons would be "comparable in effectiveness to the weapons used by the United States." Further, the committee reported that these thefts were the "results of decades of intelligence operations against U.S. weapons laboratories." The Chinese intelligence service further obtained from private U.S. defense contractors through cyber espionage important elements of the stealth technology used in advanced planes and submarines. China shared (or exchanged) the fruits of its espionage on nuclear warhead design with North Korea, Pakistan, Iran, and Russia.

Despite its formidable intelligence coups in the United States, the Chinese intelligence service managed to remain among the most elusive of America's intelligence adversaries. Its espionage organizations are hidden behind layers of bureaucracy in the Ministry of State Security, Chinese Communist Party structures, and the second, third, and fourth department of the General Staff of the People's Liberation Army. Much of its cyber-espionage units are concealed on the campuses of its universities. Its hierarchy is also obscure. Few traces have been uncovered of any conventional espionage networks in the United States, and no major Chinese spy has ever been arrested. Part of the reason that Chinese espionage has proved so elusive to the eyes of Western counterintelligence is that, unlike Russia, it did not ordinarily rely on intelligence officers in its embassies to recruit penetration agents to steal secrets. It did not even have an embassy in the United States during most of the Cold War. Instead, its services specialize in mosaics of intelligence assembled from a wide variety of sources, including nonclassified documents, returning graduate students, scientific conferences, exchanges with allies, and a vast operation of hacking into computers, or cyber espionage.

Such espionage is indeed a vast enterprise in China. Graduating over 150,000 computer science engineers in the 1990s, it had no shortage of personnel. It had also developed the cyber tool kit to gain access to the computer networks of U.S. government contractors and consultants in the private sector and government agencies, planting "sleeper" bugs in networked computers. Like human sleeper agents, these hidden programs can be activated when needed for operational purposes. Chinese controllers can often retrieve e-mails and documents and can turn on the cameras and microphones of personal computers, tablets, and smart phones.

By 2007, Paul Strassmann, a top U.S. defense expert on cyber espionage, reported that China had inserted "zombie" programs in some 700,000 computers in the United States, which could be used to mount cyber attacks to retrieve e-mails from other computers. The Chinese service also reportedly penetrated companies that provide Internet services, including Google, Yahoo!, Symantec, and Adobe, which allowed it to track e-mails and enclosures of individuals. With such an invisible army of zombie computers, it is not entirely surprising that China finds little need to employ human sleeper agents.

Chinese cyber specialists used this capability to hack into the computers of outside contractors, including Booz Allen and other companies that supplied technologists to the NSA. It also had notable successes in obtaining the dossiers of U.S. employees and independent contractors at the NSA, the CIA, and other intelligence services. Its intrusions, as previously noted, into computer networks at the Office of Personnel Management traced back to 2009. Eventually, by 2015, according to U.S. estimates, the cyber attack had harvested over twenty million personnel files of past and present federal government employees. In addition, it reaped over fourteen million background checks of intelligence workers done by the Federal Investigative Services.

All intelligence workers with a sensitive compartmented information clearance, such as Snowden, were required to provide information on these forms about all their foreign acquaintances, including any non-U.S. officials whom the applicant knew or had had relationships with in the past. They also had to list their foreign travel, family members, police encounters, mental health issues, and credit history. For good measure, Chinese hackers obtained the confidential medical histories of government employees by hacking into the computers of Anthem and other giant health-care companies. If China's intelligence services consolidated the fruits of these hacking attacks, it would have a searchable database of almost everyone working in the American defense and intelligence complex. From this database, it could track individuals with high security clearances vulnerable to being bribed, blackmailed, or tricked into cooperating. No one doubted that the Chinese would use their cyber capabilities to take advantage of opportunities presented in foreign computer systems.

General Hayden said of the massive theft of intelligence personnel records, "Those records are a legitimate foreign intelligence target." He added, "If I, as director of the NSA or CIA, would have had the opportunity to grab the equivalent in the Chinese system, I would not have thought twice." If that opportunity did not arise for the NSA or the CIA during Hayden's tenure, it might have been because no insider in the Chinese intelligence services provided U.S. intelligence with a road map to it.

Cyber espionage was not the Chinese intelligence service's only powerful resource in the intelligence war. To get both electronic intelligence and human intelligence about the United States, China also had a highly productive intelligence-sharing treaty with Russia. It was signed in 1992 after the Soviet Union was dissolved. Although the terms of this exchange remain secret, defectors from the Russian KGB and SVR reported that Chinese intelligence received from Russia a continuous stream of communications intelligence about the United States in the late twentieth and early twenty-first centuries. Russia's intelligence resources during this period were formidable. They included geosynchronous satellites, listening stations in Cuba, sleeper agents, and embassy-based spy networks. Presumably, this relationship further deepened under President Putin's regime. Putin asserted in speeches in 2014 that Russia and China continued to share a key strategic objective: countering the United States' domination of international relations, or what Putin terms "a unipolar world order." China's president, Xi Jinping, expressed a very similar view, saying in 2014 in a thinly veiled reference to the United States that any attempt to "monopolize" international affairs will not succeed.

Since the end of the Cold War, Russia has been the major supplier of almost all of China's modern weaponry. It licenses for manufacture in China avionics, air defense systems, missile launchers, stealth technology, and submarine warfare equipment. To make these arms effective, it also provides China with up-to-date intelligence about the ability of the United States and its allies to counter them. While such intelligence cooperation may be limited by the reality that China and Russia still compete in many areas, they still have reason to share much of the fruits of their cyber and conventional espionage against the NSA in accordance with their intelligence. After all, the NSA works to intercept the military and political secrets of both these allies. Moreover, as the CIA's former deputy director Morell points out in his book, NSA secrets are a form of currency for adversaries in the global intelligence war, saying that part of Snowden's cache could be traded by a country that acquired it to the intelligence services of Iran and North Korea.

Snowden's stay in Hong Kong from May 20 to June 23 in 2013 made the Chinese intelligence service, willy-nilly, a potential player in whatever game he was involved in. China's full responsibility for Hong Kong's national security and foreign affairs includes monitoring foreign intelligence operatives. Chinese intelligence maintains there its largest intelligence base outside mainland China. A large contingent of its officers are stationed officially in the Prince of Wales skyscraper in central Hong Kong and unofficially maintain informers in Hong Kong's police, governing authority, airport administration, and other levers of power. It checks the computerized visitors entering Hong Kong and has the capability to ferret names that match those in the immense database its global cyber espionage has amassed. When it detects the entry of any person of possible intelligence interest, it can use its sophisticated array of cyber tools to attempt to remotely steal data from that individual. Such remote surveillance was so effective in 2013 that the U.S. State Department had instructed all its personnel in Hong Kong to avoid using their iPhones, Androids, BlackBerry phones, and other smart phones when traveling to Hong Kong or China. Instead, it supplied them with specially altered phones that disable location tracking and have a remotely activated switch to completely cut off power to its circuitry. No one in the intelligence community doubts the prudence of taking such precautions in China, and it is nearly inconceivable that Snowden, whose prior position at the NSA included teaching military personnel about Chinese capacities, could himself be unaware of Chinese intelligence service capabilities to acquire travelers' data in Hong Kong.

Once Hong Kong had served as a window into China for Western intelligence, but in the first decade of this century the Chinese intelligence service had achieved such a pervasive presence in Hong Kong, and such ubiquitous electronic coverage of diplomats and other foreigners even suspected of involvement in foreign intelligence work, that the CIA and British intelligence found it almost as difficult to operate in Hong Kong as in mainland China. Even though the CIA kept officers there in 2013, it was considered "hostile territory," according to the former CIA officer Tyler Drumheller.

Snowden apparently knew the limits of CIA operations in Hong Kong, which provided him with an envelope of protection. He told Greenwald that he was counting on the Chinese presence in Hong Kong to deter the CIA from intruding on their meetings.

When he flew to Hong Kong in May 2013, he took with him NSA secrets, which he knew would be of great interest to China.

CHAPTER 23

A Single Point of Failure

A single point of failure (SPOF) is a part of a system that, if it
fails, will stop the entire system from working.

—*Wikipedia*

SNOWDEN DESCRIBED anyone who was the sole repository of
secrets that could undo the NSA's intelligence gathering as "the
single point of failure." While still shielding his own identity in May
2013, he wrote to Gellman that U.S. intelligence "will most certainly
kill you if they think you are the single point of failure that could
stop this disclosure and make them the sole owner of this information." Such a person of course would be of even greater interest to
adversary intelligence services if they were aware of the payload of
secrets that person was carrying because they could use it to unravel
the NSA's sources and methods.

Snowden saw himself as that "single point of failure." We know
that while still in Hong Kong he said he had obtained access to computers that the NSA had penetrated throughout the world and in
Moscow he added that he had had "access to every [NSA] target,
every [NSA] active operation," against the Chinese. "Full lists of
them," which, if he chose to share them, could make China "go
dark." To be sure, he did not refer to Russian intelligence activity in

any interview that he ever gave in Moscow under Russian protection, but he had similar access to NSA operations against Russia in his job at the NSA's Threat Operations Center.

The enormous power of the NSA rested in its ability to keep its sources and methods secret from its foes. A queen on the chessboard could be captured by a lowly pawn if it was well-placed. In this case, the person who had it in his power to expose the NSA's critical sources and methods would no doubt be considered fair game by America's adversaries, including the Chinese and Russian cyber services. Indeed, how could they resist such a prize?

Snowden might have believed that he was in control, but the CIA believed that confidence was misinformed. "Snowden thinks he is smart," Morell said, after reviewing the case on a panel appointed by President Obama, "but he was never in a position in his previous jobs to fully understand the immense capabilities of our Russian and Chinese counterparts." He could adopt a cocky tone in his postmortem conversations with journalists in Moscow, but in truth he had no means to block the efforts of the Chinese or Russian services in Hong Kong. Even before Snowden contacted its diplomats in Hong Kong, the Russian intelligence service would swing into action to determine his intelligence value.

How many days he planned to be in Hong Kong depended on how speedily he could arrange a meeting with journalists. "The purpose of my [Hong Kong] mission was to get the information to journalists," he told the editor of *The Guardian* after he was safely ensconced in Moscow. He indicates that he was working under a tight clock. The time pressure resulted in his e-mailing an ultimatum to Gellman on May 24: either Gellman would publish the selected documents in *The Washington Post* within seventy-two hours, or he would lose the exclusive scoop. Snowden wanted the story to break on May 27, without his true identity (which Gellman did not know) attached to it. His identity would be known to a foreign mission in Hong Kong if Gellman acceded to his demands, because, as previously mentioned, Gellman's story would enclose an encoded signal he planned to use as proof of his bona fides. So even before the *Guardian* reporters had agreed to come to Hong Kong, Snowden had plans to deal with a foreign mission. If the *Post* had accepted his terms, Snowden would have been in a very different position. The story would have broken before Poitras or Greenwald even knew about Snowden's presence in Hong Kong, and his identity would be secret except for whatever foreign mission he had contacted. But, as we know, the *Post* turned down his ultimatum.

Time was running out if he was to break the story and leave Hong Kong before the NSA realized he was missing. At best, he was safe until June 3, when he was supposed to return from his medical leave. If he failed to show up in Hawaii on June 3, alarm bells at the NSA would go off, and it would not take long to find him. Airline records would show that he had flown to Hong Kong. Snowden told Poitras that NSA security would ask, "This guy isn't where he says he's supposed to be. He's supposed to be getting medical treatment. Why the hell is he in Hong Kong?" It would not take long to determine that he had lied about his medical treatment, and then the hunt would begin.

He had, remember, already sent Poitras an enciphered file and told her she would get the key once she followed his instructions. Greenwald had still not committed himself to meeting Snowden. Greenwald was, however, willing to publish the documents once Snowden provided them. That Snowden remained in Hong Kong suggests that his reason for going to and remaining in Hong Kong went beyond just delivering documents to journalists, which he could have done over the Internet. What he could not do in America, without risking arrest, was to make and release a video.

In any event, after his attempt to pressure the *Post*, Snowden asked Greenwald to fly immediately to Hong Kong. Presumably, he still wanted Greenwald's story and the video done in Hong Kong before he became a suspect. If Greenwald and Poitras had immediately flown to Hong Kong, it still might have left Snowden an escape window.

But of course things do not always go as planned. Greenwald, although agreeing to come to Hong Kong, waited in New York for two days while the *Guardian* editors completed their due diligence. Poitras waited with him. As a result of this delay, as we know, Greenwald and Poitras did not arrive at his hotel in Hong Kong until June 3, only hours before Snowden became suspect at the NSA. "It was a nervous period," Snowden recalled. Although he bravely told *The Guardian* "there was no risk" that the information he carried had been compromised by other parties in Hong Kong, that claim was, at best, wishful thinking on his part.

By this time, he had registered at the hotel under his true name and provided his credit card; he was in contact with three high-profile journalists, two well-known hacktivists, and, as he suggested to Gellman, a foreign diplomatic mission.

The mission's interest would likely be piqued when the newspaper published its first story on June 6. Greenwald then went on TV in Hong Kong, revealing to every interested intelligence service that a defector from the NSA was in Hong Kong providing secret documents.

Poitras released the famous video showing Snowden and secret NSA documents three days later. At this point, Snowden shone brightly as a beacon to NSA secrets to every player in the intelligence game, even if they did not know the extent of the damage he could inflict on American intelligence.

Snowden fogged over his travel plans to the media by telling reporters that he intended to remain in Hong Kong and fight extradition, but certainly the Russian officials whom he contacted became aware that he had other plans, having relayed his request to go to Russia to their superiors in Moscow. And, unlike the media, any sophisticated intelligence service was well aware of his movements. In Hong Kong, cell phones emit their GPS location every three seconds; even if Snowden disabled his own phone, lawyers and helpers could be tracked with ease.

China's president, Xi Jinping, who was meeting President Obama for the first time in Rancho Mirage, California, on June 8, would have been keenly interested in the unfolding Snowden affair. Obama had publicly called Xi to task for Chinese cyber espionage, and now that charge was undermined by Snowden's accusation that the United States was engaged in massive cyber espionage. U.S. intelligence verified that China instituted a full-court press of Snowden in Hong Kong immediately after the release of the video. From that moment on, any communication or movement Snowden made during his next fifteen days in Hong Kong would not likely escape China's scrutiny.

The United States had the ability to also follow Snowden's movements via the cell phones of his lawyers and other confederates after he surfaced. All tracking could be done by the NSA. What the United States lacked was any practical means to capture a high-profile intelligence defector in a city that was part of China. By this time, U.S. intelligence had established that Chinese and Hong Kong security services were monitoring Snowden's every move. This left few options in the game for the United States. "I'm not going to be scrambling jets to get a twenty-nine-year-old hacker," President Obama said on June 27.

The real prize, in any case, was not Snowden but the NSA's secret documents that he had with him. When Snowden was observed entering the Russian consulate, the game was all but over. U.S. diplomats could protest over back channels to Moscow, as they did, but with a trove of NSA secrets at stake there was little expectation that would stop the Russians. Two days later, the "single point of failure," as Snowden described himself, was on his way to Russia, where his hosts would be calling the shots.

When a victory is obtained in a major sports event, it is cause for public celebrations. The opposite is true in espionage. An intelligence victory involving secret documents, even if it cannot be entirely hidden, is kept veiled, as far as is possible, to increase the value of the coup. "The final move in any sophisticated intelligence game," Angleton told me in relation to espionage intelligence, is "obscuring a success."

Following Angleton's precept, the Russian or Chinese intelligence services, if they had a role in acquiring the product of the self-described "single point of failure," would work to cover their tracks in the affair even before the Aeroflot plane carrying Snowden touched down at Sheremetyevo International Airport on June 23. If any false flag operations had been used to trick, mislead, or otherwise induce Snowden to come to Hong Kong, they would be disbanded. If any safe house had been used to quarter Snowden in his first eleven days in Hong Kong, it would be shut down. If any operatives had been used in Hawaii to guide or assist Snowden, they would be put back into sleeper mode. If any telltale traces had been left in chat rooms or social media, they would be systematically deleted. Even more important to the ultimate success of such a communications intelligence coup, measures would be taken to conceal the extent of the damage done by the "single point of failure" by not precipitously closing down compromised sources. Snowden might believe that the power of the information he held was so great that if disclosed by him, all the NSA's sources would immediately go dark in Russia and China, but Russia might not wish to provide such clarity to its adversaries. An intelligence service need not close down channels it discovers are compromised by an adversary. Instead, it can elect to continue to use them and furnish through them bits of sensitive or misleading information to advance its own national interest. The real danger here was not that the NSA's "lights" would dramatically be extinguished but that all the future messages illuminated by those lights would be less reliable sources of intelligence. The game of nations is, after all, merely a competition among adversaries to gain advantages by the surreptitious exchange of both twisted and straight information.

To review: When the NSA asserted in the summer of 2013 that over one million documents had been compromised, it was recognizing the most massive failure in its sixty-year history. Not only were NSA secrets taken, but secret files from the CIA, the British GCHQ, and America's cyber military commands had been compromised. It was, as Sir David Omand, the former head of the British GCHQ, described it, a "huge strategic setback" for the West. The genie could not be put back into the bottle. There is not a reset button in this game. The best that the NSA could do now was damage control while its adversaries took full advantage of the setback. Several hundred U.S. and British intelligence officers worked around the clock in Washington, D.C., Fort Meade, Maryland, and Cheltenham, England, for months on end to determine which parts of the most powerful communications intelligence system in the world could be salvaged from what had been the Snowden breach.

Adding insult to injury, Snowden, speaking from his new perch in Moscow, told applauding audiences that the entire purpose of the U.S. exercise, including deliberately "trapping" him in Moscow, was to "demonize" him. "There was no question that I was going to be subject to a demonization campaign." Snowden said in Moscow, "They [Greenwald and Poitras] actually recorded me on camera saying this before I revealed my identity." Snowden asserted this "demonization" was to divert attention from the government's own crimes. By providing Snowden with this platform to rail against the putative machinations of the United States, Putin laid claim to the moral high ground.

Snowden's motive in requesting documents from other foreign intelligence services, such as the GCHQ, and copying lists of NSA sources remains unexplained. It is difficult to believe that his motive was whistle-blowing, because these documents were not among those he gave to journalists in Hong Kong. Indeed, he did not provide the journalists with the lists of sources that were particularly relevant to the NSA's surveillance of Russia. His legal representative in Moscow, Kucherena, confirmed that Snowden had taken secret "material" to Russia and had access to NSA documents that he had not given to journalists. Those unrevealed documents would be prized by many an adversary service. Did he use those documents as leverage in his transformation? The role that Moscow might have played in Snowden's defection clearly requires a closer examination of the machinations that brought Snowden to Russia. That is why I visited Moscow in October 2015.

PART FOUR

MOSCOW CALLING

Deception is a state of mind—and the mind of the state.

—JAMES JESUS ANGLETON

CHAPTER 24

Off to Moscow

They talk about Russia like it's the worst place on earth. Russia's great.

—EDWARD SNOWDEN, Moscow, 2015

BEFORE FLYING TO MOSCOW, I arranged to have dinner with Oliver Stone at an Italian restaurant on the Upper East Side of New York. I had greatly respected Stone's ability as a film director after watching him work on *Wall Street: Money Never Sleeps*, a film in which I had a cameo role. I had also debated Stone about the historical accuracy of his 1991 movie *JFK* at Town Hall in New York.

When we dined, he had just written, produced, and directed *Snowden*, an independently financed film depicting Snowden, as Stone put it, as "one of the great heroes of the twenty-first century." In preparing for it, Stone had seen Snowden in 2013 and 2014 and had had a six-hour meeting with Putin.

I wanted to talk to Stone not to learn about the film but to learn how he had gained access to Snowden in Moscow. I knew from the documents taken from Sony Pictures Entertainment—allegedly by North Korea—that Stone had paid *The Guardian* $700,000 for the film rights to *The Snowden Files*, a book written by Luke Harding.

These documents also revealed that Stone had paid Anatoly Kucherena, Snowden's legal representative in Moscow, $1 million, supposedly for the rights to his novel, *Time of the Octopus*. Even by Hollywood standards, $1 million was an extraordinary sum to pay for a yet-to-be-published work of Russian fiction, and it was especially striking because Stone was making a fact-based movie using the actual names of the characters, and he had already bought the rights to *The Snowden Files*.

"Is your script based on Kucherena's *Time of the Octopus*?" I asked.

"No," Stone replied. "I haven't used it."

He said that the payment was for what he termed "total access." He explained that Barbara Broccoli and Michael G. Wilson, the producers of the James Bond franchise, had optioned Greenwald's book *No Place to Hide* to make into a movie about Snowden for Sony. Stone said that the million-dollar deal with Kucherena effectively guaranteed that any competing project would not have access to Snowden. Sony consequently put the competing film on hold.

Lawyers often negotiate deals on behalf of a client, but blocking a competing film requires considerably more influence with the powers that be in Russia. Kucherena, though, was no ordinary lawyer. Among other influential positions, I noted earlier, he was on the public board of the Russian federal security bureau, which had assumed the domestic operations of the defunct KGB in April 1995. In light of such connections, Stone said Kucherena might be acting as an intermediary for other parties who controlled access to Snowden in Russia. In any case, his concern was making a movie, and Kucherena delivered the exclusive access to Snowden.

Aside from being a skilled director, Stone is a shrewd producer who knows how to close a deal. He assessed, correctly as it turned out, that his project coupled with the payment to Kucherena would effectively block Sony's competing project. Where the money went was far less clear.

Toward the end of our dinner, Stone told me that he did not know I was writing a book about Snowden until a few weeks earlier. He learned of my book from Snowden himself. He said Snowden had expressed concern to him about the direction of the book I was writing. "What is it about?" Stone asked me.

I was taken aback. I had no idea that Snowden was aware of my book. (I had not tried to contact him.) I told Stone that I considered Snowden an extraordinary man who had changed history and was intentionally vague in my description of my book's contents. Stone seemed to be reassured, so I asked him about the possibility of my seeing Snowden in Moscow. He said that I "might want to speak to Anatoly [Kucherena]." Kucherena, it seemed to me, was clearly Snowden's gatekeeper.

In Snowden's two years in Moscow, he, or his handlers, had granted only a handful of face-to-face press interviews. Most of these were with the journalists who had published his story, but one was with James Bamford for his 2014 *Wired* piece. According to Bamford, it took nearly nine months to arrange the meeting. "I have been trying to set up an interview with him [Snowden]—traveling to Berlin, Rio de Janeiro twice, and New York multiple times to talk with the handful of his confidants who can arrange a meeting," Bamford recounted in *Wired*. After my dinner with Stone, I hoped to find a quicker route.

I was advised by a Moscow-based journalist that I needed a "fixer," the curious term that journalists commonly use to describe a local intermediary who arranges appointments in foreign countries. I retained Zamir Gotta, a highly respected TV producer in Moscow, who I was told had helped "fix" the Bamford interview with Snowden.

"There is only one door to Snowden," Zamir wrote to me. "His name is Kucherena." Zamir said Kucherena rarely saw journalists, but he had a contact in his office. He further told me Kucherena required any journalist seeking an interview with Snowden to submit his questions to the lawyer two weeks in advance and, if approved, to sign a document stating he would not deviate from the questions. Next, my questions had to be translated from English to Russian (even though Snowden does not speak Russian) and then vetted by Kucherena's staff. Zamir also suggested I stay at the Hotel National in Red Square because Snowden had gone there for previous meetings with Bamford. So I sent Kucherena, via Zamir, ten questions that I wanted to ask Snowden.

I next obtained a multi-entry Russian visa from the Russian consulate in New York and booked myself a room in the Hotel National.

My night flight from New York to Moscow took just less than eight hours and landed at Terminal D of Sheremetyevo International Airport at 7:40 a.m. on October 29, 2015. I did not immediately proceed through passport control, in part because I wanted to explore the transit zone in which Snowden was supposedly trapped for six weeks.

Sheremetyevo Two, where all international flights land, was built in the waning days of the Cold War for international passengers arriving for the Moscow 1980 Summer Olympics. It was modernized in 2010, including opening a walkway that connects Terminals D, E, and F for transit passengers.

With the exception of the staged press conference on July 12, Snowden had vanished from public view for nearly six weeks in the summer of 2013. His explanation to journalists, as will be recalled, was two part. First, he said he had planned to board the next fight to Cuba and from there proceed to Ecuador. He said that he was unable to board this flight because his passport had been invalidated by the U.S. government while he was flying to Russia. Second, after discovering his passport had been revoked, he stayed in a capsule hotel in the transit zone for the next thirty-nine days. To better understand the plausibility of his version of those events, I proceeded through the transit passage to Terminal F, where Snowden's plane from Hong Kong had landed at 5:15 p.m. Moscow time on June 23, 2013.

Snowden did not go through passport control upon arrival. Before any of the other passengers were allowed to disembark from the plane, Russian plainclothes officers from the special services boarded the plane and asked both Snowden and Sarah Harrison, his WikiLeaks-supplied "ninja," to accompany them to a waiting car that whisked them away. According to the account in *Izvestia*, "A special operation was conducted for his reception and evacuation." It further said, "Snowden's flight to Moscow was coordinated with the Russian authorities and intelligence services."

If not for the "special operation," he could have easily gone by foot to Terminal E. It is a nine-minute walk through the transit passageway. Snowden, though, had one good reason for not going to Ecuador, even if Russia had permitted it. He believed that he would be vulnerable to rendition by the U.S. government in Ecuador. "If they [the U.S. government] really wanted to capture me, they would've allowed me to travel to Latin America, because the CIA can operate with impunity down there," he explained in the previously cited interview with Katrina vanden Heuvel, the editor of *The Nation*, in 2014. He had already discussed the likelihood of his being captured in Ecuador with Assange before his departure for Moscow. He later told Alan Rusbridger, the editor of *The Guardian*, that he considered himself at risk in Latin America. So why would Snowden, who told Greenwald that his "first priority" was his own "physical safety," leave the comparative safety of Russia to put himself in jeopardy in Ecuador?

He had not obtained a visa to Ecuador at its consulate in Hong Kong, as Kucherena confirmed. The Ecuador destination was, as we have seen, a cover story put out by Assange and his associates, and it worked with the press.

Over a hundred reporters and photographers scrambled aboard Aeroflot Flight SU150 to Cuba the next morning in response to this anonymous tip on a website, but Snowden was not aboard that flight and was not seen in Terminal E. By the time the plane landed in Cuba, Aeroflot denied that anyone named Snowden had ever been booked on any of its flights to Cuba, a denial it continued to repeat to every reporter who queried the airline for the next six weeks.

The first news that Snowden was still in Russia came on July 1, 2013. A statement posted on the WikiLeaks website—and signed "Edward Snowden"—after thanking "friends new and old" for his "continued liberty," accused President Obama of pressuring "leaders of nations from which I have requested protection to deny my asylum petitions." It added, "This kind of deception from a world leader is not justice, and neither is the extralegal penalty of exile. These are the old, bad tools of political aggression." In fact, Snowden had not suffered a "penalty of exile," because his passport was still valid for returning to the United States, but that was not an option for him as the statement made clear.

Because the Aeroflot flight to Cuba was the only means of getting directly from Moscow to Latin America, Russian reporters, encouraged by WikiLeaks posts, continued taking the daily eleven-hour flight to Cuba until August 1. The charade only ended when Kucherena said in a press conference at the airport that Snowden would be taking up residency at an undisclosed location in Moscow and walked out of the airport with Snowden.

Sarah Harrison, Snowden's companion on the plane to Moscow, told *Vogue* that she and Snowden for thirty-nine days had shared a windowless room in the transit zone of the airport where they watched TV, washed their clothes in a sink basin, and ate meals from the nearby Burger King. The only hotel with windowless rooms in the transit zone in 2013 was the Vozdushny V-Express Capsule Hotel, located next to a newly opened Burger King.

The polite V-Express desk clerk, who spoke English, showed me the standard windowless double room. It was approximately twenty-four square feet in area. Most of the floor space was taken up by twin beds. Across from the bed, behind a plastic curtain, was a stall with a shower, a toilet, and a sink. It would be very cramped quarters for two people to share for such an extended period. It cost 850 rubles an hour (about $18 in 2013). For thirty-nine days, that hourly charge would have added up to $16,600. Snowden claimed to the BBC that he brought a large cache of cash to Russia, which he could have used to pay the hotel. But such a long stay was not allowed, according to the desk clerk. The maximum stay allowed by the hotel was twenty-four hours. So either the rule was waived for Snowden, or Harrison did not tell the full truth.

I learned from a former KGB officer that there are VIP quarters beyond the confines of the airport, including suites at the four-hundred-room Novotel hotel, which is located about seven miles away, that are used for debriefing and other purposes by the security services. According to him, the security services are not restricted from entering and leaving the transit zone.

The possibility that Snowden was staying elsewhere would help explain the futile search for him by a large number of reporters over those thirty-nine days. When they learned from tweets that Snowden was not aboard the plane to Havana on June 24, for weeks they aggressively questioned all the restaurant employees, security guards, and airport personnel they could find. They also bought business-class tickets on flights just to gain access to VIP lounges in the transit zones. Despite this intensive search, none of them found a single person who had seen Snowden, although his image was constantly shown on airport TV screens. Egor Piskunov, a reporter for RT television, even rented a room in the V-Express Capsule Hotel and "tipped" hotel employees, trying, without success, to get information. Piskunov told me, "It was a total vanishing act."

CHAPTER 25

Through the Looking Glass

There's definitely a deep state. Trust me, I've been there.

—EDWARD SNOWDEN, Moscow, 2014

WHILE WAITING to hear back from Kucherena's office, I arranged to meet with Victor Cherkashin, who had been one of the most successful KGB spy handlers in the Cold War. Cherkashin, born in 1932, had served in the KGB's espionage branch from 1952 until 1991 and now operated a private security firm in Moscow. I was particularly interested in his recruitment of three top American intelligence officers: Aldrich Ames of the CIA, Robert Hanssen of the FBI, and Ronald Pelton of the NSA. I hoped that seeing these intelligence coups through the eyes, and mind-set, of their KGB handler might provide some historical context for the Snowden defection. So I invited Cherkashin to lunch at Gusto, a quiet Italian restaurant, located near the Chekhov Theater in Moscow.

Cherkashin, a tall thin man with silver hair, showed up promptly at 1:00 p.m., wearing an elegant gray suit and dark tie. He walked with a spry step. Because he had served in counterintelligence in the Soviet embassy in Washington, D.C., for nearly a decade, he spoke flawless English.

I began by asking him about one of the more celebrated cases he had handled for the KGB, that of Ames, who had acted as a Russian mole in the CIA between April 1985 and January 1994. In those nine years, he rose, or was maneuvered by the KGB, into a top position in the CIA's highly sensitive Counterintelligence Center Analysis Group, which allowed him to deliver hundreds of top secrets to the KGB. In return, according to Cherkashin, Ames received between $20,000 and $50,000 in cash for each delivery, which amounted to $4.6 million over the nine years.

I asked Cherkashin about the weakness the KGB looked for in an American intelligence worker that might lead him to copy and steal top secret documents. How did he spot a potential Ames? Was it a financial problem? Was it a sexual vulnerability? Was it an ideological leaning?

"Nothing so dramatic," he answered. When assessing Ames's biographical data, Cherkashin said he was looking for a well-placed intelligence officer who was both dissatisfied with and antagonistic to the service for which he worked.

"The classic disgruntled employee," I interjected.

"Any intelligence officer who strongly feels that his superiors are not listening to him, and that they are doing stupid things, is a candidate," he continued. He said he had found that the flaw in a prospect that could be most dependably exploited was not his greed, lust, or deviant behavior but his resentment over the way he was being treated.

"Is that how you spotted Ames?"

"Actually, he approached us, not vice versa." It was his job in the CIA to approach opposition KGB officers. "But, yes, we saw the potential," he said.

Because Ames had been paid $50,000 in cash by Cherkashin for his first delivery, I asked whether he fit into the category of a disgruntled employee.

"Wasn't he just a mercenary?" I asked.

"I knew from our intelligence reports that he needed money for debts stemming from his divorce," he answered. "But he was also angry at the stupidity and paranoia of those running the CIA. Ames told me at our first secret meeting that they were misleading

Congress by exaggerating the Soviet threat." Cherkashin evaluated Ames as a man who felt not only slighted by his superiors but "helpless to do anything about it" within the bureaucracy of the CIA. "The money we gave, even if he could spend only a small portion of it, gave him a sense of worth." He explained that the KGB had an entire team of psychologists in Moscow that worked on further exploiting Ames's resentment against his superiors.

The search for an adversary intelligence officer who resents his service was not limited to KGB recruiters. It was also the "classic attitude" that the CIA sought to exploit in its adversaries, according to a former deputy director. "You find someone working for the other side and tell him that he is not receiving the proper recognition, pay, and honors due him," Morell said, pointing out that the same "psychological dynamic" could be used to motivate someone to "act alone" in gathering espionage material.

I next turned to an even more important KGB coup with Cherkashin: the Robert Hanssen case. From the KGB's perspective, Hanssen was an extraordinary espionage source. He was a walk-in who never entered the Soviet embassy or met with KGB case officers, but in working as a KGB mole between 1979 and 2001, he had delivered even more documents to the Russian intelligence services than Ames. Cherkashin learned of this potential spy when he received an anonymous letter from him identifying an FBI source in the Soviet embassy. When that tip proved to be accurate, Cherkashin got the resources he needed from the KGB to develop this source. From the start of his work for the KGB, Hanssen laid down his own rules. The KGB would deliver cash from which all the fingerprints were removed to locations, or "dead drops," he specified. He would deliver documents exposing FBI, CIA, and NSA sources and methods in another dead drop. The KGB would precisely follow his instructions.

Cherkashin told me that Hanssen's "astounding self-recruitment" was executed in such a way that the KGB never actually controlled him. "He was our most important mole and we didn't ever know his identity, where he worked, or how he had access to FBI, CIA, and NSA files." Even so, the KGB (and later the SVR) paid him $600,000 in cash. In return, the anonymous spy delivered twenty-seven computer disks containing hundreds of secret documents revealing the sources and methods of American intelligence. According to Cherkashin, it was the largest haul of top secret documents ever obtained by the KGB (although it was only a small fraction of the number of top secret NSA, Department of Defense, and CIA documents taken by Snowden in 2013). Cherkashin told me the price paid by Moscow was a great bargain because it helped compromise "the NSA's most advanced electronic interception technology," including a tunnel under the Soviet embassy.

Yet it was only after newspapers reported that Hanssen had been arrested by the FBI in February 2001 that Cherkashin learned the name and position of the spy he had recruited. Cherkashin told me that what mattered to the KGB was not "control" of an agent but the value of the secrets he or she delivered. "Control is not necessary in espionage as long as we manage to obtain the documents." So in the eyes of the KGB, anyone who elected to provide it with U.S. secrets was a spy.

"All we knew was that he delivered valuable documents to us and asked for cash in return," he said. "We didn't control him; he controlled us."

An uncontrolled mole who provided secrets to the KGB and the SVR for twenty-two years was very different from fictional moles in the spy movies. I asked whether it would have been better if the KGB had him under its control.

"Possibly," Cherkashin answered. "But as it turned out, Hanssen was by far our most valuable penetration in the Cold War."

"Could Hanssen really be called a mole?" I asked.

"A 'mole' is a term used in spy fiction," he said. "We prefer the more general term 'espionage source.' "

"So anyone who delivers state secrets to the KGB, for whatever reason, is an espionage source?" I asked.

"Certainly, if the information is valuable to us," Cherkashin answered.

"If some unknown person simply delivered a trove of communications secrets to the doorstep of Russia, would it be accepted?" I asked with Snowden in mind.

"I can't say what the SVR would do today. I am long retired," he said, with a nostalgic shake of his head. "But in my day, we needed some reason to believe the gift was genuine."

"Would you need to vet the person delivering it?"

"With Hanssen we did not have that opportunity," he said. "If we believed the documents were genuine, we would of course grab them."

The final recruitment I asked Cherkashin about was that of Ronald Pelton, the civilian employee of the NSA who had retired in 1979. Pelton had left the NSA without taking any classified documents with him. After retiring, he had financial difficulties, and he sought to get money from the KGB. On January 14, 1980, he walked into the Soviet embassy in Washington, D.C., and asked to see an intelligence officer. After he was ushered into a secure debriefing room, he said that he had information that Russia would find interesting, but he wanted money in return. What interested me about the Pelton case was that Cherkashin proceeded to recruit Pelton, even though he was no longer working at the NSA and no longer had access to the NSA. In addition, because the FBI had twenty-four-hour surveillance on the embassy, Pelton had almost certainly been photographed entering it and had also possibly been recorded asking for an intelligence officer by electronic bugs that the KGB suspected the NSA had planted there. What did the KGB do in a situation in which a former civilian employee at the NSA possessed no documents?

Despite the risks involved, Cherkashin decided Pelton had to be debriefed by communications intelligence specialists. So he had him disguised as a utility worker and smuggled out in a van to the residential compound of the ambassador in Georgetown. A few days later, he was dropped off at a shopping mall.

"Why did you go to such effort if Pelton had neither documents nor access to the NSA?" I asked.

"It was the information in his head that we wanted." Cherkashin said that because the KGB rarely got access to any NSA officer, it was worth the risk. So Pelton was given $5,000 in cash and a plane ticket to Vienna, where he was domiciled at the residence of the Soviet ambassador to Austria. A KGB electronic communications expert, Anatoly Slavnov, was then sent to Vienna to supervise the

Pelton debriefings. The debriefing sessions, which went on for fifteen days, were from 8:00 a.m. to 6:00 p.m. In them, Pelton managed to recall Project A, a joint NSA-CIA-navy operation in which submarines surreptitiously tapped into Soviet undersea cables in the Sea of Okhotsk, which connected to the Soviet Pacific Fleet's mainland headquarters at Vladivostok. Pelton received another $30,000 from the KGB.

"Did the information in his head prove valuable?" I asked.

"As long as the NSA didn't know the tap was compromised by Pelton, we could use the cable to send the NSA the information we wanted it to intercept." He said that while actual NSA documents would have proved more useful than someone's memories, "Our job is to take advantage of whatever we can get."

Two years later, Pelton was again flown to Vienna for another debriefing to see if he could recall any further details. According to Cherkashin, the KGB's job was to leave no stone unturned when it came to the NSA's sources. In 1985, the KGB's task ended when Pelton was arrested by the FBI. Like Ames and Hanssen, Pelton was sentenced to life imprisonment.

Looking at his watch, Cherkashin politely excused himself.

I subsequently spoke to Colonel Oleg Nechiporenko, who had been a foreign intelligence officer in the KGB between 1958 and 1985 and continued his intelligence work until recently as chief counterterrorism expert of the Russian-led Collective Security Treaty Organization. Over a leisurely coffee in the bar of the Hotel National, he told me that many "walk-ins" who contacted Soviet officials in his time were emotionally disturbed, but all of them had to be assessed for possible intelligence value. "Our job was to find espionage sources," he said with a twinkle in his eye. "The Internet has changed the espionage business since secret documents can be massively downloaded by an unhappy employee," he said, "but they still need to be assessed by a professional."

Through the eyes of the KGB, a penetration of American intelligence was clearly opportunistic. If these practices continued, they put Snowden's situation in a new light for me. If Russian intelligence considered it worthwhile to send a former civilian worker at the NSA, such as Ronald Pelton, two thousand miles from Washington, D.C., to Austria so that its specialists could debrief him on the secrets he held in his head, it would have an even greater interest in exfiltrating Snowden from Hong Kong to get, aside from his documents, whatever secrets he held in his head. If Russian intelligence were willing to opportunistically accept the delivery of U.S. secrets from an unknown espionage source that it neither recruited nor controlled, such as Hanssen, it would obviously have little hesitancy in acquiring the secrets that Snowden had stolen of his own volition, even if Snowden had acted for idealistic reasons.

If Russian intelligence focused its search pattern on disgruntled American intelligence workers, such as Ames, it is plausible that it spotted Snowden through his Internet rants against U.S. surveillance. Even if it had missed Snowden in Hawaii, a disgruntled former civilian employee at the NSA would have received its full attention after he contacted Russian officials in Hong Kong. While the tactics of the SVR might have changed since Cherkashin retired, its objectives remained the same. And the NSA remained its principal target. Nor is there any reason to doubt that it still measures success in its ability to obtain, by whatever means, the secret sources and methods of its adversaries. Snowden was in a position, with both the documents he had taken and the knowledge he had in his head, to deliver the KGB such a coup.

CHAPTER 26

The Handler

As for [Snowden's] communication with the outside world, yes, I am his main contact.

—ANATOLY KUCHERENA, Moscow, 2013

O N NOVEMBER 1, I still had not been able to make contact with Anatoly Kucherena, and my flight back to New York was in five days. My fixer, Zamir, had been trying to arrange an appointment for three weeks, but he had only received one callback from Kucherena's assistant, Valentina Kvirvova. She wanted to know how I knew Oliver Stone. Zamir told her of my part in Stone's movie. That was the last he had heard from her. Meanwhile, a Moscow-based journalist told me that she had waited eighteen months to hear back from Kucherena before giving up. I also learned from a Russian researcher that Kucherena had not given a single interview since his television interview with Sophie Shevardnadze on September 23, 2013. And no Russian journalist, or any Moscow-based foreign journalist, had ever obtained an interview with Snowden. At this point, Zamir was becoming increasingly doubtful about my getting access to either Kucherena or Snowden.

I turned to another contact in Moscow. When I had been investigating the 2006 polonium poisoning of the former KGB officer

Alexander Litvinenko, I had interviewed Andrei Lugovoy. A former KGB officer assigned to protecting the Kremlin's top members in the 1990s, Lugovoy later opened his own security company. In 2005, he became a business associate of Litvinenko's in gathering information and made regular trips to London to meet with him. Because he had tea with Litvinenko at the Pine Bar of the Millennium Hotel in London on November 1, 2006, the day Litvinenko was poisoned, he became the main suspect in the British investigation. He could not be extradited, however. After reconstructing the chronology of the crime, I established that Litvinenko had been contaminated with polonium at a Japanese restaurant some four hours before his tea with Lugovoy. I therefore wrote that the crime scene might not have been at the Pine Bar, a finding that he said he greatly appreciated.

Lugovoy was elected to the Duma in 2007 and also hosted a twenty-four-part television series on espionage for which Putin personally decorated him. He was also now reputed to be in the inner circle of power in Moscow. So I called him.

We arranged to meet in the bar of the Hotel National. A short but well-built man with a bullet-style haircut, Lugovoy showed up promptly at 1:00 p.m. After discussing some of the subsequent developments in the still-lingering polonium investigation, I asked him if he knew Kucherena.

"I don't know him, but I know someone who does," he answered. "Why are you interested in seeing Kucherena?"

I told him that I wanted to speak to him about Snowden but I had been unable to arrange a meeting.

"That's no problem," he said, raising his cell phone (which never left his hand). He hit a number on the speed dial and spoke rapidly in Russian (which I do not understand). He cupped his hand over the phone and asked how long I would be in Moscow. After I told him that I was leaving that Friday, he spoke again in Russian to the person on the other end. "You will have an appointment on Thursday," he said.

Later that afternoon, Valentina, Kucherena's assistant, called to say that Kucherena would be happy to see me at his office at 6:00 p.m. on Thursday. I didn't ask Lugovoy whom he had called. Whomever Lugovoy called obviously had the power to arrange the meeting.

When I arrived at Kucherena's office, I was with my translator Zamir. (Kucherena did not speak English.) I arrived ten minutes early, and a receptionist showed me into a well-lit square room with an elegant table in the center. There was a sumptuous basket of exotic fruits on the table and large portraits of racehorses on the walls. Another door opened, and a tall, graceful woman came into the room and introduced herself as Valentina. She was wearing a well-fitting black dress, a striking jade necklace, and high heels. When she asked whether we would like anything to drink, it seemed more like the prelude to an elegant dinner party than an interview about Snowden.

Valentina spoke very good English. She apologized for the delay in responding to my requests, explaining that she received "thousands of requests" for interviews and did not have time to answer them. When I asked how many were answered, she shrugged and said, "Not many."

At that moment, Kucherena entered with a jaunty step, a cherubic face, and untamed white hair. He was wearing gray slacks, a partially buttoned cashmere polo sweater, and a fully engaging smile.

As I had learned from his entry in *Wikipedia*, he was born in a small village in the Soviet Socialist Republic of Moldavia in 1960 and had obtained his law degree from the All-Union Correspondence Law Institute in 1991. He opened his own law firm in Moscow in 1995. Kucherena's well-known friendship with Putin had evidently not hurt his law practice. His clients had included such well-connected defendants as Viktor Yanukovych, the president of Ukraine overthrown in 2014; Grigory Leps, a Russian singer blacklisted by the United States for allegedly acting as a money courier for a Eurasian criminal organization; Valentine Kovalev, a former Russian minister of justice charged with corruption; and Suleyman Kerimov, a civil servant from Dagestan who had amassed an estimated fortune of $7.1 billion. Kerimov had recently been charged for manipulating the price of potash in Belarus. Most of these clients were reputed to be part of Putin's inner circle.

To break the ice, I asked Kucherena about Oliver Stone. I knew he had a small role in Stone's forthcoming movie, in which he plays Snowden's lawyer in Moscow.

"I was impressed by how few takes he needed to shoot my scene," he answered.

"How did you come to be Snowden's lawyer?" I asked.

"Snowden picked me from a roster of fifteen lawyers with which he had been provided."

Because Snowden did not speak or read Russian, I asked Kucherena about how Snowden had come to pick him from the roster. Could he have known about his connections?

"I suppose it was because of my record in defending human rights," Kucherena replied with a broad smile.

Kucherena went to Sheremetyevo International Airport to meet his new client on the morning of Friday, July 12, 2013. At that point, he said that Snowden had been held virtually incommunicado for twenty days. Other than Russian officials, the only person he had been allowed to see during this period was Assange's aide, Sarah Harrison.

"Where in the airport did you meet him?" I asked. "Was it in a VIP lounge?"

"It was in the transit zone," he replied coyly. "That is all I can say."

They spoke through a translator. By this time, Harrison had sent twenty-one countries petitions for asylum that were signed by Snowden. Whatever their purpose, Kucherena did not consider them helpful.

"I told him that if he wanted to get sanctuary in Russia, he would have to immediately withdraw all the petitions in which he had asked other countries for asylum." Kucherena said that otherwise he could not represent him. Snowden agreed to that condition.

Shortly before 5:00 p.m., Kucherena accompanied Snowden, who was wearing an open-neck blue shirt and a badly creased jacket, to area G9 in the transit zone, where they emerged from a door marked "Authorized Personnel Only." A number of officials in dark suits, who Kucherena assumed were from the "special services" to protect Snowden, were already in the room. Snowden and Harrison seated themselves at a table. A Russian translator was also seated at the table. At this point, thirteen invitees were ushered into the room to witness Snowden's first public appearance in Russia. It was rare if not unprecedented for an American intelligence worker to seek asylum in Russia.

These invitees included some of Putin's close associates, pro-government activists, and representatives of both Amnesty International and Human Rights Watch. "It was totally bizarre," said Tanya Lokshina, the deputy director of Human Rights Watch, who attended. "Although it was billed as a press conference," she recalled, "there was no press or photographers allowed in the room." Nor was anyone allowed to photograph or record the event.

Snowden read from a prepared statement accusing the U.S. government of violating the Universal Declaration of Human Rights, saying he was a victim of political persecution, and concluding, "I will be submitting my request to Russia today [for asylum], and hope it will be accepted favorably." After answering a few questions posed by the audience, he left the room with Kucherena and Harrison by the same door they had entered.

In discussing this meeting, Kucherena told me that Snowden had not intended to seek asylum in Russia when he arrived on June 23. Because he also said he had not met Snowden prior to the day of the conference, I asked how he knew Snowden's intentions.

"When I accepted the case, I received Snowden's dossier," he answered. "I was able to see all his interviews."

Presumably, Snowden's dossier included his interviews with the FSB, the SVR, and other Russian security services. If so, it would explain how Kucherena could be so certain that Snowden had brought "material" with him to Russia that he had not provided to journalists in Hong Kong. Before meeting with Kucherena, I had met with Sophie Shevardnadze, who told me that Kucherena had personally approved the translation of their interview into English. So I asked Kucherena about the interview. It will be recalled that in response to a question about whether Snowden had secret material with him in Russia, Kucherena had said "certainly." Was this exchange accurate?

"It was accurate," he answered.

Snowden, as we know, had said in Hong Kong that he had only given journalists some of the state secrets he had stolen and that he deemed others too sensitive for journalists. So I wanted to find out from Kucherena which documents Snowden had taken to Russia. I went about it in a roundabout way. When Shevardnadze asked him about the secret material Snowden might reveal in Russia, Kucherena pointedly called her attention to Snowden's CIA service, suggesting that he might possess CIA files. I also knew that in Kucherena's roman à clef, he had Joshua Frost, the thinly veiled Snowden-based character, steal a vast number of CIA documents that could do great damage to U.S. intelligence. By retaining them, Frost made himself a prime target of the CIA.

So I asked, "Is Joshua Frost fact or fiction?"

"I can't tell you that," he said. "If I said he was Snowden, it would violate the attorney-client privilege."

"I understand," I said. "But did Snowden do what Frost did in your book?"

"That is for you to decide," he answered with a sly smile. "It's my first novel."

When I asked if he could arrange for me to see Snowden, he said that first I would have to submit my questions to Ben Wizner, Snowden's American lawyer at the ACLU. He made it clear to me that the exposure of Snowden to journalists, or at least the vetting of journalists, had been outsourced to Wizner. Kucherena was handling Snowden's liaisons with the Russian authorities while Wizner was handling the Snowden narrative, including selecting the media outlets. Presumably, Wizner had handpicked Snowden's past interviewers in Moscow, including Barton Gellmna, James Bamford, Brian Williams, John Oliver, Alan Rusbridger, and Katrina vanden Heuvel.

"After that, the final decision is up to Snowden," he said. That seemed to conclude the interview, but as I got up to leave, he added, "His legal defense is fairly expensive."

Snowden had said in a BBC interview in 2015, as previously mentioned, that he had brought enough cash to Hong Kong and Russia to cover all of his expenses. So I asked Kucherena if Snowden had brought his own funds.

"He was penniless when he arrived," he replied. I found that answer plausible because the FBI reportedly had not found a large cash withdrawal from his account before his departure and it seemed to me too risky for him to carry a large sum of undeclared cash through three airports. Because large sums of cash must be declared, the detection of the money could compromise his plan to deliver his NSA documents. Snowden might have told the BBC he had brought cash to allay suspicions about who was financing his stay in Moscow.

I was intrigued by this remark. Snowden, as far as I knew, didn't need a legal defense, because he was not charged with a crime in Russia and the United States had no extradition treaty with Russia.

While Kucherena unfortunately did not arrange an interview with Snowden, he did something I considered more important. He confirmed the accuracy of his September 2013 assertion that Snowden had brought secret material to Russia, material he had not given to journalists in Hong Kong. After what I had learned from Cherkashin about the lengths that Russian intelligence would go to obtain U.S. communications intelligence secrets, I viewed Snowden's access to this material to be a crucially important part of the mystery.

That day, I immediately sent my questions to Ben Wizner, and I offered to fly back to Moscow if Snowden would grant me an interview. In March 2016, Wizner answered that Snowden had "respectfully declined."

PART FIVE

CONCLUSIONS: WALKING THE CAT BACK

In solving a problem of this sort, the grand thing is to be able to reason backward.

—SHERLOCK HOLMES, *A Study in Scarlet*

CHAPTER 27

Snowden's Choices

It is the choices we make that show who we truly are.

—J. K. ROWLING, *Harry Potter and the Sorcerer's Stone*

RUSSIAN AUTHORITIES had the opportunity to thoroughly debrief Snowden as to his motive for stealing state secrets, whereas U.S. authorities did not. It cannot be assumed that he had a single consistent motive in 2013. Snowden has shown, if nothing else, that he was adaptable to changing circumstances. He might have begun taking documents for one reason and found other reasons as he proceeded in his quest. Many of the reported circumstances of his activities, including his probes, contacts, theft, and escape, are disputed by his supporters. Many of his other activities are shrouded by the secrecy of the NSA. We do know, though, that Snowden made four extraordinary choices during the nine-month period in 2013. If, as is said, actions speak louder than words, Snowden's four choices illuminate the underlying concerns guiding his acts. In the case of a classified intelligence breach, as in the post-action analysis of a masterful chess game, the sequence of moves a player makes provides an important clue to his strategy. Let us review what we have already learned about these decisions.

The First Decision

The initial move that Snowden made in preparation for the Level 3 breach was switching jobs on March 15. Snowden chose to leave his job as a system administrator at Dell to take one at Booz Allen as an analyst in training. His motive could not have been money, because it was a lower-paying position. At the time he made this choice, he had already set up an encrypted channel with Laura Poitras for the purpose of sending her secret material. But he did not have to change jobs to send her important secrets. So what was his purpose in making this fateful choice?

The job change was not necessary to expose NSA domestic activities. If he had only wanted to be a whistle-blower, there were ample documents about the NSA's activities already available to him on the NSANet. He also had access at Dell to the administrative file that contained the FISA court orders issued every three months to Verizon. In addition, as the NSA's damage assessment established, before switching jobs, Snowden had already taken most of the documents pertaining to the NSA's domestic operations that he could have supplied to Poitras and Greenwald for whistle-blowing purposes. Indeed, while still at Dell, he had told Poitras he had a copy of Presidential Policy Directive 20, a document in which President Obama authorized the NSA to tap into fiber cables crossing the United States. Snowden described it to her as "a kind of martial law for cyber operations, created by the White House." True, he took a more recently issued FISA order and PRISM presentation in April after switching jobs, but he could just as easily have taken the January 2013 version of the FISA order from the administrative file of Dell. It would have had the same explosive effect in the media.

Nor did he switch jobs to lessen the risk of getting caught. Actually, the change put him in far greater jeopardy. At Dell, he was relatively safe from apprehension because he could take documents, such as the Presidential Policy Directive 20, from access points at the NSA shared by many of his peers, making it difficult to trace the theft. Indeed, if he just wanted to expose the NSA's domestic operations, he could have done the entire operation at Dell. He could even have sent Poitras documents anonymously over his own Tor software and server. And he could have remained in his self-described "paradise" in Hawaii with his girlfriend.

When he chose to move to Booz Allen, the risk of exposure greatly increased because of its auditing system. Any documents he took without authorization could be traced back to him (though not in real time). As he later told Greenwald and Poitras, he knew that stealing documents at the Booz Allen job meant that he would either go to prison or escape from America. He didn't want to face prison time, so the job change required an escape plan. As part of that plan, soon after he started work at the Booz Allen–managed facility, he submitted a request for a medical leave of absence.

We can safely assume that the reason he made this risky switch in employment was that he wanted something beyond the whistle-blowing documents. He wanted documents that were not available at the Dell job. One such document he took was the top secret *Congressional Budget Justification* book for fiscal year 2013. This "black budget," as it is called in Congress, contained the entire intelligence community's priorities for, among other things, monitoring the activities of potential adversaries and terrorist organizations. It specified the money requested not only by the NSA but by the CIA, the DIA, the National Reconnaissance Office, and other intelligence services. Snowden could not have objected to the budget's being somehow secret or illegitimate, because it was duly approved by both houses of Congress and the president. If it was not for purposes of whistle-blowing, presumably he had another purpose for taking such a document. It certainly held value to other actors. "For our enemies, having it [the black budget] is like having the playbook of the opposing NFL team," said the former CIA deputy director Morell in 2015. "I guarantee you that the SVR, the Russian foreign intelligence service, would have paid millions of dollars for such a document." If unlike Ames, Hanssen, and Pelton, Snowden was not after acquiring money, he must have seen another value in taking it.

The documents he stole at Booz Allen certainly increased his value to adversary nations, because they included lists revealing the NSA's sources in Russia, China, and other foreign countries.

Snowden wanted more than just NSA secrets. He used his new position and widened access at Booz Allen to go after secret documents from the intelligence services of Britain, Australia, New Zealand, and Israel. He revealed this operation only after receiving sanctuary in Russia. He told an interviewer that by moving to his new Booz Allen job as an infrastructure analyst, he gained the ability to pry secrets out of the allies of the NSA. "I had a special level of clearance, called 'Priv Ac,' " he said. This "priv ac" status did not allow him to bypass the password protection at sealed-off compartments at the NSA, but it did allow him to request files from foreign services cooperating with U.S. intelligence.

By way of example, he described one file from the British GCHQ cipher service that he copied, stole, and provided to other parties. It exposed a legally authorized British operation to collect electronic data on terrorist matters in Pakistan by tapping into Cisco routers used by telecom companies in Asia. This GCHQ operation, as Snowden knew, violated neither British nor American law. He told a BBC interviewer in regard to that file, "What's scariest is not what the government is doing that's unlawful, but what they're doing that is completely lawful." So his criteria for taking such documents were not their illegality. In his five weeks at this Booz Allen job, he also used this same newly acquired "priv ac" at the NSA to steal files from the Israeli, Canadian, and Australian intelligence services.

Jumping from one outside contracting firm to another for the purpose of penetrating other Western intelligence services is not the conventional mission of a whistle-blower. In the parlance of CIA counterintelligence, the actions of an employee of an intelligence service who changes his jobs solely to steal the more valuable secrets of this service is called an "expanding penetration." It is not possible to believe that Snowden did not know the immense damage that the highly sensitive documents he was taking from the NSA and its allies could cause.

His choice to switch jobs did not come out of the blue. It was not based on serendipitously discovering the documents after he began working at Booz Allen. As he told Lana Lam, he knew in advance that by switching to the job at Booz Allen, he would gain the opportunity to take the lists of NSA sources. He knew that the NSA's secretive National Threat Operations Center's chief business was, as its name suggests, countering direct threats from China, Russia, and other adversary states and that to deal with these threats, the NSA had used sophisticated methods to hack into the computers of adversaries. The NSA was even able to remotely gain entry to adversary computers that were not hooked into a network. "It's no secret that we hack China very aggressively," Snowden later said from Moscow. He had a planned target: getting the lists of the enemy computers that the NSA had hacked into.

He also knew he was undertaking a dangerous enterprise. He even mentioned the possibility that he would be "in an orange jumpsuit, super-max prison in isolation or Guantánamo," perhaps even assassinated.

He knowingly chose this course presumably because he believed the value of the secrets he would obtain by switching jobs outweighed the risk of imprisonment. Or worse. Part of his calculus might have been the belief that the NSA lists, GCHQ documents, and other material in his possession could give him great leverage, if he chose to exert it, in his future dealings with intelligence services (including the NSA). His choice to widen his access was made, if not to get rich, to empower himself.

The Second Decision

The second choice of consequence that Snowden made was to make Hong Kong his first stop. He had many other options. He could have remained in America, as almost all previous whistle-blowers had chosen to do. If he did that, he would have to make his case in court (and, in that case, the Level 3 documents he took might have been retrieved before they fell into unauthorized hands). He could have also chosen to make an escape to a country that did not have an active extradition treaty with the United States. He could have, for example, taken a direct flight to Brazil, which has no extradition treaty with the United States. Brazil also had the advantage of being the home country of Glenn Greenwald, whose cooperation he sought. Snowden could have gone to many other countries without extradition treaties with the United States. Yet, instead, he flew to Hong Kong, which had an extradition agreement that had been enforced throughout the past decade with Hong Kong courts ordering the arrest of almost every fugitive charged by U.S. authorities. He could expect that when the United States filed a criminal complaint, Hong Kong authorities would seize him and the alleged stolen property of the U.S. government in his possession. Even if he were released on bail and successfully defeated extradition in a Hong Kong court, the Hong Kong authorities would almost certainly retain all the NSA and GCHQ files he had gone to such lengths to steal.

His reason, as he told Greenwald, was that China could provide him with physical protection from any countermeasures by U.S. intelligence agencies such as "American agents . . . breaking down the door" of the hotel room and seizing him. China also had sway over Hong Kong's security activities.

Hong Kong was therefore merely a protected stopover en route to his next destination. If he had gone directly to Moscow and provided the same journalists with the same documents at a press conference in Moscow, his status as a whistle-blower might have been viewed with less sympathy in the media. Even *The Guardian*, for example, might have been reluctant to publish a Moscow-based story revealing British and American communications intelligence secrets.

The Third Decision

The third choice Snowden made, and the choice that most effectively defined him to the public, was to reveal himself as the man behind the leak in a video in Hong Kong. He not only identified himself as the person who stole the government documents published by *The Guardian* and *The Washington Post* but also incriminated himself further on camera by allowing Poitras to film him actually disclosing the NSA's secret operations to Greenwald. By disclosing classified data to Greenwald, an unauthorized person, he intentionally burned his bridges.

What makes this choice intriguing is that there was no evident need for him to expose himself in this way. If he merely wanted to be a whistle-blower, he could have, as Bradley Manning did, anonymously sent the documents to journalists as "Citizen Four." In fact, in late May 2013, that was exactly what he did. He anonymously sent Gellman the PRISM scoop, which the *Post* published on June 6. He also sent Greenwald and Poitras documents while he was still the anonymous Citizen Four. Neither Gellman nor Greenwald had suggested the need for a face-to-face meeting with Snowden. Even after he had revealed his true identity to Poitras and Greenwald on June 3, the *Guardian* editor Ewen MacAskill offered him the option of remaining an unnamed source for the stories. He said, as he later told *Vanity Fair*, "You should remain anonymous; the stories are just as good without you." However, anonymity was not part of Snowden's long game.

The reason he gave Greenwald in Hong Kong for going public in this way was to avoid having any suspicion fall on his co-workers at the NSA. Yet in the initial stories published by Greenwald, Poitras, and Gellman, Snowden had not allowed the reporters to identify him by either name or position. If he did not act to deflect suspicion from his co-workers for the initial investigation, why do it a week later? In the intervening week, the FBI had already launched its criminal investigation. In any case, he did not need to be the subject of a documentary film to take sole responsibility for stealing state secrets. He could have simply allowed Greenwald to identify him by name as the source in the stories.

One thing that Snowden could not accomplish by anonymously transferring the documents to journalists was a starring role in the drama. If he had appeared digitally masked in Poitras's video with an altered voice, he would not achieve fame. To do that, he needed to allow Poitras to film him committing the crime of turning over NSA documents to Greenwald. This video was also part of his advance planning. Indeed, one reason he chose Poitras was that she was a prizewinning documentary filmmaker. Snowden, while he was still working at the NSA in March 2013, made it clear how he intended to use Poitras's filmmaking skills. He told her, "My personal desire is that you paint the target directly on my back." Making himself the on-camera star of a twenty-hour-long reality show, edited first into a video and then a full-length documentary, transformed him in the public's mind into a hero.

It would be a mistake to assume that the central role he gave himself was simply an exercise in narcissism. After the video was released, he was no longer a near nonentity servicing a computer system at a backwater NSA base in Hawaii. He had emerged from the shadowy world of electronic intelligence to become one of the most famous whistle-blowers in modern history. It was a mantle that would allow him to also become a leading advocate of privacy and encryption rights, as well as the leading opponent of NSA spying. While this remarkable transformation might not have been his entire motive, it was certainly the result of the choice he made to go public.

The Fourth Decision

The final choice he made was to board a nonstop flight to Moscow on June 23. Once the U.S. criminal complaint was unsealed on June 21, he needed to leave Hong Kong; his continued presence would have been a complication for the Chinese president, Xi, scheduled soon to meet President Obama. His only route out of Hong Kong went through two adversaries of the United States: China and Russia. China, as far as is known, did not offer him sanctuary. According to one U.S. diplomat cited by *The New York Times,* China might have already obtained copies of Snowden's NSA files and did not want the problem of having Snowden defect to Beijing. In any case, if it had not already acquired the files, it could assume it would receive that intelligence data from its Russian ally in the intelligence war. Whatever its reason, China did not use its considerable power in Hong Kong to block Snowden's exit.

Nor did Snowden obtain a visa to any country in Latin America or elsewhere during his monthlong stay in Hong Kong. As in the oft-cited Sherlock Holmes clue of the dog that did not bark, Snowden's lack of any visas in his passport strongly suggests that he had not made plans to go anyplace but where he actually went: Moscow. His actions here, including his contacts with Russian officials in Hong Kong, speak louder than his words.

Just as he believed the Chinese intelligence service could protect him in Hong Kong from a physical attack by agents of the United States, he could assume that the FSB could protect him from them in Moscow. He was not entirely naive about its capabilities. During his service in the CIA, he had taken a monthlong training course at the CIA's "farm" at Fort Peary, in which counterintelligence officers taught about the capabilities of the Russian security services. He couldn't have believed that Russia would allow a defector from the NSA who claimed to have had access to the NSA's sources in Russia and China to leave Moscow before its security services obtained that information.

It is not uncommon for a defector to change sides in order to find a better life for himself in another country. Some defectors flee to escape a repressive government or to find one in which they believe they are more closely attuned to its values. Russia, however, is ordinarily not the country of choice for someone such as Snowden seeking greater civil liberties and personal freedom. So why did Snowden choose Russia for his new life?

The four choices just discussed that Snowden made, taken together, show that Snowden was determined to succeed where others before him had failed. He not only wanted to take full credit for stealing files from the NSA but also wanted to escape any American retribution for his act. His decision suggests to me a highly intelligent, carefully calculating man who was hell-bent on finding a new life for himself in a foreign country. A common thread that runs through these four choices is a willingness to do whatever was necessary to achieve this new life, including disregarding his oath to protect secrets and instead transporting them on thumb drives to a foreign country. To protect himself, he was also willing to rely on the influence of adversary intelligence services in Hong Kong and put himself in the hands of Russian authorities in Moscow. He was also willing to use some of his classified documents as a medium of exchange, if not bait, with journalists to get the public attention he sought.

These choices paid off for Snowden, the new hero of millions. In

Moscow, he could enjoy a safe life, free from the threats of a CIA rendition team dropping from the sky or extradition proceedings. He was now under the protection of Putin's Russia. The press had a field day with the domestic surveillance documents that he gave them. As far as Snowden was concerned, as he told Gellman on December 21, 2013, in Moscow, "The mission's already accomplished."

CHAPTER 28

The Espionage Source

The government's investigation failed. [It] didn't know what was
taken.

—EDWARD SNOWDEN, Moscow, 2014

IN MOSCOW, I had learned that Russian intelligence services use
the broad, umbrella term "espionage source" to describe moles,
volunteers, and anyone else who delivers another state's secrets
to it. It applies not only to documents but to the secret knowledge
that such a source is able to recall and includes both controlled and
uncontrolled bearers of secrets. It is also a job description that fit
Edward Snowden in June 2013.

Unless one is willing to believe that the Putin regime acted out of
purely altruistic motives in exfiltrating this American intelligence
worker to Moscow, the only plausible explanation for its actions
in Hong Kong was that it recognized Snowden's potential as an
espionage source. Snowden's open disillusionment with the NSA
presented the very situation that the Russian intelligence services
specialized in exploiting. He had also revealed to reporters in Hong
Kong that he had deliberately gained access to the NSA's sources
and methods and that he had taken highly classified documents to
Hong Kong. He further disclosed that before leaving the NSA, he

had gained access to the lists of computers that the NSA had penetrated in foreign countries. He even went so far as to describe to these journalists the secrets that he had taken as a "single point of failure" for the NSA. And aside from the documents he had copied, he claimed that the secret knowledge in his head, if he disclosed it, would wreak havoc on U.S. intelligence. "If I were providing information that I know, that's in my head, to some foreign government, the US intelligence community would ... see sources go dark that were previously productive," he told the editor of *The Guardian* in Moscow.

In short, he advertised possessing priceless data that the Russian intelligence services had been seeking, with little success, for the past six decades. These electronic files could provide it with the keys to unlock the NSA's entire kingdom of electronic spying. Could any world-class intelligence service ignore such a prize? To miss the opportunity to get its hands on such a potential espionage source would be nothing short of gross negligence.

In fact, this golden opportunity was not missed in Hong Kong. Even if the Russian intelligence service had not previously had him in its sights—which, as discussed earlier, appears to me to be extremely unlikely—he made contact with Russian officials in Hong Kong, and Putin personally approved allowing Snowden to come to Russia.

This decision made it possible for Snowden, without an entry visa to Russia, or, for that matter, any other country, to check in and board an Aeroflot flight to Moscow. We also know that a special operation was mounted to take Snowden off the plane once it landed in Moscow. Such an operation could not have been executed without advance planning. Nor would he be removed from the plane without a plan for his stay in Russia. Once Putin approved it, there is little reason to doubt that the plans to get Snowden to Moscow, and whatever cover stories were deemed necessary to obscure them, had been carried out professionally by Russia's special services.

When an intelligence service makes such elaborate preparations for extracting a foreign intelligence worker, it presumably also expects to debrief him or her on arrival. Pelton, for example, who had access to far less valuable information than had Snowden, was held incommunicado in Vienna for two weeks during his debriefing. It would be inconceivable for an intelligence service to bring a potential espionage source such as Snowden to Russia and allow him to catch the next plane to Latin America. The false report provided to the press that Snowden was flying there was likely nothing more than a smoke screen to confuse foreign observers while he was receiving his initial debriefing and evaluation.

When it comes to the esoteric enterprise of reconstructing the work of U.S. communications intelligence, military as well as civilian experts in cryptology, computer sciences, and communications are necessary. Snowden had secret material in his possession. That he brought part of this material to Moscow is confirmed in recorded interviews by two Kremlin insiders, Kucherena and Klintsevich. The House Select Committee on Intelligence also reached that conclusion based on still-secret U.S. intelligence. Snowden's interpretation of the material would be part of the debriefing because intelligence data needs to be put in context.

"This debriefing could not be done overnight," according to a former high-ranking officer in the GRU, the Russian military intelligence service. "There is no way that Snowden would not be fully debriefed," he said. He also said GRU specialists in signals intelligence would be called in.

Putin's approval of the Snowden operation was not without consequences. Not only did Obama make good on his threat to cancel the pre-Olympics summit with Putin, but also, as it turned out, the Snowden exfiltration proved a turning point in the "reset" of U.S.-Russian relations. Having to accept the onus of declining relations with the Obama administration, Putin, it seems safe to assume, attempted to get the bonus of the NSA's communications intelligence from Snowden. The GRU, the SVR, and other Russian intelligence services would not stop questioning Snowden, even if it took years, until they had squeezed out of him whatever state secrets he had. Because Snowden was rewarded with sanctuary, a residence, and bodyguards, there is no reason to doubt that he refused to accommodate his hosts. While he might continue to see himself as a whistleblower on a supranational scale, as far as Russian intelligence was concerned, he was an espionage source.

For an intelligence service, the game is not over when it obtains state secrets. It still needs to fog over the extent of its coup, as said earlier, to prolong the value of the espionage. Hence it is likely that the story that Snowden had thoroughly destroyed all the stolen data in the month prior to departing for Russia, as well as the story that he had turned down all requests to be questioned by the FSB and other Russian intelligence officials, was part of the legend constructed for him. The repetitions of these uncorroborated claims in his press interviews might also have enhanced his public image for the ACLU effort to get clemency for him. Even so, in view of the importance of such communications intelligence to Russia, it would be the height of naïveté for U.S. or British intelligence to accept such claims as anything more than camouflage.

As for Snowden's motive, I see no reason to doubt his explanation that he stole NSA documents to expose its surveillance because he believed that it was an illicit intrusion into the privacy of individuals. Such disaffection is not a unique situation in the intelligence business. Many of Russia's worldwide espionage sources before Snowden were also dissatisfied employees who had access to classified secrets. Like some of them, Snowden used his privileged access to reveal what he considered the improper activities of the organization for which he worked. In that sense, I fully accept that he began as a whistle-blower, not as a spy. It was also as a whistle-blower that he contacted Laura Poitras, Glenn Greenwald, and Barton Gellman, who published the scoops he provided in *Der Spiegel*, *The Guardian*, and *The Washington Post*.

Snowden's penetration went beyond whistle-blowing, however. In the vast number of files he copied were documents that contained the NSA's most sensitive sources and methods that had little if anything to do with domestic surveillance or whistle-blowing.

Snowden could not have acted entirely alone. It will be recalled that the deepest part of his penetration was during the five weeks he worked at the National Threat Operations Center in Hawaii as a contract employee of Booz Allen Hamilton. It was there that he copied Level 3 files, including the so-called road map to the gaps in American intelligence. During this period, Snowden had neither the passwords nor the system administrator's privileges that would allow him to copy, transfer, and steal the electronic files. He therefore must have obtained that assistance from someone who had the passwords and privileges. Other workers there might have shared his sensibilities and antipathy toward NSA surveillance. It therefore seems entirely plausible that he found a co-worker willing to cooperate or, vice versa, a co-worker found him. Snowden might not have been aware of his new accomplice's true motives or affiliations, but without some co-worker's providing him with entry to the sealed-off computers, he could not have carried out the penetration. To our knowledge, whoever helped him evidently did not want to expose himself to prosecution or defect from the NSA. That was Snowden's role. By accepting the sole blame in the video that Poitras made about him in Hong Kong, Snowden shielded anyone else from suspicion, which was, as he told Poitras, his purpose. Whoever helped him may still be working at the NSA.

To be sure, there remains that other glaring gap in the chain of events that led Snowden to Moscow: his whereabouts and activities during his first eleven days in Hong Kong. Mike Rogers, the chairman of the House Select Committee on Intelligence, even suggested, without any evidence, that Snowden might have been taken to mainland China during this period. What drove his speculation was the admission of U.S. intelligence that despite its vast global resources for searching credit card charges, banking transactions, hotel registrations, e-mails, police records, and even CCTV cameras, neither it nor its allies were able to find a trace of Snowden during that time. It was, in a phrase made famous by the former secretary of defense Donald Rumsfeld, "a known unknown." Just as likely he could have been staying in a well-prepared safe house anywhere in Hong Kong or even at the home of an unknown associate. All that is really known is that soon after he emerged from this venue, moved to the Mira hotel, and gave his celebrated interview to journalists, he was safely settled in Russia.

Snowden's actions appear squarely at odds with his assertions of serving his country's interests. Even accepting that he began with a sincere desire to be a world-class whistle-blower, his mission evolved,

CHAPTER 29

The "War on Terror" After Snowden

Because of a number of unauthorized disclosures and a lot of hand-wringing over the government's role in the effort to try to uncover these terrorists, there have been some policy and legal and other actions that make our ability collectively, internationally, to find these terrorists much more challenging.

—CIA DIRECTOR JOHN BRENNAN,
in response to the Paris terrorist attack, November 2015

O N THE EVENING of November 13, 2015, nine jihadist terrorists acting on behalf of ISIS brought normal life in Paris to a screeching halt. Three suicide bombers blew themselves up at the stadium at Saint-Denis while President Hollande was inside attending a match between France and Germany. Other terrorists that night killed 130 people at cafés, restaurants, and a theater. Three hundred and eighty-eight others were wounded in the carnage. Abdelhamid Abaaoud, a twenty-eight-year-old Belgian citizen of Moroccan origins who served ISIS as a logistics officer in Syria in 2014, planned the attack over many months with the help of others in Syria. To organize it, they smuggled three suicide bombers into Europe through Greece, raised financing, set up a base in the Molenbeek section of Brussels, imported deactivated assault weapons from Slovenia that were restored by a technician, bought ammunition, acquired suicide vests, obtained "burner" cell phones, rented cars, and, two months before the attack, rented three additional apartments under fake identities to conceal the operation. Finally, in

November, they made online bookings for quarters in Paris for the nine attackers. Even though Abaaoud was well-known to Western intelligence services, none of the communications surrounding the preparations for the attack came to the attention of the NSA or its allied services in Europe. A critical find for the investigators enabled them to unravel the chain that eventually led them to the perpetrators, but it had nothing to do with electronic surveillance. A cell phone belonging to one of them was found by the security forces, following a broad search they conducted, which included trash cans situated in the vicinity of the concert halls. So this breakthrough in the investigation had nothing to do with systematic data analysis conducted prior to the attack.

Indeed, in the sequence of the Paris events, as in other terror events, the challenge is not just bringing culprits to justice. It is preventing the terrorists from carrying out their attack to begin with. Police cannot constantly protect "soft targets" such as restaurants, cafés, theaters, and street gatherings. The only practical means by which a government can prevent such attacks is to learn in advance their planning and preparations. One means of acquiring this information is by listening in on the channels through which members of loosely knit terrorist organizations, such as ISIS, communicate. This form of intelligence gathering obviously works best so long as the terrorists remain unaware that the communication channels they are using are being monitored. Once they find out that their messages and conversations are being intercepted, they will likely find a safer means to communicate important information. For that reason, communications intelligence organizations keep the sources and methods they employ for monitoring these channels in a tightly sealed envelope of secrecy.

Yet, in June 2013, the NSA found that envelope had been breached by Snowden, who knowingly compromised three programs that it used to keep track of terrorist organizations around the world. The first system he divulged, and the one that received the most public attention, was what the NSA called the "215" program because it had been authorized by Section 215 of the Patriot Act of 2001. This program compiled the billing records of every phone call made in America. The data included the number called and the duration of the call but not the name of the caller. This anonymous data was archived into a huge database. The idea was that when any foreigner on the FBI's watch list of terrorists called any number in the United States, the FBI could trace that person's entire chain of telephone contacts to try to determine if he or she was connected to a known terrorist cell. There was, however, a major flaw in this program: it did not cover e-mail and other Internet messaging, which by 2013 had largely replaced telephone calls. In addition, terrorist organizations, after the tracking down of Osama bin Laden in 2011, had become fully aware of the vulnerability of telephoning overseas. So although the NSA could cite a handful of early successes that "215" yielded, Snowden's exposure of it did only limited damage.

Snowden did vastly more damage by revealing the PRISM program, also called "702" because it was authorized in 2008 by Section 702 of the Foreign Intelligence Surveillance Act. Its effectiveness proceeded from the misplaced confidence that terrorist organizations in Iraq, Syria, Afghanistan, and Pakistan had in the encryption and other safeguards used by giant Internet companies, such as Apple, Google, Twitter, and WhatsApp. They evidently had not known that in 2007 the NSA found a way to intercept this data before it was encrypted. The Internet, despite metaphors such as "the cloud" and "cyberspace," initially travels through fiber cables, almost all of which run through the United States and its Five Eyes allies. So by 2013 the NSA was able to access 91 percent of the Internet *before* it was encrypted. This so-called upstream data included Google searches, tweets on Twitter, social media postings, Skype conversations, messages on Xbox Live, instant messages sent over WhatsApp, and e-mails sent via the Internet. The NSA could also read concealed messages in photographs and online game moves. According to a declassified 2015 inspector general's analysis, the actual interceptions in this program in 2013 were mainly limited to the communications of preselected foreign terrorists.

Until the Snowden breach was revealed on June 6, 2013, this program gave U.S. intelligence a valuable tool for gathering unexpected intelligence. Snowden must have been aware of how highly the NSA valued this program because, according to the documents he released, PRISM was "the number one source of raw intelligence used for

NSA analytic reports." From the continued use of these intercepted channels by suspected terrorists on the NSA's watch lists, it could be reasonably assumed that these users were unaware of the NSA's capacity to intercept their messages on the unencrypted Internet.

Unlike the telephone program that Snowden revealed, the PRISM program produced actionable intelligence until the time when Snowden blew it. General Hayden, who was NSA director during the three years following the 9/11 attack, wrote that these surveillance powers, among other things, "uncovered illicit financing networks, detected suspect travel, discovered ties to aviation schools, linked transportation employees to associates of terrorists, drew connections to the illicit purchases of arms, tied U.S. persons to Khalid Sheikh Mohammed, and discovered a suspect terrorist on the no-fly list who was already in the United States." More specifically, just between 2007 and 2013, according to the testimony of NSA and FBI officials, it resulted in the preempting of at least forty-five terrorist attacks. Almost all of the thwarted attacks occurred outside the jurisdiction of the United States, and therefore did not result in U.S. prosecutions. One of the plots that targeted Americans was a planned attack using high explosives on the subways in Grand Central station and the Times Square station at rush hour in New York City in 2009. It was averted after British intelligence supplied the NSA with the e-mail address of the terrorist suspect Najibullah Zazi in Aurora, Colorado. The PRISM surveillance program then traced it to an IP address on the watch list associated with Rashid Rauf, an al-Qaeda bomb maker in Pakistan. Zazi, evidently unaware that e-mails sent via Yahoo! could be intercepted before they were encrypted by Yahoo!, continued sending e-mails to Rauf as he prepared to assemble the bombs in early September 2009. As a result, the NSA search of its database yielded e-mails from Zazi discussing the proportions of explosives to be used. These e-mails recovered through the PRISM program, according to an analysis done for the Senate Judiciary Committee in 2014, provided the "critical lead" that led to the arrest of Zazi and his confederates before they could detonate bombs in the subways of New York City. The members of the House and Senate Select Committees on Intelligence had no doubt that the 702 program played a key role in aborting this plot they had been secretly briefed on in 2009. Dianne Feinstein, the chair of the Senate Select Committee, pointed out with privileged knowledge that it saved "subway cars stuffed to the gunwales with people"; Representative Mike Rogers also spoke with privileged knowledge when he said on June 9, 2013, referring to the 702 program, "I can tell you in the Zazi case in New York, it's exactly the program that was used."

The third NSA program of interest to terrorists that Snowden revealed was called XKeyscore. Using Internet data from PRISM, the NSA had created the equivalent of digital fingerprints for suspected foreign terrorists on watch lists. The "fingerprint" for each suspect was based on his or her search pattern on the Internet. These algorithms made it difficult for suspects to hide on the Internet by using aliases. Once a suspect was "fingerprinted," any attempt to evade surveillance by using a different computer and another user name would be detected by the XKeyscore algorithms. The "fingerprints" only worked so long as XKeyscore remained secret from those on the watch list. After Snowden exposed it, suspects could evade surveillance by changing their search patterns when they changed their aliases.

Further enabling furtive Internet users to evade the surveillance of the government, Snowden offered specific tips about the secret sources and methods used by both the NSA and the British GCHQ. He revealed in a public interview, for example, that the GCHQ had deployed the first "full-take" Internet interceptor that "snarfs everything, in a rolling buffer to allow retroactive investigation without missing a single bit." When asked how to circumvent it, he replied, "You should never route through or peer with the UK under any circumstances. Their fibers are radioactive, and even the Queen's selfies to the pool boy get logged." Aside from this warning about using Internet providers whose wiring passes through Britain, he also warned Internet users about trusting the encryption of any U.S.-based Internet company because of their secret relationships with the NSA. He added that the NSA considered "telecom collaborators to be the jewels in their crown of omniscience." He also gave a warning about the attention the NSA was paying to "jihadi forums." He said that to avoid being automatically "targeted" by the NSA, one needed to avoid them.

These precise tips for evading U.S. and British surveillance were not accidentally leaked. Snowden supplied them in written answers to interrogatives sent to him by Poitras and Appelbaum in May 2013 while he was still at the NSA. He also carefully orchestrated the exposure of the PRISM surveillance programs, precisely specifying, as Greenwald writes in his book *No Place to Hide*, who was to release the "scoops" in which newspapers. He gave Gellman a seventy-two-hour ultimatum for exposing PRISM, as we know. He further provided Poitras with well-organized files for publications revealing, among other things, that the NSA had paid RSA, a leading computer security provider, to build flawed encryption protocols, which allowed the NSA to read encrypted messages on computers and online video games. In short, he used these journalists to accomplish his purpose. In light of the way he micromanaged the leaks, it is difficult to conclude that he did not deliberately plan to compromise and render useless these U.S. and British operations.

Whatever he intended, he clearly succeeded in blowing the cover off NSA's operations authorized under the Foreign Intelligence Surveillance Act for monitoring terrorists' activities. After all, terrorist groups are no different from other criminal enterprises in their need to keep their communications secret from the authorities pursuing them. If they find out that the police are tapping their phone lines or intercepting other channels of communication, they can be expected to either stop using them or use them to divert attention away from their real plans.

In addition, Snowden suggested an alternative means to those who wanted to evade government surveillance. He recommended that they use end-to-end encryption, which results in messages being encrypted before they are sent over the Internet. He told Greenwald, for example, that encryption was "critically necessary" for anyone to evade NSA surveillance. Just as Robert Hanssen had deliberately compromised the NSA's interception of Soviet communications in Washington, D.C., in the 1990s, Snowden deliberately compromised the NSA's interception of concealed messages by potential terrorists on the Internet. We cannot know whether or not any of the jihadists involved in subsequent terrorist attacks (such as those in Paris or San Bernardino, California, in 2015) would have used the Internet or phone lines more freely if Snowden had not divulged the NSA's surveillance of them, but there can be little doubt that his breach of the secrecy envelope had serious consequences for U.S., French, and British intelligence. For example, François Molins, the former head prosecutor of Paris, pointed out that after the Paris attacks the French investigation had run into an obstacle: end-to-end encryption. "We can't penetrate into certain conversations," he said about "Telegram," the end-to-end encryption program that Snowden had repeatedly recommended, and as a result "we're dealing with this gigantic black hole, a dark zone where there are just so many dangerous things going on."

The effects of Snowden's intervention were soon realized by the CIA, according to Michael Morell, who had closely followed intelligence about terrorist groups in the Middle East ever since he had acted as the CIA's briefer for the president on the day of the 9/11 attack. "Terrorist organizations around the world were already starting to modify their actions in light of what Snowden disclosed," Morell wrote in 2015. "Within weeks of the [Snowden] leaks, communications sources dried up, tactics were changed." Even more disturbing, suspects on the CIA's watch list began switching to an "encryption platform." Instead of continuing to rely on the Internet to protect their messages, they increased their use of end-to-end encryption, which defeated the effectiveness of PRISM's capturing Internet traffic before it was encrypted by Internet companies. Indeed, after the Snowden breach, ISIS even provided a tutorial on its websites about using end-to-end encryption. So Morell and others at the CIA helplessly watched as this previous source of unexpected intelligence went dark.

What further heightened Morell's concern about this sudden loss of NSA intelligence from these sources was the discovery by the CIA in January 2014 of two documents, one 26 pages and the other 19 pages, on a captured ISIS computer in Syria. These documents discussed the advantages of using bubonic plague germs and other biological weapons against Western civilian populations. They even provided a religious justification for using biological warfare against civilian targets in the West. In addition, evidence uncovered from the safe house used by the ISIS terrorists involved in the Paris attack suggested they had been interested in acquiring radioactive isotopes. Without the advance warning that the NSA's surveillance of the pre-encrypted Internet had provided in the past, could the CIA now contend with such unconventional threats?

The NSA also saw its sources disappearing from its surveillance. Before the Snowden breach, the FBI, the CIA, and the DIA, which were the NSA's partners in the PRISM program, had compiled a watch list of highly active foreign terrorist targets for the NSA's PRISM program. These "targets" included logistics officers, bomb builders, weapons specialists, and suicide bomber recruiters. Until June 6, 2013, many of these targets had frequently used Internet services, such as Twitter, Facebook, and Xbox Live, to send what they believed would be hidden messages. After the PRISM story broke in *The Washington Post* on June 6, the NSA "saw one after another target go dark," according to a senior NSA executive involved in that surveillance. The NSA has watched about one thousand of these targets take "steps to remove themselves from our visibility." According to the NSA's deputy director, Richard Ledgett, in 2016, the vanishings included a group planning attacks in Europe and the United States.

Admiral Rogers, the new NSA director, discussed the damage done by Snowden. He was blunt and direct. Asked in February 2015 whether or not the disclosures by Snowden had reduced the NSA's ability to pursue terrorists, he answered, "Have I lost capability that we had prior to the revelations? Yes."

Epilogue

The Snowden Effect

Governments can reduce our dignity to something like that of tagged animals.

—EDWARD SNOWDEN, Moscow, 2016

THE ENORMOUS EFFECT that Snowden has had on America can be divided into three categories: the good, the bad, and the ugly. The good proceeds from the national conversation on the issue of surveillance in 2013 that his disclosures ignited. There is no denying that Snowden's dramatic disclosures, despite the damage they did to U.S. intelligence, accomplished a salutary service in alerting both the public and the government to the potential danger of a surveillance leviathan. The steady expansion of the NSA's collection of telephone billing records under the cloak of secrecy, for example, revealed a bureaucratic mission creep that badly needed to be brought under closer oversight by Congress. Snowden's breach provided another benefit. It pointed to the security dangers proceeding from the NSA's headlong rush to outsource its computer servicing to private contractors. Opening this back door, as Snowden amply demonstrated, greatly increased the risk that America's secrets would fall into the hands of its enemies. An intelligence service has little if any value if it cannot keep secret its sources from its adversaries.

The conversation that Snowden began is necessary for another reason. The relentless growth of data-collection technology had come to endanger personal privacy. Smart phones in our pockets, GPS recorders in our cars, fitness bands on our wrists, CCTV monitors in stores, and network-connected devices in our homes leave a digital trail of every move we make. The government can subpoena as part of an investigation, as we know, our personal data, including our Internet searches, social media postings, electronic communications, and credit card records. In addition, the government has its own tools of surveillance. Snowden, by disclosing that the government was vacuuming in phone billing records and Internet activities, hit a sore spot in the public's consciousness. How far did the surveillance state extend? Did an Orwellian government intercept private conversations of American citizens? Should Apple, Google, and other Internet giants use a doomsday system of encryption to prevent court-ordered searches for data? Were there adequate safeguards against government snooping?

In popular culture, surveillance is often associated with the sinister measures taken by a totalitarian government to suppress individual dissidence. On television we see government agents in black vans operating arrays of tape recorders, following people on the street, and breaking into homes to steal files and tap telephone lines. In the 2006 Academy Award–winning film *The Lives of Others*, for example, East Germany's Stasi police use listening devices to gather information to blackmail intellectuals to assist in the eradication of dissent. East Germany was not the only place in the Cold War era using surveillance to suppress dissent. Even in the United States in the 1950s and 1960s, J. Edgar Hoover's FBI bugged the phones of civil rights leaders, including Martin Luther King Jr., to root out suspected subversive elements. Most Americans viewed this as a reprehensible use of government surveillance, and the very mention of the word, even before Snowden's disclosure, evoked disquiet among the public. But what Snowden exposed was not any sort of rogue operation but programs authorized by the president and Congress and approved by fifteen federal judges. If one accepts that the nation's security remains a legitimate function of government, the issue is not surveillance itself; it is the proper way such surveillance is conducted.

The NSA surveillance of telephone records that Snowden exposed was different in its intent from the surveillance of the Cold War. Its target was a selected list of 300 to 400 foreign jihadists living abroad. Many of these individuals residing in Syria, Iraq, and Pakistan had been identified by the FBI and the CIA as active bomb makers, assassins, and weapon specialists. This was not domestic surveillance, but when any of these suspects telephoned a phone number in the United States, the NSA checked the billing records of the domestic phone number that had been called to determine all the calls emanating from it. The purpose of this search was to assemble for the FBI a list of contacts that a foreign suspect might have in the United States. To expedite this task, it obtained from telephone companies the billing records, without any names attached, of all their users and stored them in a single archive under its control. While this surveillance targeted foreign terrorists, not domestic dissent, the bulk collection of phone records had the potential for more nefarious use, a danger that Snowden brought to the public's attention. As a result, Congress modified the Patriot Act so that billing records would remain on the computers of the phone companies for a limited time rather than on those of the NSA. The NSA could still search them after obtaining an order from the FISA court, though it could not archive the data for future use, so little harm to individual privacy could be done. Snowden deserves a large share of the credit not only for this change but for making the public aware of domestic surveillance.

The bad part of the equation is that Snowden deeply damaged an intelligence system that American presidents have relied on for over six decades. The heart of that system was the sources and methods used to intercept other nations' communications. Until Snowden, the NSA's wall of secrecy kept these nations from knowing about them or, in some cases, even realizing that they were vulnerable to interception. For example, as previously discussed, the NSA had developed the remarkable ability to tap into an adversary nation's computers, even though they had been isolated from any network. This innovation had provided President Obama and his national security team an edge of which our adversaries were unaware from 2008 to 2013. However, Snowden deliberately nullified this advantage in 2013 by revealing this technology (which was published in *The New York Times* and other newspapers). The vast number of documents that he compromised contained many other secret sources and methods.

The full extent of the damage Snowden did may never be fully known, even though the Department of Defense spent the better part of a year, and tens of thousands of investigative man-hours, trying to sort out just the compromised sources and methods pertaining to military and cyber-defense operations. In addition to the direct and significant cost to taxpayers represented by this investigation, one measure of how serious the loss has been was revealed by Michael McConnell, the vice-chairman of the company for which Snowden had worked at the time of the breach. McConnell stated publicly, "Snowden has compromised more capability than any spy in U.S. history." McConnell had no obvious reason to exaggerate the loss because his company, Booz Allen Hamilton, was partly responsible for the damage. It hired Snowden, as will be recalled, even after its vetters had detected an untruthful statement in his application. McConnell said, "This will have impact on our ability to do our mission for the next twenty to thirty years." By any measure, two decades of lost intelligence is a steep price to pay.

To be sure, the practical value of peacetime intelligence about the activities of adversary states is not always evident. What is far clearer to the public is the value of intelligence that can thwart terrorist attacks against subways, theaters, and other civilian targets. We have seen that Snowden also deprived the NSA of much of the effectiveness of its PRISM program by revealing it, through the articles published at his specific behest in *The Guardian* and *The Washington Post* that explained how it worked. This single revelation compromised a system, duly authorized by Congress and the president, that had been the government's single most effective tool for learning in advance about attacks in America and Europe by jihadist terrorists.

The ugly part of the equation is the rampant growth of the public's distrust of the institutions of government in America. According to recent polls, 4 out of 5 Americans distrust the government. Snowden did not create this new age of distrust, but his disclosures greatly contributed to it, as well as to the worldwide distrust of the U.S. government. This post-Snowden distrust is especially powerful in the section of the international media that assisted Snowden in his release of NSA documents. In defending Snowden, it questions the truthfulness of any government official or member of Congress who discloses information contradicting Snowden's claims or showing that there was some benefit to the multibillion-dollar intelligence system that he compromised. Even Senator Dianne Feinstein, who herself fought the secrecy of the CIA for years, was not exempt from such distrust when she asserted in June 2013 that the program that Snowden had compromised had helped avert a bloody carnage on the New York subways in September 2009, as mentioned earlier. That she was the ranking Democrat on the Senate Select Committee on Intelligence, and briefed on the program at the time of the attack, did not prevent a distrustful press from attempting to impeach her credibility and that of the fourteen other members of the Senate Select Committee and the twenty members of the House Select Committee on Intelligence who had affirmed her assertion.

In this culture of distrust, any claim that any of the secrets that Snowden disclosed could have caused any harm is preemptively dismissed as government propaganda. Snowden's word also is taken over that of government officials because, as *The Nation* explained, Snowden speaks "truth to power." Such a formulation of distrust allows those who accept it to dismiss all assertions of government officials representing power who contradict Snowden's version of reality. Such is Snowden's glorified aura that even when his revelations expose purported U.S. government actions in foreign lands, including the alleged tapping of friendly government officials' conversations, such as Angela Merkel's, these are implicitly conflated with the NSA's domestic surveillance program, around which a popular movement has emerged questioning its purpose and methods. As a result, a legitimate debate on what should constitute our domestic liberties—and potential limits to those when facing significant security concerns—has largely obfuscated in this mind-set the reality of Snowden's weakening, durably and structurally, the critical ability of the United States and its allies to address their mounting external security challenges. In this culture of distrust, whatever contradicts the innocent whistle-blower narrative can be preemptively dismissed because Snowden, even though he remains ensconced in Moscow at an unknown location, remains the ultimate truth teller.

I do not accept either this formulation of Snowden or his version of the events in which he was the hero. Opening a Pandora's box of government secrets is a dangerous undertaking. Whether Snowden's theft of state secrets proceeded from an idealistic attempt to right a wrong, a narcissistic drive to obtain personal recognition, an intent to weaken the foundations of the surveillance infrastructure in which he worked, or a combination of such factors, by the time he arrived in Moscow, it had evolved, deliberately or not, but necessarily, into a mission of disclosing key national secrets to a foreign power. In the end, such conjectures about Snowden's motives matter less than that he was helped, consciously or not, by others with interests that differed from those of the United States. The effects on America of such a massive breach of confidence will not easily be reversible.

Author's Note

Since it was created by the House of Representatives in 1977, the United States House Permanent Select Committee on Intelligence has had the responsibility of overseeing the secret activities of the NSA, CIA, FBI, and other agencies of the intelligence community and, to carry out this charge, the congressmen on it have been given security clearance necessary to examine its classified material. The importance of its bipartisan report on the Snowden breach that was declassified in December 2016 proceeds from the access to material not available to the realm of journalism, including both the damage assessment reports done by the NSA and the far more extensive investigation of the Pentagon in which all 1.5 million files that Snowden removed were examined. Signed by all its Democratic and Republican members, it concluded that the narrative that Snowden supplied to journalists was not true, and that the claims that Snowden made were, in the words of Adam Schiff, the committee's ranking Democrat, "self-serving and false, and the damage done to our national security . . . profound." Even more ominously, it found that "Since his arrival in Moscow, Snowden has had, and continues to have, contact with Russian Intelligence services."

EXECUTIVE SUMMARY OF REVIEW OF THE

UNAUTHORIZED DISCLOSURES OF FORMER NATIONAL

SECURITY AGENCY CONTRACTOR EDWARD SNOWDEN

September 15, 2016

In June 2013, former National Security Agency (NSA) contractor Edward Snowden perpetrated the largest and most damaging public release of classified information in U.S. intelligence history. In August 2014, the Chairman and Ranking Member of the House Permanent Select Committee on Intelligence (HPSCI) directed Committee staff to carry out a comprehensive review of the unauthorized disclosures. The aim of the review was to allow the Committee to explain to other Members of Congress—and, where possible, the American people—how this breach occurred, what the U.S. Government knows about the man who committed it, and whether the security shortfalls it highlighted had been remedied.

Over the next two years, Committee staff requested hundreds of documents from the Intelligence Community (IC), participated in dozens of briefings and meetings with IC personnel, conducted several interviews with key individuals with knowledge of Snowden's background and actions, and traveled to NSA Hawaii to visit Snowden's last two work locations. The review focused on Snowden's background, how he was able to remove more than 1.5 million classified documents from secure NSA networks, what the 1.5 million documents contained, and the damage their removal caused to national security.

The Committee's review was careful not to disturb any criminal investigation or future prosecution of Snowden, who has remained in Russia since he fled there on June 23, 2013. Accordingly, the Committee did not interview individuals whom the Department of Justice identified as possible witnesses at Snowden's trial, including Snowden himself, nor did the Committee request any matters that may have occurred before a grand jury. Instead, the Committee had access to other individuals who possessed substantively similar knowledge as the possible witnesses. Similarly, rather than interview Snowden's NSA coworkers and supervisors directly, Committee staff interviewed IC personnel who had reviewed reports of interviews with Snowden's co-workers and supervisors. The Committee remains hopeful that Snowden will return to the United States to face justice.

The bulk of the Committee's 36-page review, which includes 230 footnotes, must remain classified to avoid causing further harm to national security; however, the Committee has made a number of unclassified findings. These findings demonstrate that the public narrative popularized by Snowden and his allies is rife with falsehoods, exaggerations, and crucial omissions, a pattern that began before he stole 1.5 million sensitive documents.

First, Snowden caused tremendous damage to national security, and the vast majority of the documents he stole have nothing to do with programs impacting individual privacy interests— they instead pertain to military, defense, and intelligence programs of great interest to America's adversaries. A review of the materials Snowden compromised makes clear that he handed over secrets that protect American troops overseas and secrets that provide vital defenses against terrorists and nation-states. Some of Snowden's disclosures exacerbated and accelerated existing trends that diminished the IC's capabilities to collect against legitimate foreign intelligence targets, while others resulted in the loss of intelligence streams that had saved American lives. Snowden insists he has not shared the full cache of 1.5 million classified documents with anyone; however, in June 2016, the deputy chairman of the Russian parliament's defense and security committee publicly conceded that "Snowden did share Intelligence" with his government. Additionally, although Snowden's professed objective may have been to inform the general public, the information he released is also available to Russian, Chinese, Iranian, and North Korean government intelligence services; any terrorist with Internet access; and many others who wish to do harm to the United States.

The full scope of the damage inflicted by Snowden remains unknown. Over the past three years, the IC and the Department of Defense (DOD) have carried out separate reviews with differing methodologies of the damage Snowden caused. Out of an abundance of caution, DOD reviewed all 1.5 million documents Snowden removed. The IC, by contrast, has carried out a damage assessment for only a small subset of the documents. The Committee is concerned that the IC does not plan to assess the damage of the vast majority of documents Snowden removed. Nevertheless, even by a conservative estimate, the U.S. Government has spent hundreds of millions of dollars, and will eventually spend billions, to attempt to mitigate the damage Snowden caused. These dollars would have been better spent on combating America's adversaries in an increasingly dangerous world.

Second, Snowden was not a whistleblower. Under the law, publicly revealing classified information does not qualify someone as a whistleblower. However, disclosing classified information that shows fraud, waste, abuse, or other illegal activity to the appropriate law enforcement or oversight personnel—including to Congress—does make someone a whistleblower and affords them with critical protections. Contrary to his public claims that he notified numerous NSA officials about what he believed to be illegal intelligence collection, the Committee found no evidence that Snowden took any official effort to express concerns about U.S. intelligence activities—legal, moral, or otherwise—to any oversight officials within the U.S. Government, despite numerous avenues for him to do so. Snowden was aware of these avenues. His only attempt to contact an NSA attorney revolved around a question about the legal precedence of executive orders, and his only contact to the Central Intelligence Agency (CIA) Inspector General (IG) revolved around his disagreements with his managers about training and retention of information technology specialists.

Despite Snowden's later public claim that he would have faced retribution for voicing concerns about intelligence activities, the Committee found that laws and regulations in effect at the time of Snowden's actions afforded him protection. The Committee routinely receives disclosures from IC contractors pursuant to the Intelligence Community Whistleblower Protection Act of 1998 (IC WPA). If Snowden had been worried about possible retaliation for voicing concerns about NSA activities, he could have made a disclosure to the Committee. He did not. Nor did Snowden remain in the United States to face the legal consequences of his actions, contrary to the tradition of civil disobedience he professes to embrace. Instead, he fled to China and Russia, two countries whose governments place scant value on their citizens' privacy or civil liberties—and whose intelligence services aggressively collect information on both the United States and their own citizens.

To gather the files he took with him when he left the country for Hong Kong, Snowden infringed on the privacy of thousands of government employees and contractors. He obtained his colleagues' security credentials through misleading means, abused his access as a systems administrator to search his co-workers' personal drives, and removed the personally identifiable information of thousands of IC employees and contractors. From Hong Kong he went to Russia, where he remains a guest of the Kremlin to this day.

It is also not clear Snowden understood the numerous privacy protections that govern the activities of the IC. He failed basic annual training for NSA employees on Section 702 of the Foreign Intelligence Surveillance Act (FISA) and complained the training was rigged to be overly difficult. This training included explanations of the privacy protections related to the PRISM program that Snowden would later disclose.

Third, two weeks before Snowden began mass downloads of classified documents, he was reprimanded after engaging in a workplace spat with NSA managers. Snowden was repeatedly counseled by his managers regarding his behavior at work. For example, in June 2012, Snowden became involved in a fiery e-mail argument with a Supervisor about how computer updates should be managed. Snowden added an NSA senior executive several levels above the supervisor to the e-mail thread, an action that earned him a swift reprimand from his contracting officer for failing to follow the proper protocol for raising grievances through the chain of command. Two weeks later, Snowden began his mass downloads of classified information from NSA networks. Despite Snowden's later claim that the March 2013 congressional testimony of Director of National Intelligence James Clapper was a "breaking point" for him, these mass downloads *predated* Director Clapper's testimony by eight months.

Fourth, Snowden was, and remains, a serial exaggerator and fabricator. A close review of Snowden's official employment records and submissions reveals a pattern of intentional lying. He claimed to have left Army basic training because of broken legs when in fact he washed out because of shin splints. He claimed to have obtained a high school degree equivalent when in fact he never did. He claimed to have worked for the CIA as a "senior advisor," which was a gross exaggeration of his entry-level duties as a computer technician. He also doctored his performance evaluations and obtained new positions at NSA by exaggerating his résumé and stealing the answers to an employment test. In May 2013, Snowden informed his supervisor that he would be out of the office to receive treatment for worsening epilepsy. In reality, he was on his way to Hong Kong with stolen secrets.

Finally, the Committee remains concerned that more than three years after the start of the unauthorized disclosures, NSA, and the IC as a whole, have not done enough to minimize the risk of another massive unauthorized disclosure. Although it is impossible to reduce the chance of another Snowden to zero, more work can and should be done to improve the security of the people and computer networks that keep America's most closely held secrets. For instance, a recent DOD Inspector General report directed by the Committee found that NSA has yet to effectively implement its post-Snowden security improvements. The Committee has taken actions to improve IC information security in the Intelligence Authorization Acts for Fiscal Years 2014, 2015, 2016, and 2017, and looks forward to working with the IC to continue to improve security.

Acknowledgments

I am deeply grateful to the many individuals who put their knowledge and expertise at my disposal during the course of writing this book. Unfortunately, I cannot give due credit to some of those people to whom I owe the greatest debt in understanding the intelligence issues, because they spoke to me on condition that I keep secret their identities.

I greatly benefited from the insights, erudition, and criticisms provided by those who read draft chapters at various stages of my investigation. I am particularly indebted in this regard to Tobias Brown, Rachelle Bergstein, Richard Bernstein, Sidney Blumenthal, David Braunschvig, Ash Carter, Susana Duncan, Joe Finder, Ben Gerson, Andrew Hacker, William Haseltine, Eli Jacobs, Bruce Kovner, Robert Loomis, Gary Lucas, John Micklethwait, Frederick Mocatta, Andrew Rosenberg, Curt Sawyer, Sean Wilentz, and Ezra Zilkha.

I am especially grateful to Harold Edgar, the Julius Silver Professor in Law, Science, and Technology at Columbia Law School; and to Jack Goldsmith, Henry L. Shattuck Professor at Harvard Law School, for sharing with me their legal perspective on the espionage statutes and other legal issues.

I thank Edward Lucas of *The Economist* for recommending Catherine A. FitzPatrick, a writer and translator at *The Interpreter* magazine as someone who "possesses a unique knowledge of the labyrinthine world of Russian disinformation." She proved a godsend for this book. With her deep understanding of the workings of the Internet, she helped me retrieve information from the dark side of the Internet that I otherwise would not have found.

Because I do not believe an investigative book should be written without the author visiting the crime scene and other pertinent venues, I undertook research in Hawaii, Japan, Hong Kong, and Moscow. Where possible, I flew the same flights that Snowden did. I am grateful to Ena and Ines Talakic for their assistance on these research trips. As talented documentarians in their own right, they filmed a number of my interviews on these trips, and generously provided photographs for this book. I thank Alexander Bitter in Hawaii, Joyce Xu in Hong Kong, Ko Shoiya in Japan, and Zamir Gotta, Natalie Filkina, and Svetlana Chervonnaya in Russia for their help in arranging my interviews in those places. I also owe special thanks to Nick Grube, an editor at *Civil Beat* in Honolulu, for accompanying me to the NSA base where Snowden was working in 2013.

I am indebted to Nancy Novick for her skill, patience and enterprise in helping me find the selection of photographs for this book.

I am grateful to Zachary Gresham for his meticulous fact-checking and proofreading, and to Ingrid Sterner for her immensely helpful copyediting skills. Because I perform all my own research, I alone am responsible for any errors that appear in this book.

Mort Janklow, who has represented me for three decades, did a superb job in arranging for Alfred A. Knopf to publish this book.

I am thankful to Julia Ringo and the team at Knopf for their help in preparing this book. Finally, I am deeply indebted to Jonathan Segal for meticulously editing this book. The manuscript gained immeasurably from both his keen eye and his wise judgment.

Notes

PROLOGUE Snowden's Trail: Hong Kong, 2014

3 "No Such Agency": The best description of the birth of the NSA can be found in Bamford, *Puzzle Palace*, 1–4.

4 the NSA learned: General Keith Alexander, interview with author.

4 twelve-minute video: This video can be seen at http://www.theguardian.com /world/video/2013/jun/09/nsa-whistleblower-edward-snowden-interview -video. All of the dozens of videos Snowden made after this initial one can be viewed in chronological order at https://nsa.gov1.info/dni/snowden.html.

5 I had written several books: My book *Inquest* examined the failure of the FBI, the Secret Service, and the CIA to establish the context of the John F. Kennedy assassination. This interest continued in other books of mine, including *Deception*, in which I investigated the vulnerability of intelligence services involved in espionage during the Cold War, and *Agency of Fear* (New York: G. P. Putnam's Sons, 1977), in which I explored intelligence failures of domestic intelligence in the war on drugs.

5 extradite Trent Martin: The FBI press statement on this case was released on March 27, 2013, less than two months before Snowden bought his ticket for Hong Kong: https://www.fbi.gov/newyork/press-releases/2013/australian -research-analyst-extradited-on-insider-trading-charges.

6 "It's very mysterious": Hayden, interview with author.

6 My first surprise: I interviewed six members of the Mira staff, all of whom asked me not to identify them. Te-Ping Chen, a journalist for the Asian edition of *The Wall Street Journal*, received similar replies when she interviewed Mira hotel employees the day Snowden left the Mira. Chen and Yung, "Snowden's Whereabouts Remain Unclear."

6 to send Greenwald: Greenwald's description of his encounters with Snowden is taken mainly from chapter 1, "Contact," and chapter 2, "Ten Days in Hong Kong," in Greenwald, *No Place to Hide*, 7–32.

7 Snowden also contacted: Gellman, "Code Name 'Verax.'"

7 He proposed we meet: Bradsher, interview with author. Bradsher wrote a number of excellent articles about Snowden and Ho. See Bradsher, "Hasty Exit Started with Pizza Inside a Hong Kong Hideout."

8   appointment with Robert Tibbo: Tibbo, interviews with author.

12 "angel descending": Snowden, interview with Brian Williams, NBC, May 28, 2014.

CHAPTER 1 Tinker

15 "It's like the boiling frog": Bamford, "Edward Snowden."

15 Lon Snowden, like his father: The best reporting on Snowden's childhood was done by Suzanne Andrews. See Burrough, Ellison, and Andrews, "Snowden Saga."

16 Brad Gunson, who knew Snowden: Carol D. Leonnig, Jenna Johnson, and Marc Fisher, "Who Is Edward Snowden?," *Washington Post*, June 15, 2013.

16 Snowden stayed home: Kinsey, interview with author.

16 Posting under the alias: Mullin, "NSA Leaker Ed Snowden's Life on Ars Technica."

16 He even went to anime conventions: Christopher Johnson, "Chatting About Japan with Snowden," *Japan Times*, June 18, 2013.

17 "body fat percentage": Leonnig, Johnson, and Fisher, "Who Is Edward Snowden?"

17 "I've always dreamed": Mullin, "NSA Leaker Ed Snowden's Life on Ars Technica."

17 Admiral Barrett: Coast Guard Biography, http://www.uscg.mil/history/people /Flags/BarrettEBio.pdf. Also, for his FBI career, see http://www1.umn.edu /humanrts/OathBetrayed/FBI%2047.pdf.

18 Army records show: Author interviews. The U.S. Army spokesman George Wright stated Snowden was enrolled in the program between May 7, 2004, and September 28, 2004. The spokesman Colonel David Patterson said, "He attempted to qualify to become a Special Forces soldier but did not complete the requisite training and was administratively discharged from the army."

18 taking a job as a security guard: Burrough, Ellison, and Andrews, "Snowden Saga."

19 "So sexxxy it hurts": The information about Snowden's modeling career comes from his posts on *Ars Technica*. See Mullin, "NSA Leaker Ed Snowden's Life on Ars Technica."

19 Jonathan Mills, Lindsay's father: Daniel Bates, "Snowden Totally Abandoned His Girlfriend When He Fled amid NSA Revelations, Her Dad Says," *Daily Mail*, Jan. 17, 2014. The information about Lindsay Mills comes from her Twitter and Instagram postings.

19 The CIA's minimum requirements in 2006: https://www.cia.gov/careers /application-process.

CHAPTER 2 Secret Agent

22 "It seems to me spies": Snowden, interview with Williams.

23 team of information technologists: Former CIA officer who requested anonymity, interview with author.

23 The only person: "Edward Snowden's Friend Mavanee Anderson Exclusive Interview," *Last Word*, MSNBC, June 12, 2013, www.youtube.com/watch?v= beQUMdolBWE.

25 "was trying to break into": Schmitt, "C.I.A. Warning on Snowden in '09 Said to Slip Through the Cracks."

26 explained the discrepancy: Former CIA officer who requested anonymity, interview with author.

26 "It was not a stellar": Drumheller, interviews with author.

26 "e-mail spat": Snowden was interviewed via the Internet by Risen, "Snowden Says He Took No Secret Files to Russia."

27 "totally incapable": Snowden, interview with Bamford, "Edward Snowden."

27 "through the system": Burrough, Ellison, and Andrews, "Snowden Saga."

CHAPTER 3 Contractor

28 "Much of what I saw": Greenwald, Poitras, and MacAskill, "Edward Snowden."

30 This "free pass": Tyler Drumheller, interview with author.

30 "So the guy with whom the CIA": Morell, *Great War of Our Time*, 284.

30 His initial job for Dell: Burrough, Ellison, and Andrews, "Snowden Saga."

31 Lindsay Mills: The information about Lindsay comes from her postings on Instagram and her blog *L's Journey*, https://twitter.com/lsjourneys. The information about her and Snowden's travel to Mount Fuji and other places in Japan comes from the *Little Red Ninja* blog written by Jennie Chamberlin: https://www.facebook.com/Little-Red-Ninja-214045021941347/timeline/.

32 working on a backup system: Burrough, Ellison, and Andrews, "Snowden Saga."

32 most of the classified data: Source who requested anonymity, interview with author.

32 spotted a major flaw: Snowden, interview with Bamford, "Edward Snowden."

32 "I actually recommended": Ibid.

33 Snowden made a ten-day trip: Harris, "What Was Edward Snowden Doing in India?" Also, Shilpa Phadnis, "Edward Snowden Sharpened His Hacking Skills in Delhi," *Times of India*, Dec. 4, 2013.

33 "It is a dead-end job": Former Booz Allen official who requested anonymity, interview with author.

33 shaded by a sakura: The description of Snowden's life in Maryland comes entirely from Lindsay Mills's Internet postings. See *L's Journey*.

34 The guest speaker was: Michael Hayden, interview with the author.

34 "They [the NSA] are intent": Greenwald, Poitras, and MacAskill, "Edward Snowden."

34 "none of whom took any action": Andrea Peterson, "Snowden: I Raised NSA Concerns Internally over 10 Times Before Going Rogue," *Washington Post*, March 7, 2014. The NSA's response came from the NSA spokesperson Vanee Vines in an author interview.

35 U.S. Investigations Services: Dion Nissenbaum, "U.S. Gives New Contract to Firm That Vetted NSA Leaker Edward Snowden," *Wall Street Journal*, July 2, 2014.

CHAPTER 4 Thief

38   In Hawaii in 2012: Former Dell executive who requested anonymity because of company policy restricting Dell employees from discussing the Snowden case, interview with author.

39   "You're in a vaulted space": Transcript of interview with Snowden in Moscow. Rusbridger and MacAskill, "I, Spy."

39   "Law is a lot like medicine": David Weigel, "Edward Snowden and Ron Paul Kick Off Libertarian Student Conference," *Bloomberg News*, Feb. 13, 2015. For Ron Paul's position on "secret government," see http://www.presstv.ir /Detail/2015/06/02/413952/US-Ron-Paul-CIA-NSA-secret-government.

40   "The [American] government": Arundhati Roy, "Edward Snowden Meets Arundhati Roy and John Cusack," *Guardian*, Nov. 28, 2015.

40   "fear and a false image": Bamford, "Edward Snowden."

40   Snowden was fully aware: Snowden in Moscow, e-mail interview with James Risen. Risen, "Snowden Says He Took No Secret Files to Russia."

41   Physical Phatness: Lindsay Mills's Facebook page, https://www.facebook.com /lindsay.mills.90/about.

42   the first known document: Ledgett revealed this in an interview with *Vanity Fair*. Burrough, Ellison, and Andrews, "Snowden Saga."

42   "He stole the [NSA] test": Snowden's obtaining the NSA examination is described by Michael McConnell. See King, "Ex-NSA Chief Details Snowden's Hiring at Agency, Booz Allen." The extended video of the interview is at www .wsj.com.

43   "It was totally unrealistic": NSA executive who requested anonymity, interview with author.

43   subsequently joking to a reporter: Bamford, "Edward Snowden."

CHAPTER 5 Crossing the Rubicon

44   "What I came to feel": Snowden quoted in Rusbridger and MacAskill, "I, Spy."

44   "was moving copies of that data": Burrough, Ellison, and Andrews, "Snowden Saga."

45   he later pointed out: Bamford, "Edward Snowden."

45   Ledgett subsequently reported: Burrough, Ellison, and Andrews, "Snowden Saga."

45   This theft was made: Michael Hayden, interview with author.

46   "I crossed that line": Burrough, Ellison, and Andrews, "Snowden Saga."

46   "We're subverting our security": Transcript of Snowden interview on PBS. James Bamford and Tim De Chant, "Edward Snowden on Cyber Warfare," *Nova*, Jan. 8, 2015, www.pbs.org/wgbh/nova/next/military/snowden-transcript.

46   bragged to James Risen: Risen, "Snowden Says He Took No Secret Files to Russia."

47   this counterculture is "tormented": Shils, *Torment of Secrecy*.

47   "[The elites] know everything": Roy, "Edward Snowden Meets Arundhati Roy and John Cusack."

47   "What do you think": Gellman, "Edward Snowden, After Months of NSA Revelations, Says His Mission's Accomplished."

48   violate U.S. espionage laws: Michael Hayden, interview with author.

CHAPTER 6 Hacktivist

49 the group Anonymous: Coleman, *Hacker, Hoaxer, Whistleblower, Spy*, 1–8.

50 "My own forays": Sue Halpern, "In the Depths of the Net," *New York Review of Books*, Oct. 8, 2015.

51 Silk Road, which acted: Holman W. Jenkins Jr., "The Anti-hero of Silk Road," *Wall Street Journal*, June 3, 2015. Also, Justice Department official who requested anonymity, interview with author.

51 "Tor's importance": Hastings, "Julian Assange." Also see Julian Assange, introduction to *Underground*, by Suelette Dreyfus and Julian Assange (Edinburgh: Canongate, 2012).

51 Tor was a creation: Fitzpatrick, *Privacy for Me and Not for Thee*, pt. 6.

52 "the state is all-powerful": Fitzpatrick, introduction to ibid.

53 "Meet the Most Dangerous Man": Appelbaum, interview with Rolling Stone, "Meet the Most Dangerous Man in Cyberspace: The American Behind WikiLeaks," *Rolling Stone*, Dec. 2, 2010.

53 In Berlin, Appelbaum: Packer, "Holder of Secrets."

54 she identified herself: Runa A. Sandvik, *Forbes*, http://www.forbes.com/sites/runasandvik/.

54 According to an anonymous: Andy Greenberg, "An NSA Coworker Remembers the Real Edward Snowden," *Forbes*, Dec. 16, 2013.

54 "Without Tor," he later wrote: Twitter, https://twitter.com/snowden/status/682257506018672640.

54 "Tor Stinks": Sean Michael Kerner, "Snowden Leaks Show NSA Targets Tor," *E Week*, Oct. 4, 2013.

55 He would later tell Sandvik: Runa A. Sandvik, "What Edward Snowden Said at the Nordic Media Festival," *Forbes*, May 10, 2015.

55 According to Sandvik's account: Sandvik did not reveal her encounter with Snowden in any of her blogs until eleven months after Snowden went public in June 2013. It was only after Greenwald disclosed in his book *No Place to Hide* that Snowden used the alias Cincinnatus that Internet investigators discovered he had hosted with Sandvik the CryptoParty. Sandvik then wrote her account of it. See Sandvik, "That One Time I Threw a CryptoParty with Edward Snowden." Also, Kevin Poulsen, "Snowden's First Move Against the NSA Was a Party in Hawaii," *Wired*, May 21, 2014.

56 owner of BoxJelly: Fujihira, interview with author.

57 "The idea was to spread": Morell, *Great War of Our Time*, 288.

58 "Snowden was not an NSA": Former NSA executive who requested anonymity, interview with author.

CHAPTER 7 String Puller

59 "It wasn't that they put": Gellman, "Edward Snowden, After Months of NSA Revelations, Says His Mission's Accomplished."

59 He used the same alias: All of Snowden's post-party activities in 2012 and 2013 come from the Twitter account of "Oahu Crypto Party."

59 The journalist to whom: The description of Snowden's attempts to contact Greenwald in December 2012 and January 2013 can be found in Greenwald, *No Place to Hide*, 7–10.

59 Greenwald had not always: Mark Memmott, "He Broke the NSA Leaks Story, but Just Who Is Glenn Greenwald?," NPR, June 11, 2013. For his part ownership of the HJ website, see Dareh Gregorian, "Glenn Greenwald, Journalist Who Broke Edward Snowden Story, Was Once Lawyer Sued over Porn Business," *Daily News*, June 26, 2013. Also, Jessica Testa, "How Glenn Greenwald Became Glenn Greenwald," *BuzzFeed*, June 26, 2013.

60 by "ordering illegal eavesdropping": Greenwald, *No Place to Hide*, 2. On Ron Paul, see ibid., 24.

60 Freedom of the Press Foundation: Michael Calderone, "Freedom of the Press Foundation Launches to Support WikiLeaks," *Huffington Post*, Dec. 16, 2012.

60 "The first serious info war": David Sarno, "'Hacktivists' Fight for Their Cause Online," *Los Angeles Times*, Dec. 11, 2010.

61 "The US operates a sprawling": Glenn Greenwald, "FBI's Abuse of the Surveillance State Is the Real Scandal Needing Investigation," *Guardian*, Nov. 13, 2012.

62 Poitras had been diligently filming: Adan Salazar, "Mini Documentary Reveals Full Extent of 'Stellarwind' Domestic Spy Program," *Infowars*, Aug. 28, 2012.

62 Poitras had other impressive credentials: "Laura Poitras: Secret No Longer," *New School News*, Aug. 14, 2013.

63 "I didn't. You chose yourself": Snowden's e-mails to Poitras were extracted from her film *Citizenfour* and published in *Wired*. See Greenberg, "These Are the Emails Snowden Sent to First Introduce His Epic NSA Leaks."

63 he wrote to Micah Lee: Lee's involvement with Snowden, although known to the journalists Greenwald and Poitras since April 2013, was not revealed to the public for some eighteen months. Lee, "Ed Snowden Taught Me to Smuggle Secrets Past Incredible Danger."

63 "I was at that point filming": Poitras, interview with Amy Goodman, *Democracy Now*, Jan. 15, 2015, http://www.democracynow.org/blog/2015/1/15/oscars_2015_laura_poitras_film_on.

64 "At this stage": Greenberg, "These Are the Emails Snowden Sent to First Introduce His Epic NSA Leaks."

65 surveillance of her communications: Glenn Greenwald, "U.S. Filmmaker Repeatedly Detained at Border," *Salon*, April 8, 2012.

65 "Kafkaesque government harassment": Ben Child, "Citizenfour Director Laura Poitras Sues US over 'Kafkaesque Harassment,'" *Guardian*, July 14, 2015.

65 "more paranoid": Snowden, interview with vanden Heuvel and Cohen, "Snowden Speaks."

66 "Is C4 a trap?": Andy Greenberg, "Snowden's Chronicler Reveals Her Own Life Under Surveillance," *Wired*, Feb. 4, 2016.

66 Stellarwind: Greenberg, "These Are the Emails Snowden Sent to First Introduce His Epic NSA Leaks."

68 "No one, not even": Ibid.

68 under enormous stress: Greenberg, "Snowden's Chronicler Reveals Her Own Life Under Surveillance."

70 he had Poitras write: "The *Frontline* Interviews," "Barton Gellman," PBS, March 7, 2014, http://www.pbs.org/wgbh/pages/frontline/government-elections-politics/united-states-of-secrets/the-frontline-interview-barton-gellman/.

70 Poitras had requested help: Karen Greenberg, interview with the author.

71 Council on American-Islamic Relations: CAIR-NY Blog, "Glenn Greenwald Speaks at CAIR-NY Annual Banquet," May 16, 2013.

71 When they finally settled: The descriptions of the initial two meetings between Greenwald and Poitras in April 2013 are provided in Greenwald's 2014 book, *No Place to Hide*, pp. 10-15.

CHAPTER 8 Raider of the Inner Sanctum

74 "They think there's a smoking gun": Bamford, "Edward Snowden."

75 system for stratifying its data: Michael McConnell, interview with King, "Ex-NSA Chief Details Snowden's Hiring at Agency, Booz Allen."

76 Snowden applied to Booz Allen: Booz Allen officer who requested anonymity, interview with author.

76 "Snowden was an IT guy": John R. Schindler, "Snowden Is a Fraud," XX Committee, June 12, 2015.

76 "get access to lists": Lana Lam, "Post Reporter Lana Lam Tells of Her Journey into the Secret World of Edward Snowden," *South China Morning Post*, June 23, 2013.

76 "He targeted my company": King, "Ex-NSA Chief Details Snowden's Hiring at Agency, Booz Allen."

76–77 he would not have password access: Former NSA executive who requested anonymity, interview with author.

77 engaged in a minor subterfuge: Hosenball, "NSA Contractor Hired Snowden Despite Concerns About Resume Discrepancies."

78 "playing with fire": Spencer Ackerman and Ewen MacAskill, "Snowden Calls for Whistleblower After Claims by New Pentagon Source," *Guardian*, May 22, 2016.

78 establish a paper trail: Director of National Intelligence, *IC on the Record* (blog on Tumblr), May 27, 2014, http://icontherecord.tumblr.com/post/87218708448 /edward-j-snowden-email-inquiry-to-the-nsa-office. Snowden response, in "Edward Snowden Responds to Release of E-mail by U.S. Officials," *Washington Post*, May 29, 2014.

78 He returned on April 13: Lindsay Mills's blog.

78 a brief medical leave: Former NSA executive who requested anonymity, interview with author.

79 needed to get passwords: Stephen Braun, "NSA to Congress: Snowden Copied Co-worker's Password," *Military Times*, Feb. 13, 2014.

79 software applications called spiders: David E. Sanger and Eric Schmitt, "Snowden Used Low-Cost Tool to Best N.S.A.," *New York Times*, Feb. 8, 2014.

79 Finally, Snowden had to: Former intelligence officer who requested anonymity, interview with author.

80 These later acquisitions: The document can be seen in the National Security Archives, http://nsarchive.gwu.edu/NSAEBB/NSAEBB436/docs/EBB-059.pdf.

CHAPTER 9 Escape Artist

81 "I'm not self-destructive": Bamford, "Edward Snowden."

81 "I took everything": Edward Snowden and Peter Taylor, "Are You a Traitor?," transcript, *Panorama*, BBC, Oct. 15, 2015 (aired on BBC Oct. 10, 2015).

81 At this point: Former DIA officer who requested anonymity, interview with author.

81 He had visited Hong Kong: Lindsay Mills's blog.

81 According to Albert Ho: Bradsher, "Hasty Exit Started with Pizza Inside a Hong Kong Hideout." Also, Keith Bradsher, interview with author.

82 for the next ten days: Former DIA officer who requested anonymity, interview with author.

82 "his first priority": Greenwald, *No Place to Hide*, 43.

82 "That whole period": Rusbridger and MacAskill, "I, Spy."

82 He e-mailed Gellman: Gellman, "Code Name 'Verax.'"

83 Gellman could not make: Greenwald, *No Place to Hide*, 51–52.

83 more pressure on Gellman: Gellman, "Code Name 'Verax.'"

83 "I've been working on": Greenwald, *No Place to Hide*, 11.

84 Continuing his string pulling : Greenberg, "These Are the Emails Snowden Sent to First Introduce His Epic NSA Leaks."

85 asked Appelbaum to help: Appelbaum, "Edward Snowden Interview."

85 Greenwald was awaiting: Greenwald, *No Place to Hide*, 16–18.

86 Gibson authorized Greenwald's trip: The description of *The Guardian's* reaction to Greenwald's offer of a scoop was reported by Luke Harding, a *Guardian* reporter commissioned to write *The Snowden Files*, a book that Oliver Stone bought the film rights for from *The Guardian* for $700,000. See Harding, *Snowden Files*, 100–115.

87 Snowden arranged for Micah Lee: Lee, "Ed Snowden Taught Me to Smuggle Secrets Past Incredible Danger."

CHAPTER 10 Whistle-blower

89 "They elected me": Gellman, "Edward Snowden, After Months of NSA Revelations, Says His Mission's Accomplished."

89 "I feel alone": Lindsay Mills's blog.

90 "so we don't have a clue": Greenberg, "These Are the Emails Snowden Sent to First Introduce His Epic NSA Leaks."

90 "On timing, regarding meeting": The description of the meetings with Snowden in Hong Kong, June 3–June 9, is taken from Poitras's documentary *Citizenfour*. The film can be found at https://thoughtmaybe.com/citizenfour/.

91 "The initial impression": Greenwald, *No Place to Hide*, 30.

91 "Minutes after meeting": Packer, "Holder of Secrets."

91 One possible reason: Snowden, interview with Williams; Bamford, "Edward Snowden"; Jane Mayer, "Snowden Calls Russian-Spy Story 'Absurd' in Exclusive Interview," *New Yorker*, Jan. 21, 2014.

93 the *Guardian* policy required: Harding, *Snowden Files*, 114–16.

95 The next morning he: Packer, "Holder of Secrets."

95 Tibbo and Man planned: Patrick Koehler, "The Hong Kong Layover in Snowden's Getaway," *New York Times*, Sept. 8, 2016.

95 "I am in a safe house": Greenwald, *No Place to Hide*, 8.

96 The journalist chosen: Lam, "Post Reporter Lana Lam Tells of Her Journey into the Secret World of Edward Snowden."

97 "I was being tailed": Corbett, "How a Snowdenista Kept the NSA Leaker Hidden in a Moscow Airport."

CHAPTER 11 Enter Assange

99 "Thanks to Russia": Julian Assange, "How 'The Guardian' Milked Edward Snowden's Story," *Newsweek*, April 20, 2015.

99 Julian Assange had made: David Leigh and Luke Harding, "Julian Assange: The Teen Hacker Who Became Insurgent in Information War," *Guardian*, Jan. 30, 2011.

100 Sarah Harrison: Sarah Ellison, "The Man Who Came to Dinner," *Vanity Fair*, Oct. 2013.

100 Snowden telephoned Assange: Assange interview, in Giles Whittell, "Julian Assange Unmasked," *Sunday Times* (London), Aug. 29, 2015.

100 "Snowden told me they had abused Manning": Michael Sontheimer, "Spiegel Interview with Julian Assange," *Spiegel Online International*, July 19, 2015.

101 Assange called Harrison: Corbett, "How a Snowdenista Kept the NSA Leaker Hidden in a Moscow Airport."

102 "We were working very hard": Ibid.

102 U.S. government informed: Jane Perlez and Keith Bradsher, "China Said to Have Made Call to Let Leaker Depart," *New York Times*, June 23, 2013.

103 Tibbo wanted Snowden to remain: Tibbo, interview with author.

104 "The purpose of my mission": Rusbridger and MacAskill, "I, Spy."

CHAPTER 12 Fugitive

105 "If I end up in chains": Snowden video on the *Guardian* site, June 17, 2013, www.theguardian.com/world/video/2014/jul/17/edward-snowden-video-interview.

105 insert an encrypted key: Gellman, "Code Name 'Verax.'"

105 "I can't help him evade": Gellman quoted in Burrough, Ellison, and Andrews, "Snowden Saga."

106 asked Fidel Narváez: Juan Forero, "Ecuador's Strange Journey from Embracing Snowden to Turning Him Away," *Washington Post*, July 2, 2013.

107 "My only comment": Lam, "Post Reporter Lana Lam Tells of Her Journey into the Secret World of Edward Snowden."

107 his passage through: Perlez and Bradsher, "China Said to Have Made Call to Let Leaker Depart."

108 Snowden first met Harrison: Corbett, "How a Snowdenista Kept the NSA Leaker Hidden in a Moscow Airport."

108 Assange continued creating: Assange interview, in Whittell, "Julian Assange Unmasked."

109 "Anyone in a three-mile radius": Corbett, "How a Snowdenista Kept the NSA Leaker Hidden in a Moscow Airport."

109 $20,000 fee: Station KGUN9, "Documents: Snowden Paid 20K for UA Skype Talk," ABC 15 Arizona, April 1, 2016, //www.abc15.com/news/region-central-southern-az/tucson/documents-snowden-paid-20k-for-ua-skype-talk.

110 first live interview in Moscow: Snowden met with James Bamford, the author of the 1982 book *The Puzzle Palace,* in Moscow in June 2014. Bamford, "Edward Snowden."

CHAPTER 13 The Great Divide

113 "That moral decision": Edward Snowden, statement, http://wikileaks/statement -from-Edward-Snowden.

114 "Sitting on his unmade bed": Packer, "Holder of Secrets."

114 This powerful narrative: See Greenwald, *No Place to Hide,* 248–54; Snowden, interview with Williams.

114 "There was no question": Emily Bell, "Snowden Interview: Why the Media Isn't Doing Its Job," *Columbia Journalism Review,* May 10, 2016.

115 When two NSA analysts: "Claim US Spy Caught with Secrets," *Los Angeles Mirror,* Aug. 2, 1960, 1. Also see Rick Anderson, "Before Edward Snowden," *Salon,* July 1, 2013.

115 "man up": Interview with John Kerry, *CBS This Morning,* May 28, 2014.

115 By the Lawfare Institute's count: https://www.lawfareblog.com/snowden -revelations.

116 British cyber service GCHQ: RT television report, "NSA, GCHQ Targeted Kaspersky, Other Cyber Security Companies," June 22, 2015, http://www.rt.com /usa/268891-nsa-gchq-software-kaspersky/.

117 six government employees: Matt Apuzzo, "C.I.A. Officer Is Found Guilty in Leak Tied to Times Reporter," *New York Times,* Jan. 26, 2015. The notable exception to the policy of seeking imprisonment of intelligence workers found guilty of passing classified information to journalists is the extraordinary case of the ex-CIA director General David Petraeus. Petraeus had given classified information from his personal notebooks to his mistress and biographer, Paula Broadwell. Although none of this information appeared in her 2012 biography, *All In: The Education of Davis Petraeus,* he had violated his oath to protect this information. Yet in a 2014 deal with the Justice Department, Petraeus was allowed to plead guilty to a misdemeanor charge and sentenced to two years' probation and a $100,000 fine. See Eli Lake, "Petraeus, Justice, and Washington's Culture of Leaks," *Bloomberg View,* March 4, 2015.

117 he posted about it: Snowden wrote in chat rooms on the *Ars Technica* site between May 2001 and May 2012. His posts are quoted by Mullin, "NSA Leaker Ed Snowden's Life on Ars Technica."

117 "an act of civil disobedience": Mayer, "Snowden Calls Russian-Spy Story 'Absurd' in Exclusive Interview."

117 Ben Wizner, a lawyer: Wizner called his representation of Snowden the "work of a lifetime." Hill, "How ACLU Lawyer Ben Wizner Became Snowden's Lawyer."

118 "We've crossed lines": Snowden quoted by Bamford, "Edward Snowden."

119 "Snowden a whistleblower": Cheryl Arvidson, "Distrust of Government Apparent in Snowden Case," *Leader's Edge,* Oct. 2013.

119 "they can trust": "Beyond Distrust: How Americans View Their Government," Pew Research Center, Nov. 23, 2015.

119 "Thanks to one man's": Rebecca Shabad, "Former Rep. Ron Paul Launches Petition for Snowden Clemency," *Hill,* Feb. 13, 2014.

119 his son Senator Rand Paul: See Katie Glueck, "Rand Paul Backs Snowden, Bashes Clapper," *Politico,* Jan. 5, 2014.

119 "We actually buy cell phones": Snowden quoted in "New *The Guardian* Interview with Edward Snowden," *Guardian,* July 17, 2014, https://www.theguardian .com/world/2014/jul/18/-sp-edward-snowden-nsa-whistleblower-interview -transcript.

121 Dominique Strauss-Kahn: Edward Jay Epstein, "What Really Happened to Strauss-Kahn," *New York Review of Books,* Dec. 22, 2011. Vance made his statement on the *Charlie Rose* show, Feb. 19, 2016.

121 Apple made headlines: Mike Isaac, "Apple Still Holds the Keys to Its Cloud Service, but Reluctantly," *New York Times,* Feb. 21, 2016.

121 Consumer Financial Protection Bureau: Newt Gingrich, "A Government Snoop That Puts the NSA to Shame," *Wall Street Journal,* July 7, 2015.

122 the FISA court: http://www.fjc.gov/history/home.nsf/page/courts_special_fisc .html.

123 "His approach was": Ellen Nakashima and Joby Warrick, "For NSA Chief, Terrorist Threat Drives Passion to 'Collect It All,' " *Washington Post,* July 14, 2013.

123 Second U.S. Circuit Court of Appeals: Charlie Savage and Jonathan Weisman, "N.S.A. Collection of Bulk Data Is Ruled Illegal," *New York Times,* May 5, 2015. This court decision was stayed three months later on August 27, 2015, by a three-judge panel of the U.S. Court of Appeals on procedural grounds. By this time, however, the legal issue was rendered moot by Congress. See http://law .justia.com/cases/federal/appellate-courts/ca2/2015/.

124 knowledge of the service providers: Timothy B. Lee, "Here's Everything We Know About PRISM to Date," *Washington Post,* June 12, 2013.

126 "Edward Snowden is not the 'whistleblower' ": Nicole Mulvaney, "NSA Director Adm. Michael Rogers Discusses Freedom, Privacy, and Security Issues at Princeton University," NJ.com, March 14, 2015.

126 "Snowden stole from the United States": Mark Hosenball, "U.S. Spy Agency Targets Changed Behavior After Snowden," Reuters, May 12, 2014.

126 "The vast majority": "Snowden Leak Could Cost Military Billions: Pentagon," NBC News, March 6, 2014.

126 "over 900,000" military files: The document was obtained via a Freedom of Information request by *Vice.* See Leopold, "Inside Washington's Quest to Bring Down Edward Snowden."

126 "has caused grave damage": Hearings Before Senate Select Committee on Intelligence, Jan. 27, 2014. See http://www.dia.mil/News/SpeechesandTestimonies /ArticleView/tabid/11449/Article/567078/dia-director-flynn-unauthorized -disclosures-have-caused-grave-damage-to-our-nat.aspx.

127 The CIA's assessment: Morell, *Great War of Our Time,* 298.

127 "the greatest damage": Transcript of interview with General Keith Alexander, *Australian Financial Review,* May 8, 2014, http://www.afr.com/technology/web /security/interview-transcriptformer-head-of-the-nsa-and-commander-of-the -us-cyber-command-general-keith-alexander-20140507-itzhw#ixzz3m6TkuRa1.

127 "I don't look at this": Jeremy Herb and Justin Sink, "Sen. Feinstein Calls Snowden's NSA Leaks an 'Act of Treason,' " *Hill,* June 6, 2013.

128 duck-rabbit cartoon: Jastrow, *Fact and Fable in Psychology,* 202–4.

129 "I haven't shot anybody": Mark McClish, "The Last Words of Lee Harvey Oswald," Statement Analysis, Jan. 3, 2013, http://www.statementanalysis.com

/lee-harvey-oswald/. Like Snowden, Oswald was a high-school dropout from a broken family who joined an elite unit of the U.S. military but failed to get an honorable discharge, became hostile to policies of the U.S. government, and defected to Russia. See Edward Jay Epstein, *Legend: The Secret World of Lee Harvey Oswald* (New York: McGraw-Hill, 1978), 64–104.

130 Clapper answered that: The transcript was published by *The Washington Post*, Jan. 29, 2014. For Clapper's earlier closed-door testimony, see Steven Aftergood, "The Clapper 'Lie' and the Senate Intelligence Committee," FAS, Jan. 6, 2014.

130 On his application to Booz Allen: Hosenball, "NSA Contractor Hired Snowden Despite Concerns About Resume Discrepancies."

130 in contacting Laura Poitras: Greenberg, "These Are the Emails Snowden Sent to First Introduce His Epic NSA Leaks."

131 "read" in the news reports: Snowden Q&A, Moscow, July 12, 2013, https://www.youtube.com/watch?v=yNQSVurlAak.

131 "Consul General–Hong Kong": James Gordon Meek et al., "NSA Leaker Edward Snowden Seeks Asylum in Ecuador," ABC News, June 23, 2013.

131 "had an enormous interest": Morell, *Great War of Our Time*, 284.

132 the Enigma machines: Sebag-Montefiore, *Enigma*, 286–94.

CHAPTER 14 The Crime Scene Investigation

134 "Any private contractor": Snowden, interview with Williams.

134 Fifteen miles northwest: U.S. Navy Information Operations Command, "History of NIOC Hawaii," http://www.public.navy.mil/fcc-c10f/niochi/Pages/AboutUs.aspx.

135 General Alexander: Alexander, interview with author.

135 The NSA had also notified: Former NSA executive who requested anonymity, interview with author.

137 NSA did not immediately share: Morell, *Great War of Our Time*, 283–88.

137 briefed by the NSA: See "Unclassified Declaration of David G. Leatherwood," U.S. District Court for the District of Columbia, Case 1:10-cv-02119-RMC Document 63-8 Filed 04/26/13, https://www.fas.org/sgp/jud/shaffer/042613-leather.pdf.

138 By late July: Former intelligence executive familiar with the initial investigation who requested anonymity, interview with author.

138 According to Ledgett: Tabassum Zakaria and Warren Strobel, "After 'Cataclysmic' Snowden Affair, NSA Faces Winds of Change," Reuters, Dec. 13, 2013.

139 "Something is not right": Transcript of interview with Alexander, *Australian Financial Review*, May 8, 2014.

139 This discovery came: "Glenn Greenwald's Partner Detained at Heathrow Airport for Nine Hours," *Guardian*, Aug. 18, 2013.

140 downloading documents: Ledgett was interviewed in this timeline by Bryan Burrough. See Burrough, Ellison, and Andrews, "Snowden Saga."

140 the chronology: NSA executive who requested anonymity, interview with author.

141 "millions of records": Snowden interview, German NDR TV, Jan. 26, 2014, http://www.tagesschau.de/snowden-interview-englisch100.pdf.

141 The FBI could assume: Former Justice Department official with knowledge of the Snowden case who requested anonymity, interview with author.

142 "I'm in exile": Former member of the national security staff who cited State Department records, interview with author. Also, Jen Psaki, the State Department spokeswoman, told AP, "As is routine and consistent with US regulations, persons with felony arrest warrants are subject to having their passport revoked." That arrest warrant was issued on June 14, 2013. The State Department Operations Center alert said "Snowden's U.S. passport was revoked on June 22, 2013," after the Justice Department unsealed the charges that had been filed in the U.S. District Court for the Eastern District of Virginia on June 14, 2013. "The Consul General in Hong Kong confirmed Hong Kong authorities were notified that Mr. Snowden's passport was revoked on June 22," according to the State Department's senior watch officer.

143 had met nearly every day: Miller, "U.S. Officials Scrambled to Nab Snowden."

143 Putin admitted: Interview, Channel One, http://en.kremlin.ru/events/president/news/19143.

144 "Vladimir Putin had personally approved": Jennifer Martinez, "Report: Snowden's US Passport Revoked," *Hill*, June 23, 2013.

CHAPTER 15 Did Snowden Act Alone?

147 "When you look at the totality": Hayden, interview with author. Also, "Hayden Interview," *Meet the Press*, NBC-TV, Dec. 15, 2013.

147 whistle-blower Bradley Birkenfeld: David Kocieniewski, "Whistle-Blower Awarded $104 Million by I.R.S.," *New York Times*, Sept. 11, 2012.

148 whistle-blower Daniel Ellsberg: Martin Arnold, "Pentagon Papers Charges Are Dismissed," *New York Times*, May 11, 1973.

148 FBI office in Media: Mark Mazzetti, "Burglars Who Took On F.B.I. Abandon Shadows," *New York Times*, Jan. 7, 2014.

148 "treasure trove": Andrew, *The Sword and the Shield*, 206.

151 "It is inconceivable to me": Former Booz Allen executive who requested anonymity, interview with author.

153 we know that Snowden: Sandvik, "That One Time I Threw a CryptoParty with Edward Snowden."

153 The FBI, which was: Senate Intelligence Committee staff member who requested anonymity, interview with author.

154 "Snowden may have carried out": Drumheller, interview with author.

154 As Snowden acknowledges: Bamford, "Edward Snowden."

155 "absence of evidence": Carl Sagan, *Cosmos* (New York: Random House, 1980), 49.

155 "The greatest trick": Cherkashin, interview with author. The quotation from *The Usual Suspects* was adopted by the movie from Charles Baudelaire's observation "La plus belle des ruses du diable est de vous persuader qu'il n'existe pas."

CHAPTER 16 The Question of When

157 "The NSA was actually": Bamford and De Chant, "Edward Snowden on Cyber Warfare."

157 The career of the KGB mole: Bagley, *Spy Wars*, 46.

158 A counterespionage review: Member of the PFIAB who requested anonymity, interview with author.

158 "in that they both used": Kevin Gosztola, "NSA Inspector General Speaks on Snowden for First Time," *Shadow Proof*, Feb. 25, 2014.

158 KGB major Anatoliy Golitsyn: Bagley, *Spy Wars*, 6–11.

159 Wang Lijun: Steven Lee Myers and Mark Landler, "Frenzied Hours for U.S. on Fate of a China Insider," *New York Times*, April 17, 2012.

160 "I think Snowden is": Vincent Kessler, "Snowden Being Manipulated by Russian Intelligence: Ex-NSA Chief," Reuters, May 7, 2014.

161 A former CIA officer: Tyler Drumheller, interview with author.

162 "It is not statistically improbable": Former NSA officer who requested anonymity, interview with author.

164 "when and how he": Morell, *Great War of Our Time*, 296.

164 "looking to capitalize on": Transcript of interview with Alexander, *Australian Financial Review*, May 8, 2014.

166 "He can compromise thousands": Carol J. Williams, "NSA Leaker Edward Snowden Seeks Return to U.S. on His Terms," *Los Angeles Times*, July 22, 2015.

166 "I am still working": Gellman, "Edward Snowden, After Months of NSA Revelations, Says His Mission's Accomplished."

166 "every facet of Snowden's communications": Reitman, "Snowden and Greenwald."

166 "his hosts": Richard Byrne Reilly, "Former KGB General: Snowden Is Cooperating with Russian Intelligence," *VentureBeat*, May 22, 2014.

167 "I would lose all respect": Richard Byrne Reilly, "Former NSA Director: 'I Would Lose All Respect for Russia if They Haven't Fully Exploited Snowden,'" *VentureBeat*, May 23, 2014.

167 He was put in contact: Kucherena, interview with *Der Spiegel*, "Snowden's Lawyer: 'Russia Will Not Hand Him Over,'" *Spiegel Online International*, June 24, 2013.

167 "Officially, he is my client": "Snowden in the Kitchen," *Interpreter*, Nov. 18, 2013.

168 an interview as "great": Bamford and De Chant, "Edward Snowden on Cyber Warfare."

168 Putin's telethon: Elias Groll, "Snowden Called in to Putin's Telethon. Does That Really Make Him a Kremlin Pawn?," *Foreign Policy*, April 17, 2014.

CHAPTER 17 The Keys to the Kingdom Are Missing

169 "There's a zero percent chance": Risen, "Snowden Says He Took No Secret Files to Russia."

169 "the instruction manual": Glenn Greenwald, "'Guardian' Journalist: Snowden Docs Contain NSA 'Blueprint,'" *USA Today*, June 15, 2013.

169 "a heart attack": *Citizenfour*.

169 "keys to the kingdom": Walter Pincus, "Snowden Still Holding 'Keys to the Kingdom,'" *Washington Post*, Dec. 18, 2013. Also, Ledgett interview, *60 Minutes*, CBS, Dec. 15, 2013.

170 "touched" documents: Former NSA official who requested anonymity, interview with author.

170 more than half the documents: Staff member of the Senate Intelligence Committee who requested anonymity, interview with author.

171 Snowden also disputed: Bamford, "Edward Snowden."

171 via a *Vice* magazine: Leopold, "Inside Washington's Quest to Bring Down Edward Snowden."

172 previously cited road map: Burrough, Ellison, and Andrews, "Snowden Saga."

172 The compartment logs showed: Former NSA official who requested anonymity, interview with author.

172 "No intelligence service": Glenn Greenwald, "Email Exchange Between Edward Snowden and Former GOP Senator Gordon Humphrey," *Guardian*, July 16, 2013.

172 An answer soon came: Sophie Shevardnadze, "'Snowden Believes He Did Everything Right': Lawyer Anatoly Kucherena," *SophieCo*, RT television, Sept. 23, 2013, //www.rt.com/shows/sophieco/snowden-russia-lawyer-kucherena-214/.

173 "all the reports": Kucherena, interview with author.

174 Russian cyber service: Former member of the staff of the national security adviser who requested anonymity, interview with author.

175 State Department explicitly told: Ibid.

176 "I had spent ten years": Hill, "How ACLU Attorney Ben Wizner Became Snowden's Lawyer."

178 In the case of Stone's movie: Irina Alexsander, "Edward Snowden's Long, Strange Journey to Hollywood," *New York Times Magazine*, Sept. 4, 2016.

178 "I went the first six months": Bell, "Edward Snowden Interview."

178 "There's nothing on it": Gellman, "Edward Snowden, After Months of NSA Revelations, Says His Mission's Accomplished."

178 former CIA officer Ray McGovern: Mark Hosenball, "Laptops Snowden Took to Hong Kong, Russia Were a 'Diversion,'" Reuters, Oct. 11, 2013.

179 "break my fingers": Snowden, interview with Williams. See also Burrough, Ellison, and Andrews, "Snowden Saga," and Bamford, "Edward Snowden."

180 "said they believed that": Perlez and Bradsher, "China Said to Have Made Call to Let Leaker Depart."

180 "Both the Chinese and the Russians": Morell, *Great War of Our Time*, 284.

181 "What I can say": Snowden interview, ARD-TV, Jan. 26, 2014, https://docs.google.com/file/d/oB95Id3joMolrdDA5WIZd11Ubjg/preview.

181 She urgently texted Snowden: *Citizenfour*.

181 Poitras's co-interrogator: Appelbaum, "Edward Snowden Interview."

182 there was no document: Former NSA official who requested anonymity, interview with author.

182 He reported that no: Bamford, "Edward Snowden."

182 another person in the NSA: Ibid.

183 Greenwald suggested to the *New York Times*: Jo Becker, Steven Erlanger and Eric Schmitt, "How Russia Often Benefits When Julian Assange Reveals the West's Secrets, " *New York Times*, Sept. 1, 2016.

183 Greenwald and Poitras: "Snowden Leak: Israeli Commandos Killed Syrian General at Dinner Party," *Jerusalem Post*, July 16, 2015.

184 Specifically, it disclosed: Cora Currier and Henrik Moltke, "Spies in the Sky," *Intercept*, Jan. 28, 2016.

184 Putin had publicly enjoined him: Interview, Channel One, http://en.kremlin .ru/events/president/news/19143. Also, former Russian intelligence officer who requested anonymity, interview with author.

185 "If Snowden didn't give": Former NSA official who requested anonymity, interview with author.

185 German federal prosecutor: Theodore Schleifer, "Germany Drops Probe into U.S. Spying on Merkel," *CNN Politics*, June 13, 2015.

186 "Russian planners might have": Adam Entous, Julian E. Barnes, and Siobhan Gorman, "U.S. Scurries to Shore Up Spying on Russia," *Wall Street Journal*, March 24, 2014.

186 Britain also discovered: Tom Harper, Richard Kerbaj, and Tim Shipman, "British Spies Betrayed to Russians and Chinese," *Sunday Times* (London), June 14, 2015.

186 "losing some of its capabilities": Chris Strohm and Gopal Ratnam, "NSA Leader Seeks Openness on Secret Surveillance Orders," *Bloomberg News*, June 13, 2013. Also, staff member of National Security Council who requested anonymity, interview with author.

CHAPTER 18 The Unheeded Warning

187 "The NSA—the world's": Morell, *Great War of Our Time*, 287.

187 Alexander Poteyev: Sergei L. Loiko, "Former Russian Spymaster Convicted of Treason," *Los Angeles Times*, June 28, 2011.

188 "live under cover in the West": Pavel Sudoplatov, *Special Tasks: The Memoirs of an Unwanted Witness* (Boston: Little, Brown, 1994), xxii.

188 The CIA learned of this: Former NSA official who requested anonymity, interview with author.

189 "the business of intelligence": Angleton, interview with author.

189 preparing these "Americans": FBI, "Operation Ghost Stories: Inside the Russian Spy Case," Oct. 31, 2011, https://www.fbi.gov/news/stories/2011/october /russian_103111/russian_103111.

190 NSA at Fort Meade: Gertz, "Counterspies Hunt Russian Mole Inside National Security Agency." Also, Bill Gertz, interview with author.

190 "They [were] looking for one": John R. Schindler, "The Painful Truth About Snowden," XX Committee, http://20committee.com/2015/07/19/the-painful -truth-about-snowden/.

190 "insider threats by trusted insiders": Gellman and Miller, "'Black Budget' Summary Details U.S. Spy Network's Successes, Failures, and Objectives."

191 The preemptive arrests: Gregory L. White, "Russia Convicts Former Spy Official for Exposing Agents in U.S. Ring," *Wall Street Journal*, June 28, 2011.

191 turned up no evidence: Former NSA executive who requested anonymity, interview with author.

192 "broke the record": Tennent H. Bagley, *Spymaster* (New York: Skyhorse, 2015), 3.

192 Russia had dispatched: Weiner, *Legacy of Ashes*, 450–51. Also, Walter Pincus, "CIA Passed Bogus News to Presidents," *Washington Post*, Oct. 31, 1995.

192 "There are no rivers": Baker, "Michael Hayden Says U.S. Is Easy Prey for Hackers."

193 "The best defense": Former NSA official who requested anonymity, interview with author.

CHAPTER 19 The Rise of the NSA

197 "There are many things": Gellman, "Edward Snowden, After Months of NSA Revelations, Says His Mission's Accomplished."

198 By 1914, the U.S. Army: National Security Agency, Pearl Harbor Review: The Black Chamber, NSA, 2009, https://www.nsa.gov/about/cryptologic_heritage /center_cryptologic_history/pearl_harbor_review/black_chamber.shtml.

198 "Its far-seeking eyes": Kahn, *Codebreakers,* 358.

200 The NSA also organized: Woodward, *Veil,* 471–75.

200 In 1980, President Ronald Reagan: David R. Shedd, "How Obama Unilaterally Chilled Surveillance," *Wall Street Journal,* Nov. 30, 2015.

200 "We are approaching": Turner, *Secrecy and Democracy,* 92.

200 "vastness": Woodward, *Veil,* 202.

201 James Bond provision: Ian Cobain, "How Secret Renditions Shed Light on MI6's Licence to Kill and Torture," *Guardian,* Feb. 13, 2012.

201 The NSA had assiduously: Kevin Poulsen, "New Snowden Leak Reports 'Groundbreaking' NSA Crypto-cracking," *Wired,* Aug. 29, 2013.

202 "Yes, my continental European friends": Woolsey, "Why We Spy on Our Allies."

202 "very foundation of U.S. intelligence": John McLaughlin, "We Need NSA to Do What It Does—It Makes Us Safer," *Press of Atlantic City,* Jan. 8, 2014.

203 It made leading hacktivists: Charlie Savage et al., "Hunting for Hackers, N.S.A. Secretly Expands Internet Spying at U.S. Border," *New York Times,* June 4, 2015.

204 "one of the most regulated": De, "Former NSA Lawyer on 'Harm' of Edward Snowden's Revelations."

205 the attack on Sony: Rob Lever, "Some Experts Still Aren't Convinced That North Korea Hacked Sony," *Business Insider,* Dec. 30, 2014.

205 "The Chinese are viewed": Alexander quoted in Kelley Vlahos, "America's Already-Failed Cyber War," *American Conservative,* July 23, 2015.

206 "We are bolstering our support": "Black Budget: Congressional Budget Justification Excerpt," *Washington Post,* Aug. 30, 2013.

207 These compartments were: Former NSA officer who requested anonymity, interview with author.

207 "The queen on our chessboard": Former NSA officer who requested anonymity, interview with author.

207 to confront flagging morale: Hayden, interview with author.

207 "the nation has lost": Mulvaney, "NSA Director Adm. Michael Rogers Discusses Freedom, Privacy, and Security Issues at Princeton University."

207 Although repairing the damage: King, "Ex-NSA Chief Details Snowden's Hiring at Agency, Booz Allen."

CHAPTER 20 The NSA's Back Door

209 "You have private for-profit": Bamford and De Chant, "Edward Snowden on Cyber Warfare."

210 According to a report: "Out of Control," NSA, http://nsarchive.gwu.edu /NSAEBB/NSAEBB424/docs/Cyber-009.pdf.

213 "All of us just fell": Baker, "Michael Hayden Says U.S. Is Easy Prey for Hackers."

214 "it stays secret": De, "Former NSA Lawyer on 'Harm' of Edward Snowden's Revelations."

214 North Korea in 1968: John Prados and Jack Cheevers, "USS *Pueblo:* LBJ Considered Nuclear Weapons," National Security Archive Electronic Briefing Book No. 453, Jan. 23, 2014.

215 Booz Allen Hamilton: Booz Allen Hamilton issued a history of its evolution in 2004. "Helping Clients Envision the Future," PDF file, 2004, https://www.booz allen.com/content/dam/boozallen/documents/90th-History-Book-Complete .pdf.

216 The private company named: Julie Creswell, "The Private Equity Firm That Grew Too Fast," *New York Times,* April 24, 2015.

216 USIS had prematurely closed: Tom Hamburger and Debbi Wilgoren, "Justice Department Says USIS Submitted 665,000 Incomplete Background Checks," *Washington Post,* Jan. 23, 2014.

217 USIS was also open to: Ellen Nakashima, "DHS Contractor Suffers Major Computer Breach, Officials Say," *Washington Post,* Aug. 6, 2014.

217 successful 2011 attack: Andy Greenberg, "Anonymous Hackers Breach Booz Allen Hamilton," *Forbes,* July 11, 2011.

217 a computer system called e-QIP: Joe Davidson, "Federal Background Check System Shut Down Because of 'Vulnerability,' " *Washington Post,* June 29, 2015.

218 this memorandum noted: Former NSA executive who requested anonymity, interview with author.

CHAPTER 21 The Russians Are Coming

220 "The collapse of the Soviet Union": Nick Allen, "Soviet Break-Up Was Geopolitical Disaster, Says Putin," *Telegraph,* April 26, 2005.

220 Russian units had managed: Entous, Barnes, and Gorman, "U.S. Scurries to Shore Up Spying on Russia."

221 Russian acronym SORM: Steven Aftergood, "The Red Web: Russia and the Internet," FAS, Oct. 5, 2015.

222 William Martin and Bernon Mitchell: David P. Mowry, "Betrayers of the Trust," Cryptologic Almanac 50th Anniversary Series (NSA), Feb. 28, 2003.

223 Victor Norris Hamilton: "American Defector Is Found in Russian Prison," *New York Times,* June 4, 1992.

223 He was found dead: Edward Jay Epstein, "The Spy Wars," *New York Times,* Sept. 28, 1980.

225 Harold Nicholson: Elizabeth Farnsworth, "Update on the Case of CIA Agent Harold Nicholson," PBS (transcript), Nov. 19, 1996. See also "Affidavit in Support of Complaint, Arrest Warrant, and Search Warrants: United States v. Harold J. Nicholson," http://www.washingtonpost.com/wp-srv/national/longterm /ciaspy/affidavt.htm.

226 When it comes to recruiting moles: Angleton, interviews with author.

227 well experienced with false flags: Epstein, *Deception,* 22–28.

227 the "Trust" deception: Ibid. Also, Raymond Rocca (the CIA's former research chief for the counterintelligence staff), interview with author.

230 "a learning experience": "Out of Control."

231 127-page Standard Form 86: David Larter and Andrew Tilghman, "Military Clearance OPM Data Breach 'Absolute Calamity,'" *Navy Times*, June 18, 2015.

232 Under Putin: Nicole Perlroth, "Online Security Experts Link More Breaches to Russian Government," *New York Times*, Oct. 28, 2014.

232 "It is next to impossible": Schneier quoted in Jenkins, "Anti-hero of Silk Road."

233 The Silk Road founder: Jenkins, "Anti-hero of Silk Road." Also, former Justice Department official who requested anonymity, interview with author.

233 "better cyber security": Morell, *Great War of Our Time*, 291.

CHAPTER 22 The Chinese Puzzle

234 "The first [false assumption]": Snowden video in Hong Kong.

234 "China its first credible": 2014 Annual Report to Congress by the U.S.-China Economic and Security Review Commission, quoted in David Tweed, "China Takes Nuclear Weapons Undersea Away from Prying Eyes," *Bloomberg Business*, Dec. 8, 2014.

235 "results of decades": Select Committee, U.S. Congress, Report, 1999, http://www.house.gov/coxreport/chapfs/over.html.

236 a vast enterprise in China: Nir Kshetri, *The Rapidly Transforming Chinese High-Technology Industry and Market* (London: Chandos, 2008), 92.

236 By 2007, Paul Strassmann: "China Has .75M 'Zombie Computers' in U.S.," UPI, Sept. 17, 2007.

237 cyber attack had harvested: David E. Sanger and Julie Hirschfeld Davis, "Hackers May Have Obtained Names," *New York Times*, June 11, 2015.

237 "Those records are": Baker, "Michael Hayden Says U.S. Is Easy Prey for Hackers."

238 any attempt to "monopolize": Patrick Goodenough, "Chinese President in Veiled Warning to the US: Don't Try to 'Monopolize Regional Affairs,'" CNS News, May 22, 2014.

238 Chinese intelligence maintains: Former U.S. intelligence officer stationed in Hong Kong who requested anonymity, interview with author.

239 "hostile territory": Drumheller, interview with author.

CHAPTER 23 A Single Point of Failure

241 "the single point of failure": Gellman, "Code Name 'Verax.'"

242 "Snowden thinks he is smart": Morell, *Great War of Our Time*, 285.

242 "The purpose of my [Hong Kong]": Rusbridger and MacAskill, "I, Spy."

243 "This guy": Ibid.

243–244 "It was a nervous period": Ibid.

245 "I'm not going to": Dave Boyer, "Obama on Snowden: 'I'm Not Going to Be Scrambling Jets to Get a 29-Year-Old Hacker,'" *Washington Times*, June 27, 2013.

246 "huge strategic setback": Harper, Kerbaj, and Shipman, "British Spies Betrayed to Russians and Chinese."

246 Adding insult to injury: Vanden Heuvel and Cohen, "Snowden Speaks."

CHAPTER 24 Off to Moscow

251 "They talk about Russia": Bamford and De Chant, "Edward Snowden on Cyber Warfare."
251 Before flying to Moscow: Stone, interview with author.
252 $1 million: Mike Fleming Jr., "Oliver Stone Buys Edward Snowden Russian Lawyer's 'Novel' About Asylum-Seeking Whistleblower," *Deadline*, June 10, 2014.
253 "I have been trying": Bamford, "Edward Snowden."
253 "There is only one door": Gotta, e-mail exchange with author.
254 "A special operation": Gridasov, Yavlyansky, and Gorkovskaya, "Secret Services in Moscow with WikiLeaks Conducted Operation Snowden."
255 "If they [the U.S. government]": Vanden Heuvel and Cohen, "Snowden Speaks."
255 Over a hundred reporters: Irina Galushka, interview with author.
255 A statement posted: "Statement from Edward Snowden in Moscow," https://WikiLeaks.org/Statement-from-Edward-Snowden-in.html.
256 Sarah Harrison, Snowden's companion: Corbett, "How a Snowdenista Kept the NSA Leaker Hidden in a Moscow Airport."
256 So either the rule: The maximum stay is listed on the hotel's website, http://www.v-exp.ru/en/price/.
257 "It was a total vanishing act": Piskunov, interview with author.

CHAPTER 25 Through the Looking Glass

258 "There's definitely a deep state": Vanden Heuvel and Cohen, "Snowden Speaks."
259 according to Cherkashin: Cherkashin, interview with author.
262 Pelton had left the NSA: George E. Curry, "Ex-intelligence Expert Guilty of Espionage," *Chicago Tribune*, June 6, 1986.

CHAPTER 26 The Handler

265 "As for [Snowden's] communication": Kucherena interview, Shevardnadze, "Snowden Believes He Did Everything Right."
265 learned from a Russian researcher: Vassili Sonkine, interview with author.
265 When I had been investigating: Edward Jay Epstein, *The Annals of Unsolved Crime* (Brooklyn: Melville House, 2013), 209–40.
266 "I don't know him": Lugovoy, interview with author.
268 It was rare: The vast majority of the fifteen American defectors to the Soviet Union in the Cold War, including Joel Barr, Morris and Lona Cohen, Victor Hamilton, Edward Lee Howard, George Koval, Bernon Mitchell, William Martin, Isaiah Oggins, Alfred Sarant, Robert E. Webster, and Flora Wovschin, were involved in espionage. The remaining three, Harold M. Koch, a Catholic priest protesting the Vietnam War; Arnold Lockshin, a Communist Party organizer; and Lee Harvey Oswald, a U.S. marine, defected for idealistic principles. All were given asylum, and two, Webster and Oswald, redefected to the United States.
269 "It was totally bizarre": Lokshina, interview with author. Also, "Meeting Edward

Snowden," *Dispatches*, July 13, 2015, https://www.hrw.org/news/2013/07/12 /dispatches-meeting-edward-snowden.

269 "I will be submitting": "Statement by Edward Snowden," July 12, 2013, https:// WikiLeaks.org/Statement-by-Edward-Snowden-to.html.

269 "When I accepted the case": Kucherena, interview with author.

269 Kucherena had personally approved: Shevardnadze, interview with author.

CHAPTER 27 Snowden's Choices

276 Presidential Policy Directive 20: Greenwald, *No Place to Hide*, 75.

276 to trace the theft: Michael Hayden, interview with author.

277 "For our enemies": Morell, *Great War of Our Time*, 294.

278 "I had a special level": Snowden and Taylor, "Are You a Traitor?"

281 "You should remain anonymous": Burrough, Ellison, and Andrews, "Snowden Saga."

283 He was also willing: Snowden and Taylor, "Are You a Traitor?"

284 "The mission's already accomplished": Gellman, "Edward Snowden, After Months of NSA Revelations, Says His Mission's Accomplished."

CHAPTER 28 The Espionage Source

285 "The government's investigation failed": Bamford, "Edward Snowden."

286 "If I were providing information": Transcript of interview with Snowden in Moscow, Rusbridger and MacAskill, "I, Spy."

286 Pelton, for example: Victor Cherkashin, interview with author.

287 "This debriefing could not": Intelligence source who requested anonymity, interview with author.

289 Mike Rogers, the chairman: "Congressman Says Snowden Planned Escape to China," UPI, June 16, 2013.

289 "a known unknown": Donald Rumsfeld, press conference at NATO headquarters, Brussels, Belgium, June 6, 2002.

CHAPTER 29 The "War on Terror" After Snowden

291 "Because of a number": Amy Davidson, "Don't Blame Edward Snowden for the Paris Attacks," *New Yorker*, Nov. 19, 2015.

291 On the evening of: David Gauthier-Villars, "Paris Attacks Show Cracks in France's Counterterrorism Effort," *Wall Street Journal*, Nov. 23, 2015.

293 According to a declassified: Charlie Savage, "NSA Discloses Inspector General Report," *New York Times*, Feb. 16, 2016.

293 "the number one source": "NSA Slides Explain the PRISM Data-Collection Program," *Washington Post*, June 6, 2013.

294 according to the testimony: Ellen Nakashima, "Officials: Surveillance Programs Foiled More Than 50 Terrorist Plots," *Washington Post*, June 18, 2013. Details of four of the plots were then released by the House Select Committee on Intelligence,

http://intelligence.house.gov/1-four-declassified-examples-more-50-attacks
-20-countries-thwarted-nsa-collection-under-fisa-section.

294 Grand Central station: Mark Hosenball, "U.S. NSA Internet Spying Foiled Plot
to Attack New York Subways: Sources," Reuters, June 7, 2013.

294 provided the "critical lead": Marshall Erwin, "Connecting the Dots," U.S. Senate
Committee on the Judiciary, Jan. 13, 2014,.

295 "I can tell you": Rogers quoted in Ed Pilkington and Nicholas Watt, "NSA Surveillance Played Little Role in Foiling Terror Plots, Experts Say," *Guardian*, June
12, 2013.

295 The third NSA program: Glenn Greenwald, "XKeyscore: NSA Tool Collects
'Nearly Everything a User Does on the Internet,' " *Guardian*, July 31, 2013.

295 Further enabling furtive Internet: Appelbaum, "Edward Snowden Interview."

296 These precise tips: Joseph Menn, "Exclusive: Secret Contract Tied NSA and
Security Industry Pioneer," Reuters, Dec. 20, 2013.

296 as Greenwald writes: Greenwald, *No Place to Hide*, 2.

297 "We can't penetrate": Rebecca Savransky, "Head Prosecutor of Paris Attacks
Encryption Program," *Hill*, March 13, 2016.

297 "Terrorist organizations": Morell, *Great War of Our Time*, 294.

297 What further heightened Morell's concern: Ibid., 315.

297 In addition, evidence: Milan Schreuer and Alissa J. Rubin, "Video Found in Belgium May Point to a Bigger Plot," *New York Times*, Feb. 18, 2016.

298 "saw one after another": Mary Louise Kelly, "NSA: Fallout from Snowden Leaks
Isn't Over, but Info Is Getting Old," NPR, March 16, 2016.

298 "Have I lost capability": Bill Gertz, "NSA Director: Snowden's Leaks Helped
Terrorists Avoid Tracking," *Washington Free Beacon*, Feb. 24, 2015.

EPILOGUE The Snowden Effect

299 "Governments can reduce our dignity": Edward Snowden, "Governments Can
Reduce Our Dignity to That of Tagged Animals," *Guardian*, May 3, 2016.

302 published in *The New York Times:* David E. Sanger and Thom Shanker, "N.S.A.
Devises Radio Pathway into Computers," *New York Times*, Jan. 14, 2014.

302 "Snowden has compromised more": McConnell interview, King, "Ex-NSA Chief
Details Snowden's Hiring at Agency, Booz Allen."

303 a distrustful press: Pilkington and Watt, "NSA Surveillance Played Little Role
in Foiling Terror Plots, Experts Say." The first "expert" was Michael Dowling, a
Denver-based attorney who acted as Zazi's defense counsel. He said he had no
access to the undisclosed basis of the government position because Zazi pleaded
guilty in 2011. The second expert was David Davis, a British MP, who was in the
shadow government of the Conservative Party. He resigned from the shadow
government in June 2008, more than a year before the Zazi arrest. In any case,
because the PRISM program was a closely held secret, he would not have had,
and does not claim to have had, access to it.

303 Snowden speaks "truth to power": Vanden Heuvel and Cohen, "Snowden
Speaks."

Selected Bibliography

SELECTED BOOKS

Andrew, Christopher. *The Sword and the Shield*. New York: Basic Books, 2000.

Bagley, Tennent H. *Spy Wars: Moles, Mysteries, and Deadly Games*. New Haven, Conn.: Yale University Press, 2008.

Bamford, James. *The Puzzle Palace*. Boston: Houghton Mifflin, 1982.

Coleman, Gabriella. *Hacker, Hoaxer, Whistleblower, Spy: The Many Faces of Anonymous*. New York: Verso, 2015.

Epstein, Edward Jay. *Deception: The Invisible War Between the KGB and the CIA*. New York: Simon & Schuster, 1989.

———. *Inquest: The Warren Commission and the Establishment of Truth*. New York: Viking Press, 1966.

Fitzpatrick, Catherine A. *Privacy for Me and Not for Thee: The Movement for Invincible Personal Encryption, Radical State Transparency, and the Snowden Hack*. New York: Catherine A. Fitzpatrick, 2014.

Greenberg, Karen J. *Rogue Justice: The Making of the Security State*. New York: Crown, 2016.

Greenwald, Glenn. *How Would a Patriot Act? Defending American Values from a President Run Amok*. San Francisco: Working Assets, 2006.

———. *No Place to Hide*. New York: Metropolitan Books, 2014.

Harding, Luke. *The Snowden Files*. New York: Vintage, 2014.

Hayden, Michael V. *Playing to the Edge*. New York: Penguin, 2016.

Jastrow, Joseph. *Fact and Fable in Psychology*. Boston: Houghton, Mifflin, 1900.

Kahn, David. *The Codebreakers*. New York: Simon & Schuster, 1967.

Lucas, Edward. *The Snowden Operation*. Seattle: Amazon Digital Services, 2015.

Morell, Michael J. *The Great War of Our Time*. New York: Twelve, 2015.

Sebag-Montefiore, Hugh. *Enigma: The Battle for the Code*. New York: John Wiley and Sons, 2001.

Shils, Edward. *The Torment of Secrecy: The Background and Consequences of American Security Policies*. Chicago: Free Press, 1956.

Turner, Stansfield. *Secrecy and Democracy: The CIA in Transition*. New York: Houghton Mifflin, 1985.

Weiner, Tim. *Legacy of Ashes*. New York: Doubleday, 2007.

Woodward, Bob. *Veil: The Secret Wars of the CIA, 1981–1987.* New York: Simon & Schuster, 2005.

SELECTED ARTICLES

Appelbaum, Jacob. "Edward Snowden Interview: The NSA and Its Willing Helpers." *Spiegel Online,* July 8, 2013.

Baker, Gerard. "Michael Hayden Says U.S. Is Easy Prey for Hackers." *Wall Street Journal,* June 22, 2015.

Bamford, James. "Edward Snowden: The Untold Story." *Wired,* Aug. 2014.

Bradsher, Keith. "Hasty Exit Started with Pizza Inside a Hong Kong Hideout." *New York Times,* June 24, 2013.

Burrough, Bryan, Sarah Ellison, and Suzanna Andrews. "The Snowden Saga." *Vanity Fair,* May 2014.

Chen, Te-Ping, and Chester Yung, "Snowden's Whereabouts Remain Unclear." *Wall Street Journal,* June 10, 2013.

Corbett, Sara. "How a Snowdenista Kept the NSA Leaker Hidden in a Moscow Airport." *Vogue,* Feb. 19, 2015.

De, Rajesh. "Former NSA Lawyer on 'Harm' of Edward Snowden's Revelations." *Bloomberg,* July 27, 2015.

Gellman, Barton. "Code Name 'Verax': Snowden, in Exchanges with Post Reporter, Made Clear He Knew Risks." *Washington Post,* June 9, 2013.

———. "Edward Snowden, After Months of NSA Revelations, Says His Mission's Accomplished." *Washington Post,* Dec. 23, 2013.

Gellman, Barton, and Greg Miller. "'Black Budget' Summary Details U.S. Spy Network's Successes, Failures, and Objectives." *Washington Post,* Aug. 25, 2013.

Gertz, Bill. "Counterspies Hunt Russian Mole Inside National Security Agency." *Washington Times,* Dec. 1, 2010.

Greenberg, Andy. "These Are the Emails Snowden Sent to First Introduce His Epic NSA Leaks." *Wired,* Oct. 13, 2014.

Greenwald, Glenn, Laura Poitras, and Ewen MacAskill. "Edward Snowden: The Whistleblower Behind the NSA Surveillance Revelations." *Guardian,* June 9, 2013.

Gridasov, Andrei, Igor Yavlyansky, and Mary Gorkovskaya. "Secret Services in Moscow with WikiLeaks Conducted Operation Snowden." *Izvestia,* June 23, 2013.

Harris, Shane. "What Was Edward Snowden Doing in India?" *Foreign Policy,* Jan. 13, 2014.

Hastings, Michael. "Julian Assange: The Rolling Stone Interview." *Rolling Stone,* Jan. 18, 2012.

Hill, Kashmir. "How ACLU Attorney Ben Wizner Became Snowden's Lawyer." *Forbes,* March 10, 2014.

Hosenball, Mark. "NSA Contractor Hired Snowden Despite Concerns About Resume Discrepancies." *Reuters,* June 20, 2013.

King, Rachael. "Ex-NSA Chief Details Snowden's Hiring at Agency, Booz Allen." *Wall Street Journal,* Feb. 4, 2014.

Lam, Lana. "Whistle-Blower Edward Snowden Talks to the South China Morning Post," *South China Morning Post,* June 23, 2013.

Lee, Micah. "Ed Snowden Taught Me to Smuggle Secrets Past Incredible Danger." *Intercept,* Oct. 28, 2014.

Leopold, Jason. "Inside Washington's Quest to Bring Down Edward Snowden." *Vice,* June 4, 2015.

Miller, Greg. "U.S. Officials Scrambled to Nab Snowden." *Washington Post,* June 14, 2014.

Mullin, Joe. "NSA Leaker Ed Snowden's Life on Ars Technica." *Ars Technica,* June 13, 2013.

Packer, George. "The Holder of Secrets." *New Yorker,* Oct. 20, 2014.

Reitman, Janet. "Snowden and Greenwald." *Rolling Stone,* Dec. 4, 2013.

Risen, James. "Snowden Says He Took No Secret Files to Russia." *New York Times,* Oct. 17, 2013.

Rusbridger, Alan, and Ewen MacAskill. "I, Spy: Edward Snowden in Exile." *Guardian,* July 18, 2014.

Sandvik, Runa A. "That One Time I Threw a CryptoParty with Edward Snowden." *Forbes,* May 27, 2014.

Schmitt, Eric. "C.I.A. Warning on Snowden in '09 Said to Slip Through the Cracks." *New York Times,* Oct. 10, 2013.

vanden Heuvel, Katrina, and Stephen F. Cohen. "Snowden Speaks: A Sneak Peek at an Exclusive Interview." *Nation,* Oct. 10, 2014.

Woolsey, R. James. "Why We Spy on Our Allies." *Wall Street Journal,* March 17, 2000.

Index